Time Out

1000

things to do in London for under £10

timeout.com

Time Out Guides Ltd
Universal House
251 Tottenham Court Road
London W1T 7AB
United Kingdom
Tel: +44 (0)20 7813 3000
Fax: +44 (0)20 7813 6001
Email: guides@timeout.com
www.timeout.com

Published by Time Out Guides Ltd, a wholly owned subsidiary of Time Out Group Ltd.
Time Out and the Time Out logo are trademarks of Time Out Group Ltd.

© **Time Out Group Ltd 2012**

10 9 8 7 6 5 4 3 2 1

This edition first published in Great Britain in 2012 by Ebury Publishing.
A Random House Group Company
20 Vauxhall Bridge Road, London SW1V 2SA

Random House Australia Pty Ltd 20 Alfred Street, Milsons Point, Sydney, New South Wales 2061, Australia

Random House New Zealand Ltd 18 Poland Road, Glenfield, Auckland 10, New Zealand

Random House South Africa (Pty) Ltd Isle of Houghton, Corner Boundary Road & Carse O'Gowrie,
Houghton 2198, South Africa

Random House UK Limited Reg. No. 954009

Distributed in USA by Publishers Group West
1700 Fourth Street, Berkeley, California 94710

Distributed in Canada by Publishers Group Canada
250A Carlton Street, Toronto, Ontario M5A 2L1

For further distribution details, see www.timeout.com.

ISBN: 978-1-84670-265-5

A CIP catalogue record for this book is available from the British Library.

Printed and bound by Firmengruppe APPL, aprinta druck, Wemding, Germany.

The Random House Group Limited supports the Forest Stewardship Council (FSC®), the leading international forest
certification organisation. Our books carrying the FSC label are printed on FSC® certified paper. FSC is the only
forest certification scheme endorsed by the leading environmental organisations, including Greenpeace. Our paper
procurement policy can be found at www.randomhouse.co.uk/environment.

Time Out carbon-offsets its flights with Trees for Cities (www.treesforcities.org).

MIX
Paper from
responsible sources
FSC® C004592

Time Out Guides Limited
Universal House
251 Tottenham Court Road
London W1T 7AB
Tel + 44 (0)20 7813 3000
Fax + 44 (0)20 7813 6001
Email guides@timeout.com
www.timeout.com

Editorial
Editor Sarah Thorowgood
Copy Editors Simon Coppock, Patrick Welch
Researchers Emily Baker, William Crow
Proofreaders Mandy Martinez, Ros Sales
Indexer Dominic Thomas

Editorial Director Sarah Guy
Series Editor Cath Phillips
Management Accountants Clare Turner, Margaret Wright

Design
Art Editor Pinelope Kourmouzoglou
Senior Designer Kei Ishimaru
Group Commercial Senior Designer Jason Tansley

Picture Desk
Picture Editor Jael Marschner
Picture Researcher Ben Rowe

Advertising
Sales Director St John Betteridge
Account Manager Deborah Maclaren & team @ The Media Sales House

Marketing
Senior Publishing Brand Manager Luthfa Begum
Circulation & Distribution Manager Dan Collins

Production
Production Manager Brendan McKeown
Production Controller Katie Mulhern-Bhudia

Time Out Group
Chairman & Founder Tony Elliott
Chief Executive Officer David King
Chief Operating Officer Aksel Van der Wal
Editor-in-Chief Tim Arthur
Group Financial Director Paul Rakkar
Group General Manager/Director Nichola Coulthard
UK Chief Commercial Officer David Pepper
Time Out International Ltd MD Cathy Runciman

Contributors Jessica Ablitt Sudbury, Dominic Addison, Sharif Ahmed, Edoardo Albert, Simone Baird, Alex Barlow, Paul Burston, Rachael Claye, Clare Considine, Simon Coppock, William Crow, Annie Dare, Amy Ellis, Anna Faherty, Mike Flynn, Grant Gillespie, Charlie Godfrey-Faussett, Hugh Graham, Sarah Guy, Derek Hammond, Ronnie Haydon, Kate Hutchinson, Serena Kutchinsky, Ben Lerwill, Jon Levene, Cathy Limb, Megha Mohan, Jenni Muir, Julie Pallot, Toby Pearce, Cath Phillips, Natasha Polyviou, Kate Riordan, Alan Rutter, Robin Saikia, Cyrus Shahrad, Andrew Shields, Bella Todd, Helen Walasek, Peter Watts, Patrick Welch, Sonia Zhuravlyova.

Interviews Nuala Calvi, Bella Todd, Sarah Thorowgood.

The Editor would like to thank Katerina Botsari, Simon Coppock, Grant Gillespie, Vincent White.

Maps London Underground map supplied by Transport for London.

Front and back cover Heloise Bergman, Andrew Brackenbury, Tricia de Courcy Ling, Guy Hills, Jitka Hynkova, Britta Jaschinski, Olivia Rutherford, Ming Tang-Evans, Alys Tomlinson, Jonathan Perugia, Anthony Webb, Marzena Zoladz.

Photography pages 3, 5 (bottom left), 7 (bottom), 13 (left), 25, 27, 74, 79 (left), 102, 115, 121, 160, 188, 205, 208, 209 (middle and bottom left), 250/251, 261, 262, 273 (top) Britta Jaschinski; pages 5 (top left), 34, 89, 124, 177, 178, 236/237, 257, 284, 309 Jonathan Perugia; pages 5 (top right), 28, 30/31, 37, 38, 90/91, 123, 194 (left), 195, 210/211 Olivia Rutherford; pages 5 (top & bottom middle), 9 (top), 53, 106, 107, 230/231, 233, 275 Jitka Hynkova; pages 5 (bottom right), 7 (left), 105 (right) Haris Artimis; pages 7 (top right), 73 (bottom), 120, 175, 249 Andrew Brackenbury; pages 9 (middle), 24, 162, 246, Michelle Grant; pages 9 (bottom), 183 Scott Wishart; pages 10/11 © simo bogdanovic/Alamy; page 13 (right) Wellcome images; pages 18, 19, 26, 42, 185, 243, 266, 277 Ben Rowe; page 33 National Maritime Museum; page 43 Idil Sukan/Draw HQ; page 46 (left) cristapper; page 46 (right) Georgios Kollidas; pages 48, 67, 77, 164 Rob Greig; pages 50/51, 245 (bottom) Alastair Muir; page 57 Dave Swindells; page 61 Libby Mor; pages 62, 63, 239 Tove K Breitstein; page 69 (right) Stephen White; pages 70/71, 264, 265, 303 Marzena Zoladz; page 73 (left) Dean and Chapter of Westminster; pages 73 (top right), 169 r.nagy; page 79 (top) Katie Peters; pages 79 (right), 129, 167, 267 (left) Alys Tomlinson; page 81 Will Pryce/www.willpryce.com; page 93 (bottom) Piers Allardyce; page 93 (bottom) WWT London Wetland Selena Sherid; page 93 (top) Kirsanov; page 95 Sarah Thorowgood; page 97 The Royal Parks; page 99 Tim Spicer; pages 100, 157, 158, 159, 170/171, 197, 198, 207 Elisabeth Blanchet; pages 105 (left), 108, 113, 127, 209 (top right), 247, 273 (bottom) Ming Tang-Evans; pages 110/111 Getty Images; pages 150/151 Kilian O'Sullivan; page 173 (top) Peter Garner; page 173 (middle) Sophie Lee; page 173 (bottom) Fung Wah-Man; pages 179, 240, 285 Heloise Bergman; pages 190/191 Shutterstock.com; page 193 Dan Breckwoldt; page 194 (right) Layton Thompson; page 203 Adrian Pancucci; page 204 David Axelbank; page 209 (top left and bottom right) Rogan Macdonald; page 214 Richard Bryant/arcaid.co.uk; page 218 Stephen Dobbi; page 220 Tristram Kenton; page 221 Esme Appleton; page 223 Ez; page 227 Michael Cockerham; page 229 BBC/Mentorn/Des Willie; page 245 (top) Bernardo Doral; page 254 fasphotographic; page 267 (top and right) Gemma Day; page 268 Nick Ballon; page 269 Anthony Webb; pages 270/271 James Perry; page 282 Nick Cobbing / www.artangel.org.uk; pages 286/287 Damian O'Hara; pages 290/291 James O Jenkins; pages 294, 295 Tricia de Courcy Ling; page 297 Philip Mould Ltd; page 306 Thomas Skovsende.

The following images were supplied by the featured establishments/artists: p15, 47, 69 (left), 83 (top), 87, 109, 122, 152, 153, 187, 206, 216, 242, 248, 293, 298.

Illustrations Ian Keltie, www.keltiecochrane.com

Contents

FLAGSHIP STORE: 66–67 COLEBROOKE ROW ISLINGTON N1
ALSO AT: 13 CHARING CROSS ROAD WC2 (NEXT TO NATIONAL GALLERY), 58–62 HEATH STREET HAMPSTEAD NW3,
220 KENSINGTON HIGH STREET W8, 24 BERWICK STREET W1. OPEN 7 DAYS A WEEK. WWW.CASSART.CO.UK

About the guide

Telephone numbers

All phone numbers listed in this guide assume that you are calling from within London. From elsewhere within the UK, prefix each number with 020. From abroad, dial your international access code, then 44 for the UK, and then 20 for London.

Disclaimer

While every effort has been made to ensure the accuracy of information within this guide, the publishers cannot accept responsibility for any errors it may contain. Businesses can change their arrangements at any time so, before you go out of your way, we strongly advise you to phone ahead to check opening times, prices and other particulars.

Advertisers

The recommendations in *1000 Things to do in London for under £10* are based on the experiences of Time Out journalists. No payment or PR invitation of any kind has secured inclusion or influenced content. The editors select which venues and activities are listed in this guide, and the list of 1,000 was compiled before any advertising space was sold. Advertising has no effect on editorial content.

Let us know what you think

Did we miss anything? We welcome tips for 'things' you consider we should include in future editions and take note of your criticism of our choices. You can email us at guides@timeout.com.

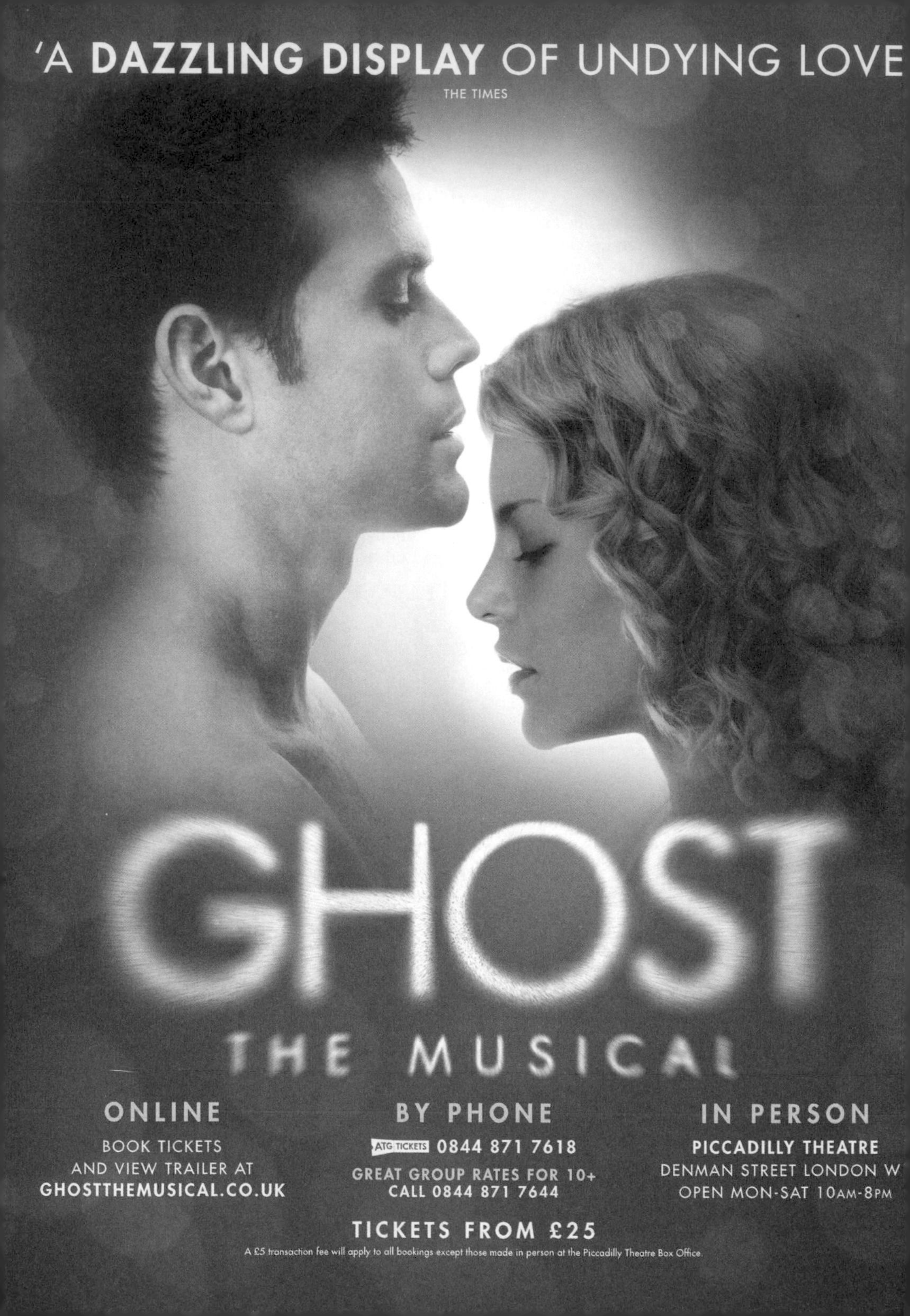
'A DAZZLING DISPLAY OF UNDYING LOVE
THE TIMES
GHOST
THE MUSICAL
ONLINE
BOOK TICKETS
AND VIEW TRAILER AT
GHOSTTHEMUSICAL.CO.UK
BY PHONE
ATG TICKETS 0844 871 7618
GREAT GROUP RATES FOR 10+
CALL 0844 871 7644
IN PERSON
PICCADILLY THEATRE
DENMAN STREET LONDON W
OPEN MON-SAT 10AM-8PM
TICKETS FROM £25
A £5 transaction fee will apply to all bookings except those made in person at the Piccadilly Theatre Box Office.

Introduction

London is a famously – some might even say reassuringly – expensive city. A place that consistently tops highest cost of living charts and which people from out of town save up to visit. There's no denying the fact that a martini at Claridge's or a box at the Royal Opera House will set you back considerably more than £10 – and that's probably the way it should be. Some things *are* worth paying a lot for. Yet despite the high rents and other costly living expenses, there is also a wealth of entertainment on offer in the city that's free – or at least attainable for less than a tenner.

When we set about compiling a list of ideas, it soon became clear that we were not going to be short of suggestions. For starters, since the great national museums threw open their doors for free after the millennium, it's been possible to spend days wandering the capital soaking up culture without paying a penny – once you've bought your travelcard. But even travelling through the city can be part of the floor show – head upstairs on a double decker bus with Peter Watts (*see p278*) and you'll see what we mean, and happy is the child that bags the front seat on a driverless DLR train (*see p238*). Then there are the hundreds of other art galleries and museums to visit, walks to take, performances to see (including opera in Covent Garden), bargains to buy, food to eat and even cocktails to sip – all for less than £10. You can use the thematic index (*see p315*) for inspiration and the A-Z one (*see p310*) if you are looking for something specific.

It's true that sometimes a little ingenuity is required to keep things ticking along for less than a tenner – we're not above a well-placed blag in the interests of research (*see p156*) – and there are some things in this book that would not be here if it weren't for the generosity of the people that run them. But, as you'll quickly discover with the help of this book, London's full to bursting with gloriously cheap thrills. Grab a crisp ten pound note and start exploring.

Sarah Thorowgood, Editor

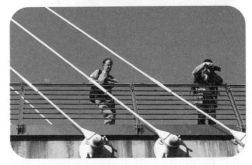

1

Refresh yourself in Battersea Park
Here's hoping for a repeat of summer
2006, when the mercury hit 36° centigrade
and London's fountains became more than
just decorative attractions. If the heatwave
comes, you'll be relieved to know that the
fountains in Battersea Park – the largest
of any London park – spring into life at
least once every hour.

2 Take tea in the British Museum

You could have a cuppa in one of the museum's various cafés, but if you have some spare time why not enjoy the free 'Way of Tea' session instead? This demonstration of the Japanese tea ceremony takes place in Room 92 roughly once a fortnight. There's also a terrific programme of free gallery talks, all linked to the vast Museum collection in some way, ranging from 'Bejewelling the male body in the Renaissance' to 'The cost of living in Roman and modern Britain'. Many of them are also timed just right (at 45 minutes) for a lunch break. Some other events, particularly family ones (such as a 'Design a game' workshop) are also free. Check the website for specific dates and details of all events.

British Museum *Great Russell Street, WC1B 3DG (7323 8299, www.britishmuseum.org).*

3 Buy Chinese food in Chinatown

Head to New Loon Moon (9A Gerrard Street, W1D 5PL, 7734 3887, www.newloonmoon.com) – a labyrinth of foodie delights – for an unrivalled range of products from different countries including China, Thailand, Vietnam, Korea, India, Japan, Indonesia, the Philippines, Malaysia and even Burma. Try fresh gai lan (Chinese broccoli), Thai pea aubergines or huge, spiky jackfruit sold by the slice (in season, otherwise tinned). Loon Fung (42-44 Gerrard Street, W1D 5QG, 7437 7332, www.loonfung.com) is one of the only oriental supermarkets in this part of town to have a butcher's counter – pork shin bones and chicken feet are offered alongside more traditional cuts. See Woon (18-20 Lisle Street, WC2H 7BE, 7439 8325, www.seewoo.com) is good for fresh vegetables and cured Chinese meats.

4 Go falcon-watching on the South Bank

The Royal Society for the Protection of Birds (RSPB) isn't all about red kites, golden eagles and puffins – high-profile species living in remote sanctuaries. From July to September, you'll find Society volunteers toting telescopes next to the Millennium Bridge just outside Tate Modern. The RSPB's Richard Bashford told us that their plan is 'to approach people and say "would you like to see a falcon", then give them binoculars and information and point them up to where they're perched up on top of the Tate Modern chimney, post breeding.' Find out more at www.rspb.org.uk/datewithnature/146957-peregrines-at-the-tate-modern.

5 See a free film

An enterprising community group that puts on free outdoor screenings in interesting public spaces in south-east London. Previous events have included *Battleship Potemkin* (with a live music soundtrack), shown on Peckham multistorey car park roof, and *Breaking Away* (a bike-powered screening) at Herne Hill Velodrome. There are also workshops, talks and walks. See www.freefilmfestivals.org for details.

6 See London through Nelson's eye

Situated in the south-west corner of Trafalgar Square, the Trafalgar Hotel's small rooftop bar, Vista (2 Spring Gardens, Trafalgar Square, SW1A 2TS, 7870 2900, www.thetrafalgar.com) overlooks the lions, the fountains, the general melée – and Nelson on his column. Up here you get pretty much the same view of the city as the great Admiral standing 170 feet up in the air. The bar serves a range of drinks (some of which cost less than a tenner), but is only open April to October and December, and may be closed for private parties – phone ahead to check before you visit.

7 Be grateful for modern medicine

The Wellcome Collection explores the connections between medicine and art through its three spaces. Upstairs, exhibits drawn from 19th-century explorer Sir Henry Wellcome's findings include a 14th-century Peruvian mummy, a used guillotine blade, Napoleon's toothbrush and a wickedly bladed torture chair. Next door, is 'Medicine Now', which contains some startling modern art on medical themes (a realistic sculpture of a man disappearing into the folds of his own obese stomach, for example). Downstairs, the series of temporary exhibitions get better and better: Skeletons – a forensic analysis of ancient bones from the Museum of London storerooms – was one of our favourite shows, as was High Society, a look at the rich history of mind-altering drugs. **Wellcome Collection** *183 Euston Road, NW1 2BE (7611 2222, www.wellcomecollection.org).*

8 Drink to George Orwell in the Fitzroy Tavern

This lively West End boozer first secured its reputation as a literary salon in the 1920s, when it provided a bolt- and watering-hole for Fitzrovia's more outré residents, including Augustus John, Jacob Epstein and Aleister Crowley. Queen of Bohemia Nina Hamnett could also be found sprawled over the bar here, trading anecdotes of her numerous adventures with Picasso in exchange for drinks. In the '50s, regulars included Dylan Thomas, George Orwell, Soho raconteur Julian McLaren-Ross and there was even the occasional visit from Lawrence Durrell when he was in the country. The Sam Smith pub still wears its history with pride – head downstairs to the Writers' and Artists' Bar, find yourself a cosy wooden booth and toast London's former literary glories. **Fitzroy Tavern** *16A Charlotte Street, W1T 2LY (7580 3714).*

Wellcome Collection

18 STAFFORD TERRACE
THE SAMBOURNE FAMILY HOME

Remarkably well-preserved and complete with its original interior decoration and contents, 18 Stafford Terrace is one of London's best kept secrets.

VISITS ARE BY GUIDED TOURS ONLY
Tickets: Adult £8, Concessions £6 and Under 16s £3.

Public Tours:
Wednesdays 11.15am and 2.15pm, Saturdays and Sundays at 11.15am, 1.00pm, 2.15pm and 3.30pm. Weekend afternoon tours are led by costumed actors.
Private Group Tours:
For adults and schools groups, different rates apply. Please call 020 7471 9158 for more information.

Address: 18 Stafford Terrace, London W8 7BH

LEIGHTON HOUSE MUSEUM
EAST MEETS WEST

One of the most extraordinary houses in the country. Built as a studio-house by the eminent artist Frederic, Lord Leighton from 1864, it grew to become a 'Private Palace of Art', famous for its exotic interiors and the collections of fine and decorative art that were displayed through its rooms.

Open daily from 10am - 5.30pm, except Tuesdays.
Tickets: £6 Adult and Concessions £3.

Public Tours:
One-hour tours of the house are available every Wednesday and Sunday at 3.00pm.

Address: 12 Holland Park Road, London W14 8LZ

CONTACT BOTH HOUSES ON:
Tel: 020 7602 3316
Email: museums@rbkc.gov.uk

 Leighton House

 @RBKCLeightonH

www.rbkc.gov.uk/museums

THE ROYAL BOROUGH OF
KENSINGTON
AND CHELSEA

A few of my favourite things

9-13

Russell Kane, comedian

If you want to see some good comedy on the cheap, the best place to go is the Greenwich venue Up The Creek (302 Creek Road, SE10 9SW, 8858 4581, www.up-the-creek.com) on a Sunday night. It's just a little local place, but the standard of comedy is always high and it'll only cost you about a fiver to get in. Another favourite of mine is the Fat Tuesdays Comedy Night at the Compass (58 Penton Street, N1 9PZ, 7837 3891, www.thecompassn1.co.uk). If you are lucky you'll sometimes see people like Frank Skinner and Eddie Izzard popping in to try out their new material.

You can't do much better than walk the half mile or so through the centre of Covent Garden to look at the jugglers, human statues and street performers – it's like a constant free theatre show out there. The other day when I was there, I saw some people having a paella cook-off. If you get a drink at the Punch and Judy pub (40 The Market, The Piazza, WC2E 8RF, 3582 4849, www.taylor-walker.co.uk) you can look down on proceedings from the upper level and have a laugh at the City types getting drunk and falling over. Something that I really love doing is going on what I call a 'human safari'. You have to head out at about 11pm, having drunk no more than one bottle of wine – you need to be lubricated but relatively sober for this – then take a tuk tuk along Great Newport Street and through Chinatown and Leicester Square. I can guarantee that you will never see such a brilliant snapshot of humanity. Every stage of inebriation and emotion will be on display – from first love right the way through to animosity and violence.

There are lots of cool places to go to see films in London, but I think that the Ritzy (Brixton Oval, Coldharbour Lane, SW2 1JG, 0871 902 5739, www.picturehouses.co.uk) is really something special. As well as having tickets for £6.50 (on a Monday) and live music for free in the café upstairs, it's also in a beautiful old building, all the movie timetables are written up on chalkboards and the staff really know their stuff. Plus it's in the heart of Brixton so it has a really great atmosphere.

I love food, and because I'm a bit hyperactive I can eat massive quantities of it without penalty. At the Stockpot (18 Old Compton Street, W1D 4TN, 7287 1066) you can get two courses, plus a drink, for under a tenner. It's the perfect place to go if you love British cooking – and if you feel like gorging yourself.

14

Take pleasure in the Palace on Bankside

As recently as the 1960s, the Bishop of Winchester's Palace on Bankside was little more than a rumour, hidden away behind Victorian warehouse walls. But now its tumbledown walls and high rose window once again add some spiritual frisson, as well as some 13th-century gravitas, to Clink Street. In the 15th and 16th centuries, Bankside was the focal point for fun in London – and who better to control the theatrical shenanigans, the dog-tossers, bear-baiters and prostitutes (aka 'Winchester geese', *see p264*) than the right honourable Bishop himself? Oh for the days when this 'private retreat from the pressures of medieval governance' featured not only 'a prison, a brewhouse and a butchery' but also the more wholesome delights of a 'tennis court, bowling alley and pleasure gardens'. No wonder the area was known as the 'Liberty of the Clink'.
Winchester Palace (*www.english-heritage.org.uk*).

Path to glory

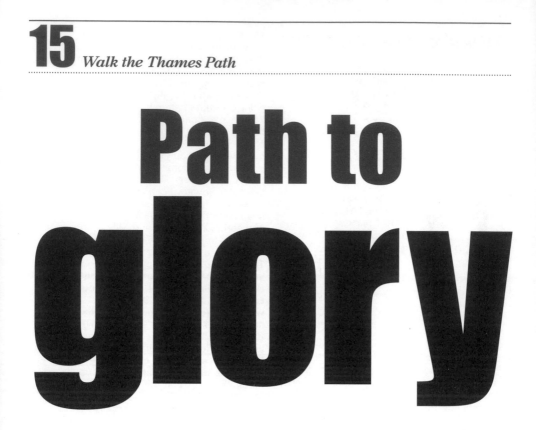

Cath Phillips packs some plasters and walks the Thames Path – all the way from the Thames Barrier to Hampton Court Palace.

The pain set in just past County Hall. The sunlight was bouncing off the water, the Houses of Parliament resplendent in the afternoon sun, and the riverside café did a mean cappuccino. But my feet were suffering: the blisters on my ankles had started to bleed, my toes were red and raw, and a strange puffy swelling had appeared on the underside of one foot. Perhaps we could call it a day, nip round the corner to Waterloo station and get the tube home? Fat chance. We were on a mission: to walk the Thames Path through London, all 36 miles of it from the Thames Barrier to Hampton Court Palace, over one weekend, and no way was the little matter of bleeding blisters going to stop us. At least I'd got some plasters and a spare pair of socks. And it was only another 23 miles to go.

It was a bright Saturday morning at the beginning of October. We'd started at 9am,

meeting at North Greenwich tube station at the top of the desolate Greenwich Peninsula, next to the 02 Centre. From there it was a bus ride to the Thames Barrier, the official 'end' of the Thames Path, which starts 184 miles away at the river's source in the Cotswolds. For us it was the beginning, however, because we were walking east to west. You can do it in either direction, of course, but we had an overnight stop in Barnes and anyway it somehow seemed more appropriate to walk west – away from the city into the countryside, the sunset and the glories of a splendid palace.

Few people walk great distances in London. Walks tend to be short and practical: to and from the tube station or bus stop, to the shops, perhaps a Sunday stroll around a park if you're lucky. There are other long-distance paths within the capital (the Capital Ring, the

London Loop, the Green Chain Walk), but the Thames Path takes you through the heart of London, not the outskirts; it reveals the ever-changing nature of the city, from the industrial east through the seats of power in the built up centre to the increasingly rural west; and it's a brilliant way to reclaim the Thames, that great thoroughfare that defines the city yet is often ignored by its inhabitants.

You don't need a map as there are signposts all along the route, but it's worth taking the three (free) mini guides to the London stretch of the Thames Path National Trail. You can download them from the Walk London website, www.walklondon.org.uk/route, or order them from the Countryside Service, Signal Court, Old Station Way, Eynsham, Oxford OX29 4TL (01865 810224). The brochures are written west to east, but they're just as useful in the opposite direction if you want sights pointed out to you, historical information and, crucially, for helping you decide which side of the river to walk on. You have no choice at the extremities, but from Greenwich to Teddington Lock the path straddles both sides of the river and it's possible to zigzag via the numerous bridges. Swapping sides gives a different perspective, but there are also lengthy and irritating detours that are best avoided, when the path is forced away from the water's edge and goes all round the houses (literally, in some instances) before getting back on course. Other essential equipment should include proper hiking boots and thick socks for cushioning, plasters, water and raingear. Binoculars are useful too.

The first ten miles, to Tower Bridge, were easy. From the shiny silver pods of the Thames Barrier to genteel Greenwich, it's a bleak but thrilling landscape of industrial decay, the path hugging the shoreline past scrapyards, derelict wharves, heaps of aggregate and mysterious metal structures dangling over the water. Rusting shopping trolleys are visible in the mud at low tide, and signs of life are few, bar the solitary Anchor & Hope pub and the occasional dog walker. In the 17th century, pirates' corpses were hung in cages at the tip of the peninsula as a deterrent to other pirates; later it became an industrial stronghold, dominated by works for guns, ships, steel, metal, cement and gas, and therefore heavily polluted. Nowadays, the

Greenwich Ecology Park and rows of colourful new apartment blocks signal the area's transformation – but it's still got a long way to go.

'The path reveals the ever-changing nature of the city: from the industrial east, through the seats of power to the increasingly rural west.'

Just past the O2 Centre is Antony Gormley's sculpture *Quantum Cloud*, a tangle of metal rods that gradually reveals the outline of a human figure. A sweet, heavy stench hangs in the air: Tate & Lyle's refinery still processes a million tonnes of sugar a year here. The brick towers of the Greenwich Power Station loom dramatically over the diminutive Trinity Hospital almshouses, founded in 1613; beyond lies the stately Royal Naval College and tourist shops of Greenwich, an ideal place for a coffee break.

At Greenwich, you can continue along the south bank, through Deptford and Rotherhithe, or traverse the Thames via the Greenwich Foot Tunnel and walk through the Isle of Dogs and Wapping. It's one or the other; there's no alternative river crossing until you reach Tower Bridge. We chose the southern route, ducking and diving around historic Rotherhithe, with changing views of the higgledy-piggledy apartment blocks and gleaming high-rises of Canary Wharf opposite as the river bends around the Isle of Dogs.

There's an awkward detour at Pepys Park in Deptford (look out for the Thames Path signs or you'll get lost). Then comes Deptford Strand, site of Henry VIII's Royal Dockyards – Drake's Steps mark the point where Francis Drake was knighted by Elizabeth after his circumnavigation of the globe in the *Golden Hind*. The docks here, once the heart of Britain's seafaring ambitions – whalers left for the Arctic from Greenland Dock – are now used by watersports enthusiasts and yachting types. Occasional danger signs warn of 'Slippery Steps. Sudden Drop. Deep Water.' Surrey Docks Farm, a ramshackle oasis with its goats, pigs, donkeys and café, is another handy refreshments stop. As the river bends to the west, you get the first glimpse of Tower Bridge.

Perhaps surprisingly, the section from Tower Bridge through the heart of the city and the tourist hotspots of the Tower of London, HMS *Belfast*, Shakespeare's Globe, Tate Modern, the South Bank Centre and the London Eye is the least interesting for the purposes of this mission. Inevitably, this is the most crowded part of the walk and it was hard to retain a sense of purpose and an air of adventure as we struggled through hordes of sightseers and office workers on their lunch break. (The northern bank, along the edge of the City, Victoria Embankment and Charing Cross, is quieter.) Eventually the throngs petered out beyond Westminster Bridge.

We crossed to the north at Lambeth Bridge (to avoid lengthy detours in Vauxhall and around the dilapidated hulk of Battersea Power Station), then crossed back again at Chelsea Bridge to take in leafy Battersea Park. We then yo-yoed once more to the north over Albert Bridge and wandered past assorted houseboats and gleaming yachts at Chelsea Harbour,

followed by a seemingly endless array of swanky new riverside apartment blocks to get to Wandsworth Bridge. By now it was getting dark and we were dog-tired; perhaps the reason that we made the mistake of continuing on the north side and had to endure a tedious longcut around the grounds of Fulham's private Hurlingham Club, before hitting Putney Bridge. We crossed the Thames once more.

From here, the most direct route to Barnes was a couple of miles, but we were walking next to the river and at this point it does one of its great meandering loops up to Hammersmith Bridge and then south again. At least the hard, foot grinding tarmac turned to gravel after the boathouses of Putney, and the tree-lined path was tranquil and increasingly pretty at we headed behind the London Wetland Centre, past playing fields and the Leg o' Mutton nature reserve. Finally, the humps of Barnes Bridge signalled the end of day one. A stiff drink, a hot bath and an early night swiftly followed. We weren't up early the following morning.

Day two started well. The stretch from Barnes to Richmond on the south bank is particularly idyllic. (It also avoids a rambling detour through the backstreets of uninteresting Brentford and, if you're counting miles – which of course we were – the southern route is more than two miles shorter than the northern one.) Trees line the gravel path, which hugs the water's edge, curving past cottages, various

pubs, the Budweiser brewery at Mortlake (the smell of hops in the west countering the sugar in the east) and a glitzy, glassy housing development just before Kew Pier and Bridge.

The weather was bright and sunny and ducks and swans paddled by on the water, keeping out of the way of the heaving rowers. Then a lovely green vista opened up as the path skirted the edge of the Royal Botanic Gardens and the Old Deer Park. It was low tide, and foxes were playing on the foreshore opposite; beyond we could see lion-topped Syon House amid the grassy expanse of Syon Park. Then came pretty Richmond Lock, Twickenham Bridge and, shortly afterwards, the White Cross pub and the smart riverside frontage of Richmond. We stopped for coffee, cake and a breather at the café nestled under the bridge.

Just after Richmond lies one of the most picturesque parts of the Thames. The buildings disappear and there's the long sweep of Petersham Meadows (where cows still graze) and a little island midstream. Handsome 17th-century Ham House on the south bank faces off against 18th-century Marble Hill House on the north (a foot ferry runs between the two). Himalayan balsam has colonised the riverbank here; it's an invasive exotic, but it's hard to resist squeezing the seedcases – which pop satisfyingly, as if alive – thus spreading it further. Then comes a series of playing fields, nature reserves and, finally, Teddington Lock.

As well as the lock (which is crammed with pleasure boats in summer), there's a weir, a summer café and footbridges to Teddington proper. The lock marks the end of the tidal Thames; from this point the river takes on a placid and unhurried air, very different from the turbulent highs and lows Londoners are used to. This is also where the path loses its double-sided character. It runs on the south bank through a grassy hinterland as far as Kingston, then you have to cross to the northern bank, following the sweeping edge of Hampton Court Park to Henry VIII's glorious Tudor palace.

Just three miles to go. Trees and bushes dangled in the water, swans floated gently past a marina; the houses of Thames Ditton across the water the only reminder that we weren't in the heart of the country. But the light was fading, and an autumnal chill had descended making our legs feel heavy and stiff. Even the gravel towpath was getting too hard underfoot, so we hobbled, staggered and stumbled on the grassy verge until the long brick wall and ornate gates of Hampton Court Palace came into view. The sense of achievement was profound and – not capable of much more – we fell into the nearest pub for a celebratory pint.

On the train home (Hampton Court station is 30 minutes from Waterloo), despite aching limbs and bleeding feet, we were already planning to do it all again, this time from west to east, filling in the gaps we'd missed this time.

Decode Da Vinci

'In London lies a knight a Pope interred…' reads the clue in Dan Brown's *The Da Vinci Code* which leads our heroes to the 'Pantheonically pagan' round nave at the 12th-century Temple Church off Fleet Street (Temple, EC4Y 7BB). There are spooky, lifelike memorial effigies of knights arrayed in the Round, where the order once held their secret initiation rites. But the hunt swiftly moves on to Westminster Abbey (20 Dean's Yard, SW1P 3NY), where fans will find Isaac Newton's tomb, complete with the orb mentioned in the next part of the clue, although on a quiet day the Chapter House may feature a distinct lack of flying cryptex cylinders, gunplay and/or damsels in distress. It turns out that Alexander Pope ('A Pope', geddit?) read Newton's funeral eulogy.

Code devotees will also enjoy the crucifixion mural by Jean Cocteau (like Da Vinci, allegedly Grand Master of the Priory of Sion) in the Notre Dame de France church off Leicester Square (5 Leicester Place, WC2H 7BX). The surreal 1950s mural features much occult symbolism, from disguised pentagrams through John the Baptist handsigns to a black sun casting black rays into the sky.

But top of the hit list has to be the hulking art deco Freemasons Hall (60 Great Queen Street, WC2B 5AZ, 7831 9811, www.ugle. org.uk), in Covent Garden – especially as it isn't common knowledge that tours are freely available. Highlights at the hall include a wealth of magickal, inexplicable regalia, walls and paraphernalia strewn with Egyptian, Hebrew and esoteric symbolism – and the 2,000-seater Grand Temple. It's stacked with Zodiacal signs, a depiction of Solomon's architect Hiram, symbols for Faith, Hope, Charity and Jacob's Ladder. There are also celestial and terrestrial globes, all-seeing eyes, charioteers and 'five-pointed stars'. Other items in the collection include the various belongings of notable masons such as Winston Churchill and Edward VII.

20 Get behind the scenes at London Transport Museum's depot

London Transport Museum has a secret horde at its depot in Acton. Normally this is closed to the public but the treasure trove of unused exhibits opens for a themed weekend twice a year (in March and October) so that the public can have a peek – a treat that includes its working model layouts of London's transport network. You can ride on the depot's miniature railway – there are steam as well as electric trains – or take a trip on full-size heritage vehicles, including the 1950s prototype of the Routemaster bus (the RM1).
London Transport Museum Depot *2 Museum Way, 118-120 Gunnersbury Lane, W3 8BQ (7565 7298, www.ltmuseum.co.uk). £10, free under-16s .*

21 Taste Trinidad at Roti Joupa

This ordinary-looking takeaway opposite Clapham North tube station has raised the bar for roti in London. This Trinidadian staple of a wholewheat flatbread wrapped around fillings originates in India but Trinidad has taken it as its own. It's also worth a trip across town for the doubles (roti stuffed with curried chick peas). There's also macaroni pie, tamarind balls, fresh coconut and other treats for homesick Trinis. It's almost impossible to spend more than £10, however hungry you are.
Roti Joupa *12 Clapham High Street, SW4 7UT (7627 8637).*

22 Make space in your diary for Open House weekend

Block out the third weekend of September and spend it visiting some of the more than 700 places – buildings of every conceivable size and type – that you can't visit the rest of the year. And, what's more, they are *all* free. See www.openhouselondon.org.uk for details.

23-31 *Head for the hills*

Alexandra Palace, N22
Alexandra Palace is famous for its splendid Victorian architecture and ice skating rink, but the view is a similarly big draw. Framed by a low brick wall and ornamental railings, and dotted with pay-per-view machines, the vista encompasses everything from the leafy Victorian terraces of Crouch End and Wood Green to the City glitter of the Gherkin. The view from below, looking back at the flamboyant 'Ally Pally', is equally majestic.

Brockwell Park, SW2
A short walk from the mean streets of Brixton, leafy Brockwell Park is worlds away in feel. Wandering amid the ancient trees, postcard lakes and gentle hills, you may feel like you're in the shires, but turn northwards and take in the vista – the Gherkin, the London Eye, Tower 42 – and suddenly the city meets the country.

Denmark Hill, SE5
Formerly Dulwich Hill, Denmark Hill was rechristened in honour of Queen Anne, wife of Prince George of Denmark, who lived on the east side. The Fox on the Hill pub stands on the site of the 'Fox under the Hill', the only building in the area shown on John Cary's 1786 map.

Forest Hill, SE23
This sleepy southern suburb is best-known for the eccentric Horniman Museum. It's a gem, to be sure, but the view from the park behind will leave an equally lasting impression – the City shimmering in the distance, rising above a canopy of leafy green.

Greenwich Park, SE10
It's quite a steep hike up to the summit of Greenwich Park from the river but the sweat is well worth it. As well as the genteel views of the Royal Park spread out before you, there's a host of graceful structures to take in on the way: from Wren and Hawksmoor's baroque Old Royal Naval College through to Inigo Jones's Queen's House and on up to the Royal Observatory. The view from the top looking back across the river is breathtaking (*see p190*).

Muswell Hill, N10
The site of a spring that was thought to have healing properties and named 'Mossy Well', Muswell Hill was a place of medieval pilgrimage. Later on, its impressive views over the Thames and Lea Valleys made it a popular rural retreat until – back in 1896 – key estates were bought by developer James Edmondson. He built new houses and shopping arcades, effectively creating a London suburb from scratch.

Parliament Hill, NW3
At the top of the wild and woody Hampstead Heath, you are a long way from the urban grit, but Parliament Hill offers a true natural high within the city. The extraordinary vista provides a medley of London's greatest landmarks – the Gherkin, the London Eye, the Houses of Parliament, St Paul's – and many harder-to-spot highlights.

Primrose Hill, NW3
The name sounds incredibly romantic, and the view from the top of Primrose Hill is just that. On a warm summer evening, this spot is a mecca for loved-up couples – it's the perfect cheap date in a neighbourhood of millionaires. London is laid out before you and its buildings are helpfully identified on a plaque. Visual highlights include Regent's Park and its zoo, the London Eye, and a couple of modernist icons: the BT Tower and Centrepoint.

Shooters Hill, SE18
At 433 feet, Shooters Hill is the highest point in south London. During the Middle Ages the lofty position was a favourite with archers and highwaymen took it to their hearts in the 17th century (because it was on the route of the mail coaches that ran between London and Dover). There was a gallows at the bottom of the hill, and the bodies of the hanged were displayed on a gibbet at the summit, close to where the Victorian gothic water tower now stands.

32-33

Ring church bells

If you thought bellringing was just a simple matter of pulling on a rope, think again. It's an art form, one that requires precision, a degree of physical exertion and team work. The current technique, known as change ringing, was developed in the 17th century. Don't expect to be able to ring perfectly straight away; there are plenty of practice sessions around London that welcome beginners. For more details, check out www.mcaldg.org.uk. We particularly recommend St John at Hackney (Lower Clapton Road, E5 0PD, www.stjohnathackney.org.uk, Mondays) and St Mary Abbots Kensington (Kensington High Street, W8 4HN, www.stmaryabbotschurch.org, Thursdays).

34-44 *Take your time in London's bookshops*

For some, there are few retail joys more unalloyed than an afternoon spent in a bookshop. And, with many now offering seating, and in some cases, cafés, it's become one of the capital's classic budget activities. Here are just a few of our favourite browsing haunts.

Big Green Bookshop

A community bookshop, run with a love and enthusiasm for books that's hard to find these days – and it has a sofa. As well as the expected local bookstore stock, it's strong on children's titles and multicultural books, and also has a second-hand department. The events programme is worth a look too; there are author events, children's storytelling sessions, a writers' group and a book group.
Unit 1 Brampton Park Road, N22 (8881 6767, www.biggreenbookshop.com).

Bolingbroke

After 30 years in the business, Bolingbroke is now as much a local communications hub as it is a bookshop. Stock is varied and includes interesting titles from publishers such as Eland and Persephone. Oh, and there's also a steam engine installation.
147 Northcote Road, SW11 6QB (7223 9344, www.bolingbrokebookshop.co.uk).

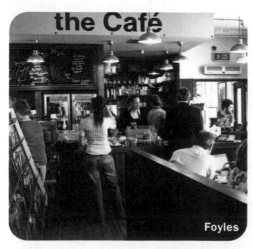

Foyles

Books for Cooks

If the range of cuisines and cookery books, plus culinary history, and food-related fiction and biographies doesn't make you hungry, then the aromatic smells coming from the tiny café at the back of the shop will. An essential browsing experience for any foodie.
4 Blenheim Crescent, W11 1NN (7221 1992, www.booksforcooks.com).

Daunt Books

A wonderful place to while away a few hours, Daunt Books is housed in a beautiful Edwardian building, complete with oak balconies, viridian walls, conservatory ceiling and a stained-glass window. The back room boasts a travel section extraordinaire but Daunt is also a good all-round bookshop: staff are well-read and dedicated, and their carefully curated picks – the best literary fiction, biography, children, design and cookery books – are dotted throughout the rest of the store.
83-84 Marylebone High Street, W1U 4QW (7224 2295, www.dauntbooks.co.uk).

Foyles

The big daddy of independent bookshops, Foyles is a London legend and a browsers' best friend. Size does matter here: 56 specialist subjects are spread across five floors. Fiction is a forte, as are music, sport, film and gay interest. Enhancing the contemplative mood is the Café at Foyles (which hosts jazz musicians every week).
113-119 Charing Cross Road, WC2H OEB (7437 5660, www.foyles.co.uk).

Hatchards

London's oldest bookshop has a refined air, but it's not too stuffy for browsing. On the contrary,

Daunt Books

the old-school charm is particularly conducive to drifting off into a literary reverie. Biography, politics, travel and fiction are strengths, and keep your eyes peeled for famous authors – the shop regularly gets in bigwigs for signings.
187 Piccadilly, W1J 9LE (7439 9921, www.hatchards.co.uk).

John Sandoe

This independent bookshop, founded in 1957, has a loyal clientele, professional staff and an enviably broad stock. New and classic releases run shoulders with more unusual items (books that have been privately printed, for example). There's a high proportion of quality hardbacks, a good travel section on the first floor and children's books in the basement. Wherever you look, the tottering piles of reading matter are a booklover's dream.
10 Blacklands Terrace, SW3 2SR (7589 9473, www.johnsandoe.com).

London Review Bookshop

In the heart of Bloomsbury, the London Review Bookshop oozes intellectual gravitas, as you'd expect from a shop owned by the esteemed periodical. If you need inspiration, you'll find it here: the impeccable selection includes politics, current affairs, history, philosophy and poetry, and the tables are piled high with cleverly chosen tomes. Walk through an archway into the adjoining London Review Cake Shop, a charming café adorned with original art.
14 Bury Place, WC1A 2JL (7269 9030, www.lrbshop.co.uk).

Magma

In some ways, design books are the ideal genre for browsing – lots of eye candy and minimal reading required. Magma is the motherlode of look-at-me coffee table books and glossy style magazines, featuring cutting-edge design, architecture and graphics. In fact, the shop's objective is to blur the boundary between bookshop and exhibition space, so quiet contemplation is highly appropriate.
117-119 Clerkenwell Road, EC1R 5BY (7242 9503, www.magmabooks.com).

Skoob

At Skoob you'll stumble across out-of-print gems, cult classics, obscure biographies and forgotten best-sellers. There are some 70,000 titles spread across 2,500 square feet and every subject under the sun is represented: from philosophy, biography, maths and science to languages, literature and criticism, art, history, economics and politics.
Unit 66, the Brunswick, WC1N 1AE (7278 8760, www.skoob.com).

Stanfords

If Daunt whets your appetite for travel, Stanfords will trigger a case of full-blown wanderlust. The shelves are bursting with books on every country, city, highway and byway. Pick up a book, a map and a latte and get planning your dream trip in the small ground floor café.
12-14 Long Acre, WC2E 9LP (7836 1321, www.stanfords.co.uk).

45-52

Look for John Soane (and find him in a telephone box)

One of Britain's greatest and most innovative architects, Sir John Soane (1753-1837) was a national treasure by the time of his death and his wonderfully idiosyncratic home, now the Sir John Soane's Museum (13 Lincoln's Inn Fields, WC2A 3BP, 7405 2107, www.soane.org), was bequeathed to the nation by Act of Parliament.

Soane believed in 'the poetry of architecture' and used his house as a testing ground for his ideas on light and space. He was a great collector, so the house is full of ingenious space-saving touches – like the panels hung with paintings that unfold from the walls. The downstairs is packed with antiquities, architectural models and art; above ground, in airy contrast, light streams through top-lit ceilings and is reflected off mirrored inserts.

But there's more to Soane than his museum – London is still full of his architectural influences. His most important commission (and the building he was most proud of) was the Bank of England. An established architectural masterpiece, it's all the more shocking that most of it was torn down after World War I.

But Soane's powerful perimeter wall remains and his first major work, the Bank Stock Office, has been reconstructed inside the Bank's Museum (Threadneedle Street, EC2R 8AH, 7601 5545, www.bankofengland.co.uk).

Purchased as Soane's country retreat in 1800, Pitzhanger Manor (Walpole Park, Mattock Lane, W5 5EQ, 8567 1227) was soon remodelled according to the architect's ideas of design and decoration and features his trademark curved ceilings and inset mirrors. Acquired by Ealing Council in 1900, the house became a library. Today the library has gone and the building has been restored to showcase Soane's work. Set in lovely Walpole Park, an extension houses a contemporary art gallery.

Dulwich Picture Gallery (Gallery Road, Dulwich, SE21 7AD, 8693 5254, www.dulwich picturegallery.org.uk) was an unlikely outcome of 18th-century European politics. Art dealers François Bourgeois and Noel Desenfans spent years gathering a spectacular assemblage of art for the King of Poland. But by 1795 Poland was partitioned, the King was kingdomless and so had no need of a royal collection. With no takers for the pictures, Bourgeois willed them to Dulwich College in 1811, stipulating that his friend Sir John Soane design a building to display them and that it be open to the public. What Soane built has been described as the most beautiful art gallery in the world and was an inspiration for countless later architects.

Set in a little Regency enclave, St Peter's Walworth (76 Tatum Road, SE17 1QR, 7703 3139) is the best preserved of Soane's three London churches, with its slim dome-topped tower, austere brick façade and Ionic portico. Its crypt is a masterful example of 19th-century brickwork. His Holy Trinity Church opposite Great Portland Street Station (Marylebone Road, NW1 4DU, www.onemarylebone.com), is now only open for events, but the exterior is eye-catching; St John's Bethnal Green (Cambridge Heath Road, E2 9PA) has been remodelled following damage in 1870 and World War II, but for Soane groupies, it's still worth a visit.

A final must-see is Soane's tomb in the atmospheric setting of St Pancras Gardens, behind St Pancras Station. Originally erected by Soane for his wife, the monument inspired the design of one of Britain's most iconic structures: Giles Gilbert Scott's K6 series of red telephone boxes.

53 *Smoke a shisha...*

Shisha, hubbly bubbly, hookah, nargileh... the names vary but the waterpipe itself is pretty much the same throughout the Middle East. London's weather may not be so congenial but there are many places where you can still sit with a friend and watch the world drift by while savouring some apple tobacco and perhaps a mint tea. The Hookah Lounge on Brick Lane is one such place; a shisha of apple tobacco here costs just £9.95.

Hookah Lounge *133 Brick Lane, E1 6SB (7033 9072).*

54 *...or snort snuff*

Meanwhile, downstairs in the confines of basement cabaret venue CellarDoor in the West End, nicotine addicts are thoughtfully offered a variety of flavours of snuff so that they don't have to go outside for a cigarette. As the venue puts it, it's 'immeasurably less antisocial than smoking and, if only someone had the foresight to ban it, infinitely cooler than coke'.

CellarDoor *Zero Aldwych WC2E 7DN (7240 8848, www.cellardoor.biz).*

55 Play skittles at the Freemasons Arms...

No, don't even mention ten-pin bowling in the same breath. That commercial, sanitised version has little to do with the ancient game and its descendent, London Skittles, which is not so much played as venerated by the Hampstead Lawn Billiard and Skittle Club. The game uses nine pins and a cheese – the wooden discus players use to knock down the pins – and involves such intricacies as the 'flying fornicator' (a cheese with bad spin) and the dreaded 'Gates of Hell' pin formation that takes expert felling. Few skittle alleys remain in London, but it's still being played, much as it has been since 1934, in the cellar at the Freemasons Arms in Hampstead. Come along on club night or book the alley for a group of friends – an experienced club member will provide help and equipment. To arrange a game contact the club at www.london skittles.co.uk.
Freemasons Arms *32 Downshire Hill, NW3 1NT (7433 6811, www.freemasonsarms.co.uk).*

56-59 ...or throw things at a 'piglet'

The Balls Brothers wine bar (Hay's Galleria, Tooley Street, SE1 2HD, 7407 4301, www.balls brothers.co.uk) runs a free pétanque pitch in the middle of the shopping arcade near London Bridge and this essential French pastime has proved such a success that there's now an annual lunchtime tournament in summer. Games are played at the Surprise pub (16 Southville, SW8 2PP, 7622 4623), on a pitch near the Chevening Road entrance to Queen's Park in north-west London (8969 5661) and, occasionally, in the square outside the Prince of Wales pub (48 Cleaver Square, SE11 4EA, 7735 9916).

The game requires no prior experience and can be played on equal terms by young and old, male and female, drunk and sober. Each of three teams or individuals has two 'boules', which they must throw in turns as near as possible to the golf ball-sized cochonnet (literally 'piglet'). The player or team whose boule is closest to the cochonnet wins. *Voilà!*

When you look at the river these days it's full of traffic – and we don't just mean day tripping cruisers. The speedy and sleek catamaran service, Thames Clippers (7001 2222, www.thames clippers.com), largely designed for commuters, is still going strong since its launch in 1999.

61 Check out 1930s gadgets at Eltham Palace

In the Domesday survey of 1086 the manor of Eltham is recorded as being in the possession of William the Conqueror's half-brother. Its estate was one of the country's largest and, for nearly six centuries, most frequented royal residences (Henry VIII spent much of his boyhood at Eltham). Gradually, however, it fell into decay, becoming a humble farm after the Civil War. In the 1930s, super-rich society couple Stephen and Virginia Courtauld built a house adjoining the 1470s Great Hall. Their new home boasted the very latest in ultra-modern art deco design and was packed with mod-cons of the day, including synchronous clocks that received a time signal direct from Greenwich; loudspeakers that piped music through all the rooms of the ground floor; a private internal telephone exchange; and a centralised vacuum cleaner system. The light-filled circular entrance hall is jaw-droppingly, cinematically glamorous, and exploring the luxurious rooms – with their wood panelling, built-in furniture, abstract carpets and decorative plaster reliefs – is enough to make Jeeves and Wooster fans swoon with delight. Even the couple's pet lemur, Mah-Jongg, enjoyed caged sleeping quarters decorated with bamboo forest murals. The extensive grounds, carefully restored to a 1930s design and complete with sunken rose garden and a rock garden with water cascades, are also well worth a wander. Admission costs £9.30 (£5.60-£8.40 reductions).

Eltham Palace *Court Yard, SE9 5QE (8294 2548, www.elthampalace.org.uk).*

62 Play tennis for free `

With some London boroughs charging nearly a tenner for an hour's worth of play, it's no wonder we're a little light on tennis talent here in the UK. Fortunately, thanks to the Tennis for Free organisation (55 Thornhill Square, N1 1BE, www.tennisforfree.com, 7609 9026), there's now no excuse for not becoming the next Andy Murray or Tim Henman. Visit the website for a list of council courts at which you can play for free.

63 Enter the Great Spitalfields Pancake Race

The pancake race is said to date back 500 years to the time when a woman, cooking at home, heard the church bells calling people to confession and ran out of her hovel, still holding her frying pan. Fast forward to the present, and there are a number of races held in London every Shrove Tuesday to mark this historic (and, let's be honest, quite possibly entirely fabricated) event. Among the best is the Great Spitalfields race: teams of four, often in fancy dress (anything from Captain Jack Sparrow to a giant bright green squid) toss pancakes as they run. Phone in advance if you want to take part (it's all done for the charity London Air Ambulance) and you'll have to bring your own frying pan (pancakes are provided). Alternatively, just show up if all you're after is the sight of daft costumes darting down the streets and pancakes hitting the pavement. There are engraved pans not only for the race winners but also for the best dressed tosser, so come imaginatively attired.

Great Spitalfields Pancake Race
7375 0441, www.alternativearts.co.uk.

64 Read a play with a playwright

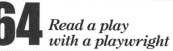

If you like your theatrical experiences interactive, then get yourself along to the Write to Play events (07973 120 270, www.inthesameboat.org.uk) hosted each month by a different modern playwright (recent writers have included Mark Ravenhill and Simon Stephens). They talk about their style and method before taking questions from the audience and – if you are so inclined – you can join in the reading of an extract from one of their plays. Tickets cost £8 and the venues change each month, so check the website for further details.

65 Explore Mars, or launch your own space probe

At the forefront of astronomy for over three centuries, the Royal Observatory now houses London's only public planetarium. Designed by architects Allies and Morrison, the RIBA-award winning concrete cone of the planetarium is clad with almost 250 bronze plates, welded together to look like a single piece. Positioning of the planetarium is minutely precise: the sloping southern side of the cone points towards the north celestial pole and pole star, the angle of the slope is the same as the degree latitude of the Royal Observatory (51° 28' 4") and the reflective glass top of the cone is sliced at an angle parallel to the celestial equator. Inside, thanks to digital laser technology, you can see Mars, Jupiter and Saturn with the untrained eye in 'The Sky Tonight' show. It's also worth saving some time for the interactive galleries upstairs where you can design and launch your very own space probe.

Royal Observatory & Planetarium
Blackheath Avenue, Greenwich Park, SE10 8XJ (8312 6565, www.nmm.ac.uk/astronomy). Planetarium £6.50.

66 Mix booze and art at Dr Sketchy's Anti Art School

Say what you want about cocaine, but the drug of choice for any artist worth their price tag has always been alcohol – a fact not lost on the organisers of Dr Sketchy's Anti Art School. This monthly craft salon manages to tuck life drawing and neo-burlesque into the same bed for a heady coitus of booze-soaked carnal whimsy. Founded in New York in 2005, this alterna-art party now has franchises in over 40 cities worldwide. Each differs in their level of conservatism – or lack thereof, some go for full nudity – but the London branch, organised by proud Chelsea Art School drop-out Ruka Johnson, follows the same format as the original: semi-naked luminaries of the burlesque scene strike unconventional poses for a happily gender-balanced class of wannabe Renoirs. Led by an irreverent host, sketchers compete in various drawing contests throughout the evening, our favourite being a challenge to interpret the model as a domestic appliance. At the end awards are handed out; prizes for the best work are, of course, bottles of alcohol – and lots of it. Tickets are £10, if you buy in advance.

Dr Sketchy's Anti Art School *various venues (www.drsketchylondon.co.uk).*

Royal Observatory & Planetarium

67-75 *Seek out 20th-century sculptures*

Great Dames of 20th-century sculpture, abstract Barbara Hepworth and figurative Elisabeth Frink, have various works sited all over the city – link them together and you've got a great day's sculpture stroll. Start your trail at Kenwood House on Hampstead Heath. After a cuppa and a scone in the tea room, in the grounds you'll find Hepworth's Monolith (*Empyrean*) from 1953, still standing proud.

Then head south-east to find Dame Elizabeth's first major public commission, *Blind Man and his Dog* (1957), at the Bethnal Green end of Roman Road. Next, it's a short hop on the Central line to St Paul's to see her *Shepherd and Sheep* (1975) in Paternoster Square, a naked man herding four Attic-looking ovine forms. Further along the Central line, near Oxford Circus, Hepworth's *Winged Figure* (1963) adorns the Holles Street façade of John Lewis on Oxford Street.

A quick walk through Mayfair to Grosvenor Square is rewarded by Frink's winged bronze bald American eagle (1986), which sits atop the World War II Eagle Squadron memorial. Head on south to find her *Horse and Rider* (1975), inspired by the stallions of the Camargue, now surrounded by the tables and chairs of Caffè Nero on Dover Street. Next, hop on a bus to Knightsbridge to see the beaten copper panels, entitled the *Four Seasons* (Frink, 1961), adorning the Jumeirah Carlton Tower Hotel on Cadogan Place.

From here, head south-west to Battersea Park, for Hepworth's lakeside *Single Form* (1961). It's a smaller version (about 10 feet tall) of her monumental piece for the United Nations in New York. One sad end note: *Two Forms* (Divided Circle), commissioned in 1970 by the Greater London Council, was stolen from Dulwich Park in December 2011.

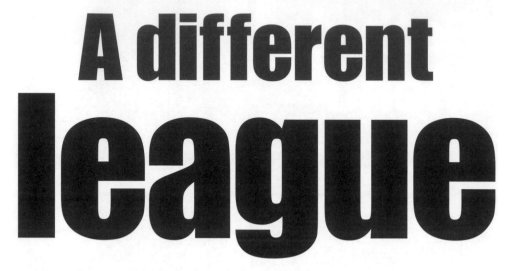

A different league

Andrew Shields gets his kicks with some cheap footie thrills.

Why pay £54 to sit behind a pillar at White Hart Lane? Or £35 to be shoehorned into Loftus Road in a plastic seat designed for a six-year-old? Professional football clubs know they have a near-stranglehold over the emotions of their fans, but control of their wallets is less secure. It's no surprise that with cash tight but the pull of live football as strong as ever, more and more supporters are acquainting themselves with London's non-league scene.

If you're used to the Premier League and are contemplating getting your fix at a lower level, you'll need to be prepared. The crowds are small – typically a couple of hundred through to a couple of thousand – and any atmosphere has to be self-generated in grounds that may be short on creature comforts. The standard of football is variable too. Even though what's known officially as 'Level 8' of the game, meaning the Ryman League Division 1, has its share of ex-pros, never-quite-made-its and young prospects, don't expect Arsenal-like wit and wizardry.

There are, however, a multitude of compensations. You will generally find camaraderie rather than antagonism among the opposing fans, and a warmth from clubs to whom your payment at the turnstile really matters. Merchandise too is rarely a rip-off. Games still kick off at the familiar time of 3pm on a Saturday afternoon and are not arbitrarily moved to suit TV schedules. You'll be up close to the action and, with none of the spectator health and safety restrictions imposed on the pro clubs' stadiums, you'll have the chance to stand rather than sit if you prefer. If you hang around afterwards, you can also probably share a pint with the big number nine you've spent 90 minutes roundly abusing.

Here are nine great non-league destinations offering history, tradition, pride, passion and a determination not merely to survive, but to thrive. And, with admission costing £10 or less at every one, you might discover that after all these years you're ditching that Spurs scarf and cheering for Enfield FC instead.

Dulwich Hamlet FC

Dulwich Hamlet FC

Hampton & Richmond FC

Steptoe & Son scriptwriter Alan Simpson is club president and has a stand named after him at the tree-fringed Beveree Stadium in the heart of salubrious Hampton village. Since the departure of former West Ham hero Alan Devonshire, the club has been led by Mark Harper, managing to stay in the Blue Square Bet Conference South. The team are saddled with one of the game's worst nicknames: the Beavers. Fans like to think of themselves as, ahem, the Beaver Patrol…

8979 2456, www.hamptonfc.net.

Enfield Town FC

Until 1999, Enfield were one of England's top amateur clubs and close to gaining admission to the Football League. Then they sold their stadium and began a series of catastrophic groundshares, which alienated most fans and led (like the well-known example of AFC Wimbledon) to the formation of fan-owned Enfield Town FC.

Christening their move to the new Queen Elizabeth II stadium in late 2011 with a win against Harefield United, the Towners are making solid progress in Division 1 North of the Ryman League. The old Enfield club was liquidated in 2007 having rebuffed a suggestion by the Enfield Town chairman that if the two clubs pooled their resources and fan base they could 'take Enfield back to the top of non-league football'. Enfield rejected the merger proposal and formed a new team of their own, competing in the Essex Senior League.

07761 814842, www.etfc.co.uk.

Carshalton Athletic FC

Surrey's oldest club (founded in 1903) and now one of the county's most active in terms of community football development, the Robins are on a mission 'to become the most friendly football club in the league pyramid'. The team's not bad either and going well in the Premier Division of the Ryman League.

8642 8658, www.carshaltonathletic.co.uk.

Clapton FC

Founder members of the Southern League along with Luton, Millwall, Reading and Southampton (Tottenham Hotspur's application was rejected), the Tons are five times winners of the FA Amateur Cup.

They became the first English team to play in Europe when they beat a Belgian XI in Antwerp way back in 1892 and then, in 1956, were the first amateur club to play under floodlights. Clapton are still based at the famous (well, slightly famous) Old Spotted Dog Ground in Forest Gate, but times are hard and they've slipped down to the modest Essex Senior League.

Bromley FC

Record attendance at the Lilywhites' Hayes Lane ground is 10,798 for a game against Nigeria, who must have been very exotic opposition back in 1950. Crowds are rather smaller these days for matches in the Blue Square Conference South (averaging around 400), but Bromley's technology is the envy of the non-league scene. The club are online pioneers in the world of London's non-league teams: they run a website carrying full video match highlights, as well as tweeting minute by minute updates on the action as it happens.
8460 5291, www.bromleyfootballclub.co.uk.

Dulwich Hamlet FC

Pink and navy striped shirts. The giants of the amateur game between the two World Wars. One of the great football addresses: Champion Hill Stadium, Dog Kennel Hill, SE22. What's not to like? When the Hamlet are playing away (they're in the Ryman League Division 1 South), you can watch tenants Fisher FC tussling in the Kent Hurlimann Football League Premier Division.
07799 500415, www.dulwichhamletfc.co.uk.

Hoddesdon Town FC

Inaugural winners of the FA Vase back in 1975, the Lilywhites (yet another club with the nickname) rather bizarrely play in the Spartan South Midlands League, despite being only 25 minutes from Liverpool Street.

They picked up last season's best programme and best pitch awards to compensate for the long away trips and have former Spurs legend Ossie Ardiles as club patron.
01992 441440, www.hoddesdontownfc.co.uk.

AFC Hornchurch

The Urchins emerged from the ruins of Hornchurch FC, who collapsed in 2004-05 when their backers went bankrupt. Grandiose plans to reach the Football League were abandoned and a roster of ex-pros on big wages proved unsustainable.

However, the reconstituted club have shown that they can be successful even with more cautious financial management. The team are currently holding their own towards the top of the Ryman League Premier Division.
01708 220080, www.afchornchurch.com.

Corinthian-Casuals FC

This is the story of a football club that has survived more than 125 years with its ideals intact.

The Corinthians were founded in 1882 (Casuals FC were established in 1878; the pair merged in 1939) as a reaction against the tide of professionalism sweeping through football in the late 19th century. They had no home ground and at first refused to enter anything as vulgar as the FA Cup. Training was outlawed and only challenge matches played. The team would refuse to take a penalty if awarded one, and would remove their goalkeeper if a spot kick was conceded, on the basis that the foul must have been serious enough to warrant a goal.

All this may sound somewhat sickly given today's style of play, but the players were genuinely talented. They inflicted Manchester United's record defeat, twice fielded the entire England side and scored 12 goals in a game against the Belgian national side.

The club spread the gospel of good sportsmanship as a globe-trotting equivalent of rugby union's Barbarians. A tour of Brazil in 1910 inspired the formation of the Corinthians Paulista club and, when they returned nearly 80 years later, the legendary international Socrates donned their kit for one game. Real Madrid adopted the Corinthians' strip in tribute and have played in white ever since.

Social change brought an end to the club's sporting superiority, though Corinthian-Casuals are battling on in Division 1 South of the Ryman League. Despite securing their first-ever home ground (King George's Field) in 1988, players are still picked off by wealthier teams.

Some things never change, though, like their spectacular chocolate and pink halved shirts. That and the first rule of the club: 'to promote fair play and sportsmanship, to play competitive football at the highest level possible whilst remaining strictly amateur and retaining the ideals of the Corinthian and the Casuals football clubs.' The greatest amateur football club ever? No contest.
8397 3368, www.corinthian-casuals.com.

ART FOR LESS

LESS THAN HALF PRICE

LESS THAN HALF PRICE

SPECIAL OFFER

HALF PRICE

£6.75
LETRASET PROMARKER
SET OF 6
RRP £13.56

SPECIAL OFFER

PREMIER PORTFOLIO
BLACK FITTINGS
A1 RRP £83.98 CASS £49.95
A2 RRP £61.43 CASS £38.50
A3 RRP £43.63 CASS £26.95
A4 RRP £31.34 CASS £21.50

£7.95
SEAWHITE A5
CONCERTINA SKETCHBOOK
70 PAGES 140GSM

£48
DALER ROWNEY
COTSWOLD EASEL
RRP £170

LESS THAN HALF PRICE

£6.95
FABER CASTELL 9000
8B-2H 12 DRAWING PENCILS
RRP £14.50

UP TO 40% OFF

ARTISTS' ACRYLIC
CADMIUM RED DEEP

SPECIAL OFFER

System 3
ACRYLIC SCREEN PRINTING SET

STEP BY STEP GUIDE
TO SCREEN PRINTING

£55
DALER-ROWNEY
SCREEN PRINTING KIT
RRP £89.50

£12.95
WINSOR & NEWTON
HENRY & WILLIAM
COLLECTION
INK SET OF 8X14ML
RRP £26.40

£60
WINSOR & NEWTON
THAMES RADIAL
EASEL RRP £190

£9.95
CASS ART
HOG BRUSH PACK
SET OF 6
RRP £21.20

£12.50
CASS ART
SYNTHETIC
BRUSH PACK
SET OF 6
RRP £28.50

£12
CASS ART
SABLE
BRUSH PACK
SET OF 5
RRP £28.50

LESS THAN HALF PRICE

WINTON
OIL COLOUR
40
Titanium White

BLANC DE TITANE
BLANC
200ml 6.75 U.S. fl.oz

FROM £4.50
WINSOR & NEWTON
ARTIST ACRYLIC 60ML

£12
WINSOR & NEWTON
WINTON OIL 200ML
TITANIUM WHITE
DOUBLE PACK
RRP £26

LESS THAN HALF PRICE

ARTISTS' BRUSHES
FOR WATERCOLOUR
OIL & ACRYLIC
SYNTHETIC

ARTISTS' BRUSHES
FOR WATERCOLOUR
SABLE

ARTISTS' BRUSHES
FOR OIL & ACRYLIC
HOG

LESS THAN HALF PRICE

LESS THAN HALF PRICE

LESS THAN HALF PRICE

£24.95
LIQUITEX
ACRYLIC BASICS SET
48 x 22ML SET
RRP £60

£4.45
DALER-ROWNEY
SYSTEM 3 ACRYLIC
250ML POT
ALL COLOURS
RRP £8.95

HALF PRICE

LESS THAN HALF PRICE

BASICS

DALER-ROWNEY
system 3
ACRYLIC

£4.50
DALER-ROWNEY
OIL PASTEL
SET OF 24
RRP £11.75

PRICE SUBJECT TO CHANGE AND AVAILABILITY. PRICES VALID AT 22/03/12.

CASS PROMISE – CREATIVITY AT THE LOWEST PRICES. WE'RE CONFIDENT OUR PRICES CAN'T BE BEATEN

CERULEAN BLUE
CADMIUM RED
LINDEN GREEN
£1 ONLY FOR OUR REUSABLE BAG!

FLAGSHIP STORE: 66-67 COLEBROOKE ROW, ISLINGTON N1
ALSO AT: 13 CHARING CROSS RD WC2 (NEXT TO THE NATIONAL GALLERY),
58-62 HEATH STREET HAMPSTEAD NW3, 220 KENSINGTON HIGH ST W8
AND 24 BERWICK ST W1. ALL STORES OPEN 7 DAYS WWW.CASSART.CO.UK

CASS ART LONDON

85

Take up orienteering

A sport that's been likened to tackling *The Times* crossword while enjoying a jog, orienteering is the art of navigating a course in the shortest possible time, using a map and compass. The British Orienteering Federation (01629 734042, www.britishorienteering.org.uk) has a list of clubs and courses and you can also buy a map of the permanent courses in London. It's a sociable sport, with regular club events (colour-coded to suit different skill levels), and an easy and family-friendly way to get some real exercise that feels just like messing about outdoors.

86-87

Attend a preview screening for free

Sites such as www.seefilmfirst.com and www.momentumsscreenings.co.uk offer the chance to see previews of new releases, without paying a penny. Sign up for a chance to catch movies such as *Shame*, *The Woman in Black* or *Haywire* (Momentum) and *Let Me In* or *Megamind 3D* (See Film First).

88

Meditate at the London Buddhist Centre

Opened in 1978 in a building that was once a Victorian fire station, this is one of the largest urban Buddhist centres in Europe. The London Buddhist Centre (51 Roman Road, E2 0HU, 8981 1225, www.lbc.org.uk) offers lunchtime and evening drop-in meditation classes (£2-£8) as well as creative writing and poetry events, retreats both on site and in the Suffolk countryside and works in the wider community through outreach projects.

89

See London by gaslight

Tired of the neon glare of the West End? Do you yearn for some ye olde city charm on your evening strolls? If so, then you'll find it, free of charge, in the parts of London still lit by gaslight. Some of the earliest street lighting in the city was established in the Royal Parks, where oil lamps were hung from the trees, but gas lighting soon followed, installed along Rotten Row in Hyde Park.

A green plaque at 100 Pall Mall commemorates Frederick Winsor, who put up London's first gas street lamps in Pall Mall in 1807 and became one of the pioneers of gas lighting in the UK and France. Born in 1763 in Brunswick, Germany, Winsor went to Paris in 1802 to investigate the 'thermo-lamp' that French engineer Phillipe Lebon had patented three years earlier. Over the next two decades, about 50,000 gaslights were installed across the city's streets.

Today, around 1,600 gaslights still illuminate central London every night. Keep your eyes peeled and in many parts of town you'll see the tell-tale bars sticking out of lampposts – before the process became automated these used to support the lamplighter's ladder. Ignore the orange glare of the city's many sodium lamps – London's standard street light – and head for the capital's grander postcodes. Fine examples of ornate lights can be seen outside Buckingham Palace, along Queen's Walk in Green Park, in St James' Park and at St James' Palace, around the Palace of Westminster and Westminster Abbey, along the Mall, in Horse Guards Parade, and at Covent Garden. Several tiny and picturesque alleys off the Strand are also still lit by gas (Bull Inn Court, Lumley Court) and there's even a gaslight in Carting Lane that is run by sewage gas – though unfortunately on recent inspection it had been bashed into by a car. Heading east into the City, the Temple is famously still gaslit, as is Charterhouse Square and the Guildhall.

90 Drive dodgems on the South Bank

If you're put off by not only the queues but the prices for the London Eye, why not nip into its neighbour, Namco Funscape (County Hall, Westminster Bridge Road, SE1 7PB, 7967 1067, www.namcofunscape-londonevents.co.uk, free admission), and drive dodgems instead. Everything at this indoor entertainment centre is token-operated, so you just pay as you go (£2.50 for the bumper cars; 1.4m height restriction applies). There are also 12 bowling lanes (£3 per person per game), US pool tables and 150 arcade games, simulators and dance machines (tokens cost 50p) and karaoke. Namco Funscape is open until midnight, and has a pub-priced bar.

91 See two for the price of one at the Riverside Studios

Better known for dance and theatre events, Riverside Studios also screens intelligently selected film retrospectives and double bills (Terence Davies, Bette Davis, Harry Potter). Ticket prices (£9.50, £8.50 reductions) come in at less than the cost of a single bill at a West End cinema.
Riverside Studios *Crisp Road, W6 9RL (8237 1111, www.riversidestudios.co.uk).*

92 Visit the Charles Dickens Museum

After the success of *The Pickwick Papers* in 1836, Dickens left his cramped chambers in Holborn and moved up to Doughty Street for three years; *Oliver Twist* and *A Christmas Carol* were written here. The building, the author's only surviving London residence, is crammed with memorabilia and artefacts. The Museum reopens in December 2012 after a £3 million redevelopment project, just in time to celebrate a Dickensian Christmas in the novelist's bicentenary year. Admission £7.
Charles Dickens Museum *48 Doughty Street, WC1N 2LX (7405 2127, www.dickens museum.com).*

93 Boost your vitamin intake at a Middle Eastern juice bar

Alongside simple orange, carrot and grapefruit and melon juices, you can sample a mixed fruit cocktail at the Lebanese Ranoush Juice (43 Edgware Road, W2 2JE, 7723 5929, www.maroush.com) for £2.50. And if juices aren't exotic enough, try *jellab* – a sweet, red-wine coloured drink with pine nuts and raisins. It's made by combining the pulp of raisins with some grape molasses, rose water and sugar, then smoking the mixture and, finally, adding the pine nuts and raisins, which float in the glass. The best time to call in at Ranoush is late on a summer night: it's an Arab London institution and the place is buzzing until closing time at 3am. There's more creative treatment of fruit over at Fresco (25 Westbourne Grove, W2 4UA, 7221 2355, www.frescojuices.co.uk), where a menu of super-healthy vegetable juices featuring the likes of cabbage, cucumber and broccoli is complemented by a huge range of fruit juices – served singly or as combos (such as mango, banana and strawberry, £2.95) – and fruity milkshakes, all served in large glasses.

Fresco

A few of my favourite things

94-99

Pappy's, comedy trio

When it's warm enough, take a trip to Tooting Bec Lido (Tooting Bec Road, SW16 1RU, 8871 7198, www.wandsworth.gov.uk), the UK's biggest outdoor swimming pool. Nothing wakes you up like a plunge in the water first thing in the morning. With the brightly painted changing cubicles and traditional atmosphere, it's the perfect place to sport a Victorian bathing suit.

Sam Smith's pubs are dotted all over central London. Here it's still possible to buy a round of drinks for under a tenner. Selling only the excellent beers produced by its own brewery, it's value and quality combined. Our favourites include the Chandos (29 St Martin's Lane, WC2N 4ER, 7836 1401) off Leicester Square and the Champion (12-13 Wells Street, W1T 3PA, 7323 1228) in Fitzrovia, with its incredible stained glass windows.

Breakfast is not only the most important meal of the day, but at the Breakfast Club (33 D'Arblay Street, W1F 8EU, 7434 2571, www.thebreakfastclubcafes.com) in Soho, by far the most enjoyable too. It does great eggs, pancakes and coffee and there is always a bustling and lively atmosphere. It's the perfect place to meet up to pretend to do some work.

Go to see the dinosaurs in Crystal Palace Park, SE20 – these enormous and haunting stone figures have dominated the lakes of Crystal Palace Park since 1854. They have since been dismissed as inaccurate representations, so now serve more as a snapshot of Victorian palaeontology than of prehistoric times. However this doesn't mean they can't still delight and terrify in equal measure.

Happy Mondays (held at the Amersham Arms, 388 New Cross Road, SE14 6TY, www.theamershamarms.com) in New Cross is a long-running comedy club that has had several different owners (ourselves included), but the one thing that hasn't changed is the fantastic line-ups and the affordable entry fee. Top TV comics such as Russell Brand, Stewart Lee, Josie Long, Stephen Merchant and Pappy's have all graced this tiny stage. In June/July you can see previews of shows headed to the Edinburgh festival for a fraction of Edinburgh prices.

Brixton Ritzy (Brixton Oval, Coldharbour Lane, SW2 1JG, 0871 704 2068, www.picturehouses.co.uk) is a gorgeous old cinema that is still in use to this day. And not just for screenings. On an average week you can expect live music, comedy, Q&As, quiz nights and events for kids. It also does excellent pizzas.

100

Watch international athletics for free at Crystal Palace

Crystal Palace's annual Grand Prix meeting gives several good reasons to head out to SE19. First, it tends to draw the niftiest movers in world athletics, from Jamaica's Usain Bolt to the UK's very own Christine Ohuruogu. Second, it takes place in late July or early August, meaning a better-than-average chance of sunshine. And third, the elevation of the surrounding park makes it possible to watch the action without a ticket. It goes without saying that you won't have a box or be in prime position with a full 400-metre panorama, but you'll be near enough to feel part of the event. And how often do you get to watch a pole vault world record attempt while walking the poodle and playing frisbee?

Crystal Palace Athletics Stadium *Crystal Palace Park, Ledrington Road, SE19 2BB (8778 0131, www.ukathletics.net).*

101-110
Pick a perfect place to picnic

There's no need to leave town to picnic in the fresh air, surrounded by trees and flowers. Concrete jungle it may be, but London is also one of the world's greenest capitals. We've rounded up ten of the city's most perfect spots from Tudor gardens to space-age parks.

Battersea Park

Once marshland and also a notorious duelling spot, the 200 acres of greenery that constitute Battersea Park (8871 7535, www.battersea park.org, free) are a far more salubrious place these days (and have also been given an £11 million Lottery-funded boost). We recommend the calming Peace Pagoda.

Fulham Palace Gardens

If you fancy sipping a crisp Chablis on the shady lawn of a lovely formal garden, head to Fulham Palace's (7736 3233, www.fulham palace.org, free) tranquil Thames-side grounds by Bishops Park. The palace and its gardens, country retreat for centuries for the medieval bishops of London, are a well-kept local picnicking secret. Full of unusual plant species, the 12 acres offer plenty to explore as well as the lawns: there's woodland, an 18th-century walled garden full of herbs, an orchard and a wisteria-clad pergola.

Ham House Gardens

Ensconce yourself on the lawns of Ham House's garden (8940 1950, www.nationaltrust.org.uk, entrance to garden only £3.30). These glorious 17th-century grounds have both formal splendour in their lavender, box and yew parterres as well as a so-called wilderness of maze-like hornbeam.

Hampstead Heath

Hampstead Heath is, of course, full of great picnic spots – and stunning views – but we especially love the slope above Highgate Pond where you can hide out in the long grass and gaze across to the City and Canary Wharf.

Holland Park

With its charmingly secluded hideaways, Holland Park has loads of great private picnic spots. If you want to make more of a splash, though, there's the Japanese garden and the lawns just north of Holland House. Just make sure you don't leave food lying around for the curious resident peacocks.

Horniman Museum Gardens

There are many good reasons to visit the Horniman Museum (8699 1872, www.horniman.ac.uk, free), but the gardens, with their roses, woodland, stange exotic shrubs and wild flowers are as enchanting a reason as any. If you are planning a trip to the museum anyway, don't forget to pack a picnic.

Regent's Park

Regent's Park can get pretty busy if the weather's good and during the holidays, but for dreamy, summer perfection, head to its northern reaches and lay out your rug near the colourful blossoms and luscious scents in the Rose Garden (www.royalparks.org.uk, 0300 061 2000, free).

Springfield Park

Hackney's Springfield Park (www.hackney.gov.uk/cp-parks-springfield.htm) is a good spot for a picnic with a view: nibble cucumber sandwiches while looking out over the River Lee, with its narrow boat marina, and the Hackney Marshes beyond.

Thames Barrier Park

A masterpiece of contemporary landscape gardening, it's worth making the effort to get to the Thames Barrier Park (7476 3741, www.thamesbarrierpark.org.uk, free). Plonk yourself in the midst of 22 acres of lawns, trees and surreal yew and maygreen topiary and look out over the mighty silver shells of the Thames Barrier.

Waterlow Park

Try the lawns of Highgate's Waterlow Park (www.waterlowpark.org.uk, free) for more exhilarating views of London as well as three spring-fed ponds. Sweeping down the steep face of Highgate Hill, the scene is dotted with elegant, mature trees framing a fabulous view of the City's skyscrapers.

Hunt for Horatio Lord Nelson

At least we know where to start: Nelson stands three-times life size – but then he was only five and a half feet tall – 145 feet up in the centre of Trafalgar Square, so named after his final, fatal victory over Napoleon's fleet in 1805. Even so, the most popular military hero in British history didn't rise to this distinction until almost 40 years after his death, when his statue was finally placed on his column in 1843. He faces south-west, into the prevailing winds, and towards the fleet at Portsmouth. Visit the National Portrait Gallery for a fine view of the back of his tricorn hat from the eighth floor bar; alternatively, go and look at one or more of its ten portraits of him in the primary collection (they have at least 57 more in the archives), which is bound to be on display somewhere in the gallery.

From here, head towards Mayfair via Soho and 33A Dean Street (now Gino's barbershop) which, as Walker's Hotel, was where Nelson spent his last night in London before heading off for Trafalgar. He set up home at 5 Cavendish Square, with his new,

and soon to be long-suffering, wife Frances. Although they only lived here for four years, much was made of the fact that his address was to be used as a YMCA for US officers towards the end of the World War I.

After this, make your way to the Royal Arcade, at 28 Old Bond Street, once the first premises of Dollond & Aitchison, the firm from which Nelson bought a telescope after losing an eye attacking Corsica in 1793. He also lodged nearby in New Bond Street on his return from the Battle of Cape St Vincent in 1797. (In the same year, he lost his right arm at the Battle of Santa Cruz, off Tenerife.) The Goat Tavern, at 3 Stafford Street, was a favourite haunt he later used for shenanigans with his mistress Lady Hamilton.

Trade in Nelson memorabilia was huge after his death and a trail of his personal effects can be tracked down around town: the shoe buckles that he wore at Trafalgar are on the wax effigy in the Westminster Abbey Museum (20 Dean's Yard, SW1P 3PA, 7222 5152, www.westminster-abbey.org),

as well as some of his clothes; his razor is in the Wellcome Museum of the History of Medicine at the Science Museum; and his solid gold, combined knife and fork, made for a left-hander and given to him by Countess Spencer, is in the Lloyd's Nelson collection exhibition. (You can see this on the trading floor during a tour of One Lime Street, EC3M 7HA, 7327 1000. Contact tours@lloyds.com or wait for Open House weekend.) The collection also includes Nelson's favourite breakfast plate, his collar for the Order of the Bath and Lady Hamilton's toothpick box. The jewel-encrusted sword, also designed for a left-hander, presented to him with the Freedom of the City in 1800, is on display in the Expanding City gallery at the Museum of London.

Nearby, you can find a fine statue of our hero, sculpted in 1810 by James Smith, in the Guildhall Art Gallery, but then it's high time you made tracks to Greenwich, the official home of Horatio worship. The Nelson Gallery at the National Maritime Museum (Romney Road, SE10 9NF, 8858 4422, www.nmm.ac.uk, free) houses the clothes he was wearing at Trafalgar (see the musket-ball-hole in the shoulder) among other fantastic artefacts. Then there's the Coade stone Nelson Pediment above the King William Block of the Old Royal Naval College, inspired by the Elgin Marbles, and showing Neptune bringing the admiral's body to Britannia.

Real devotees should also visit Southside House (Woodhayes Road, SW19 4RJ, 8946 7643, www.southsidehouse.com), which he enjoyed visiting with Emma Hamilton when she was living nearby at Merton Place. Also check out the Marine Society & Sea Cadets headquarters (202 Lambeth Road, SE1 7JW, 7654 7000, www.ms-sc.org), where one of Nelson's flags is kept.

Finally, no hunt for Horatio would be complete without visiting his tomb in St Paul's Cathedral. His black marble sarcophagus was originally designed for Cardinal Wolsey, who had died over 200 years earlier.

Meet the author

You can listen to, and perhaps even meet, your favourite writers at book signings, author readings and in-store discussions. All bookshops, from tiny local ones to giant chains, hold these events as a way of encouraging sales. Waterstones, for example, has details of 'an evening with…' events on their website, (www.waterstones.com). The Piccadilly flagship branch has seen names ranging from Scandinavian crime writer Håkan Nesser to Prue Leith; tickets are usually £5. Daunt Books (www.dauntbooks.co.uk) has regular events with authors such as William Boyd and Alexander McCall Smith (£8 including wine).

MasterCard Priceless Tip

Get exclusive access to the very best London has to offer with your MasterCard. From theatre to music, dining to shopping, museums to days out at www.pricelesslondon.co.uk

113

Eat pie and mash at Manze's

You only need to glance briefly at the seedier burger joints around town to understand that cheap food often also means cheap decor. We know London's got loads of good-value places to eat, but it's rare that you'll be spending less than a fiver on food in as lovely surroundings as those at Manze's on Tower Bridge Road. London's oldest pie and mash shop (eels – jellied and stewed – also available, of course) was established in 1902 by the present owner's grandfather, Michele Manze, of Ravello in southern Italy, and the same art nouveau-style green and cream tiles grace the walls as did back then. Those solid wooden benches also look like they've done decades' worth of sterling service propping up hungry folk.

M Manze's *87 Tower Bridge Road, SE1 4TW (7407 2985, www.manze.co.uk).*

EAT

PIE & LIQUOR
PIE 1 MASH
PIE 2 MASH
PIE 1 MASH
PIE 2 MASH
EELS & MASH
JELLIED EELS
DRINKS

114-118 Tour the capital's breweries

Mass-produced lagers are not only a burden on your taste buds but on your wallet as well. By way of therapy, we recommend a visit to one of London's breweries to get you in the mood for cheaper and tastier ales. The Fuller's brewery in Chiswick (Chiswick Lane South, W4 2QB, 8996 2175, www.fullers.co.uk) is open for two-hour guided tours at £10 a pop. At the other end of the scale, Brodie's Beers (816a High Road Leyton, E10 6AE, 07976 122 853, www.brodiesbeers.co.uk) is a tiny operation run by brother and sister team James and Lizzie Brodie, who concoct a variety of beers in all sorts of styles. Tours are free. Sambrooks Brewery (Unit 1 & 2 Yelverton Road, SW11 3QG, 7228 0598, www.sambrooksbrewery.co.uk) sources all ingredients from within 100 miles and holds open evenings (7pm Mon-Thur, 1pm, 3pm Sat; £10 Mon Thur, £12 Sat). Kernel Brewery (98 Druid Street, SE1 2HQ, 07757 552636, www.thekernelbrewery.com), makes award-winning ales that can be sampled in situ on Saturdays. Zero Degrees in Blackheath (29-31 Montpelier Vale, SE3 0TJ, 8852 5619, www.zerodegrees.co.uk) is a bar with it's own microbrewery – phone for details of free tours.

119 Visit Ernö Goldfinger's House

James Bond author and Hampstead resident Ian Fleming was so enraged by this modernist creation on Willow Road that he used the name of its architect – Ernö Goldfinger – for one of his greatest villains. Built in 1939, 2 Willow Road was the architect's home until his death (Goldfinger had fled Hitler's Europe and, like many émigré artists and intellectuals of the time, settled in leafy Hampstead). The furniture was designed specially for the house and there is lots of clever living space and plenty of storage. And with Goldfinger's books and art collection still in place you'll feel as though the man has just stepped out for a stroll on the Heath.
2 Willow Road *NW3 1TH (7435 6166, www.nationaltrust.org.uk). £5.80.*

120 Spot a stenchpipe

Stenchpipes, AKA stinkpipes, can be spotted all over London. They're Victorian, built at the same time as the city's sewerage system, to allow noxious gases to escape (well above head height). Once you've noticed one, you'll see them everywhere – if you don't believe us, just check out http://stinkpipes.blogspot.com. Try finding the one in Addison Square, Camberwell, or the fine crowned one on Kennington Road. Some are even listed, such as the one near Parliament Fields Lido, at the entrance to the park off Gordon House Road.

121

People-watch at the National Portrait Gallery...

Possibly your best bet for celebrity spotting – on canvas and film – this is one of our favourite London galleries. The prestigious BP Portrait Award and the Taylor Wessing Photographic Portrait Prize are both annual highlights. The permanent collection is free, although some exhibitions carry an entrance fee.
National Portrait Gallery *St Martin's Place, WC2H 0HE (recorded information 7312 2463, www.npg.org.uk).*

122

...then animal-watch at the Natural History Museum

From October to March, the Natural History Museum hosts the annual Wildlife Photographer of the Year exhibition, which attracts submissions from all over the world. The winning shots, displayed for around six months, have interesting explanations of the conditions under which they were taken. Admission to the exhibition costs £9 (the museum is free).
Natural History Museum *Cromwell Road, SW7 5BD (7942 5000, www.nhm.ac.uk).*

123

See the world at the Greenwich and Docklands International Festival

Billed not unreasonably as 'London's most spectacular free festival', the Greenwich and Docklands International Festival (8305 1818, www.festival.org) throws up all the eccentricities of urban multiculturalism. A host of different venues – from the O2 and Cutty Sark Gardens to the Royal Observatory – have welcomed giant French caterpillars, tango demonstrations and a South Asian dance/football fusion. A June slot makes it a colourful portal into the summer.

124
Hear voices at the British Library Sound Archive

There are 3.5 million recordings in the British Library's Sound Archive, which is one of the most extensive facilities of its kind in the world and includes published and unpublished material dating back to the late 19th century. Founded in 1955, the collections are now divided into six main sections: classical music, featuring many rare and unpublished recordings; literature (including the voices of James Joyce, Antonin Artaud, Leo Tolstoy, William Burroughs, Kurt Schwitters and Sylvia Plath) and drama (which also holds video recordings); oral history, including unpublished interviews with historic figures like Churchill as well as commercial recordings (there's an oral history of Tesco); wildlife sounds, including the work of the RSPB; and popular, international and traditional music (published and unpublished). It's also the main point of public access to archived BBC Radio broadcasts. The easiest way to get a flavour of the extraordinary scope of the collection is to visit a SoundServer in Humanities, Floor 2, or, if you have specific requests, make a listening appointment beforehand. The Sound Archive also accepts published and unpublished recordings from the public if they are suitable (in three of the basic categories – spoken word, music, wildlife). If you are interested, send recordings to the address below.

Sound Archive Information Service *British Library, Sound Archive, 96 Euston Road, NW1 2DB (7412 7447, www.bl.uk).*

125
Catch the BP Summer Big Screens

In an attempt to bring opera out of its elite closet, the Royal Opera House is continuing its annual tradition of screening its most popular work for free in Trafalgar Square and other locations around central London. Screenings happen on various dates between May and July. Check the website for details. *www.roh.org.uk.*

126 Get a handle on Handel

The baroque composer George Frederic Handel moved from Germany to Britain in 1710, aged just 25, having secured the position of *kappelmeister* to George, Elector of Hanover and soon to be King George I of England. He received an annual salary of £200 and by 1723 had established himself comfortably in his London home, where he lived for 36 years until his death in 1759. The house, in Mayfair, is now a museum and provides a good opportunity to get under the skin of the great man.

The interior has been lovingly restored and includes some beautiful replica instruments. The best way to get the feel for it is at the recitals of baroque music that take place every Thursday (and occasionally on Tuesday) and regularly at the weekends (£9, reductions £5).

Handel House Museum *25 Brook Street, W1K 4HB (7495 1685, www.handelhouse.org).*

127
Hear leather on willow at Walker Ground

Back in cricket's heyday, crowds of up to 10,000 would flock to watch United All England XI play titanic matches at Walker Ground. Established in 1855 by the seven cricket-mad Walker brothers who lived locally and who went on to found Marylebone Cricket Club (MCC) and Lord's, Walker Ground is one of the capital's oldest and perhaps most idyllic cricket fields. Today the it's home of Southgate Cricket Club, and located as it is by pretty Southgate Green, surrounded by tall oaks with the spire of Christ Church rising above the treetops, you can squint and imagine that you're deep in the English countryside. Post match, head for Ye Old Cherry Tree on the Green for refreshments. The MCC play regularly at the ground, check the website for match schedules.

Southgate CC *Walker Ground, Waterfall Road N14 7JZ (8886 8381, www.southgatecc.com).*

128 *Go bargain hunting in Bermondsey*

Up until 1995, Bermondsey Market enjoyed *marché ouvert* status thanks to a medieval loophole law, which handily made it legal to buy and sell goods of dodgy provenance during the hours of darkness. Now, with the rise of eBay, changing fashions in antiques and the redevelopment of Bermondsey Square, the market stallholders have to work harder to earn a crust – and so do punters looking for a bargain. But Bermondsey is still a market traders' market, where antiques change hands between traders from all over the country, and there are still some great deals to be had. If you're up at dawn, have a root around in the 'everything £1' boxes, which are full of pre-loved, worn out and eminently curious vintage knick-knackery.

Bermondsey Antiques Market *Bermondsey Square, SE1 3UN (www.bermondseysquare.co.uk).*

129
Have a cup of rosie with a cabbie

If you look carefully you'll find a few curious little green huts scattered across the city. Like stray (if rather posh) garden sheds, these are Cabman's Shelters – London institutions that date back to the 1870s, when the Earl of Shaftesbury and his philanthropist chums set up a charity to provide cabbies with 'wholesome refreshments at moderate prices'. Of the 61 original shelters, only a dozen remain (among them those at Chelsea Embankment, Hanover Square, Russell Square, Temple Place, and opposite the Victoria & Albert Museum). You'll wonder how they can possibly accommodate a working kitchen plus up to ten cab drivers. Pop by for a chat and eyebrow-raising tales of recent celebrity fares. If you ask nicely you may be served a cup of Rosie Lee (tea), for the absolutely princely sum of 50p.

130

Eat in Brixton Village

Once a rundown arcade, Brixton Village is now home to more than 20 new cafés, restaurants and takeaways and has become Brixton's culinary and cultural hub. Not all eateries here will leave you with a bill for under £10 a head, but many manage this feat, including Elephant (07590 389 684), a tiny Pakistani café (own-made samosas, curries, three types of thali); Honest Burgers (7733 7963, www.honest burgers.co.uk), which uses beef from Ginger Pig; French & Grace (http://saladclub.word press.com), where the short Mediterranean menu lists a selection of salads, wraps and the odd hot dish (lamb stew on our last visit); and vintage-minded Relay Tea Room (www.relay-boutique.blogspot.com), which specialises in tea served in mismatched crockery, and own-made bakes, open sandwiches, quiches and soups. **Brixton Village** *Atlantic Road & Coldharbour Lane, SW9.*

131
Visit London's loveliest public lavatory

Featuring heavily in Joe Orton biopic *Prick up your Ears*, the palatial grade II-listed public loos next to the bus terminus at South End Green, NW3, were the recent benefactor of a £50,000 renovation courtesy of the National Lottery. Built in 1897 by the London and North Western Railway, it's now a positive pleasure to visit such a historic temple of convenience, all vaulted ceilings and cream and green Doulton tiles. If you don't think it's worth trekking across town just to visit a loo, it's also conveniently located for Hampstead Heath.

132
Get shown the money at the Bank of England Museum

Attached to the Bank of England itself, this museum is housed in a replica of the original 18th-century bank's interior, designed by Sir John Soane. As part of the exhibition you can test the weight of a real-life gold bar (28lbs). You can also discover how *Wind in the Willows* creator Kenneth Grahame foiled an armed bank robber in a permanent display on the author who worked here for 30 years and was Secretary of the Bank from 1898 to 1908. **Bank of England Museum** *Bartholomew Lane, EC2R 8AH (7601 5545, www.bankofengland.co.uk). Free.*

133
Tour the BBC

For your £9.95 (£9.25 concessions) you get an award-winning visit to the TV studios and BBC News, and, intriguingly, 'a play in the interactive studio'. Plus, in the two hours or so that you're in White City's giant television centre there's always the potential added bonus of bumping into your favourite Beeb star in the hallowed broadcasting corridors. *www.bbc.co.uk/tours.*

Crunch clubbing

The gloomy economic future signals good times ahead for London's clubbers, argues Kate Hutchinson.

While the economic climate is ominous, credit crises have often proved a catalyst for radical change in clubland. Look at 1920-1930s New York with its now iconic speakeasy culture and frenetic jazz sessions. At the same time Berlin saw the birth of bohemian and sexually ambiguous cabaret – another trend currently very much in favour in London. In the UK raving took off in the wake of the Black Monday financial crisis, a disaster that tarred Thatcher's Britain.

You only have to step outside in east London to witness the effects that rave culture has had. Crowds congregate outside every conceivable clubbing space, from converted railways arches and old pubs to deserted tube stations and shop fronts, and you can find groups of ravers bent over their smartphones and scratching their heads as they try and devise a trail to parties at secret warehouse locations across the district.

Because, as Shoreditch becomes more and more like a true sister to Soho, with neon signs advertising cocktails and troupes of hen dos storming the streets in neon wigs and tutus, its trendsetters are still redefining how we go out. And, as in the 1980s, when acid house culture took off, today's trendsetters are throwing parties at any illicit or alternative large venue they can find.

The number of available underground warehouses-style spaces has boomed in the past two years and party peddlers have looked away from Shoreditch and out into far edgier parts of Hackney for deserted venues to take over. Netil House in London Fields is one such licensed and in-demand warehouse space, and its new sister venue, Hackney Downs Studio, is a whopping 70,000 square feet of hedonist heaven on the outskirts of Stoke Newington. Meanwhile, in London Bridge and Borough, car park raves are all the rage at vast concrete spaces on Great Suffolk Street and Ewer Street.

But back in Hackney, Dalston, is the sparkling new pearl of London's clubbing scene, with its thrilling balance of underground basement dives and established party haunts. Clubbing on the cheap has not always been the norm in the capital – traditionally, partying in London meant carrying wads of cash to get you

Notting Hill Arts Club

past the velvet rope – but here you'll rarely find a party that costs more than a fiver to get into.

The age of superclubs with extortionate cover charges – in London, anyway – is drawing to a close. Only Fabric and Ministry of Sound can rival the size and quality, not to mention entry fees, of the clubs that have gone before them. And even if they wanted to party in bigger venues, with the disappearance of legendary large-scale clubs such as the Cross, Canvas, the Key, Turnmills, the Astoria and the End in the last five years, Londoners have become accustomed to expecting a great night out, with superb DJs and live music, for next to nothing. And with travel costing almost as much as the entrance fee, people are looking for nights out that are closer to home. For that reason we've split up our selection of top venues by area.

East

East London is a well-established, but still vibrant, after-dark playground for art school types, up-and-coming musicians, artists and armies of media monkeys, and it's also the new frontier for London's alternative gay scene. Competition for crowds is fierce and so it's easy to find an inexpensive nightspot.

Shoreditch is an obvious starting point. Head first to the Old Blue Last (7739 7033,

www.theoldbluelast.com) where the hipster mix of heavy rock, electronic and R&B party jams encapsulates Shoreditch's trendy, youthful style. It's owned by *Vice* magazine so expect an above average quota of so-over-it coolsters. On the plus side there are great bands, and DJs from the best music blogs, until late and for free most nights. Of the varied and ever-changing programme, exciting electro-edged party crew Deadly People throw their club showcases here every month with a forward-thinking bevy of live laptop-manglers, while, at the noisier end of the scale, in-house nights such as Pink Mist go for punk, hardcore and metal.

Likewise, the sticky-floored Catch bar (7729 6097, www.thecatchbar.com) is a lasting bastion of Hoxton cool. It still has a clutch of reliably great club nights, like baile funk mainstay Yo Mama! and eclectic pop party the Trilogy, but ravers have migrated back towards Old Street and the allure of new venues XOYO (7490 1198, www.xoyo.co.uk) and the Camp (7253 2443, www.thecamplondon.com). The former (run by the people behind long-running electronic party/label Bugged Out, groundbreaking acid house fanzine and party Boys Own and Field Day festival), attracts some of the best clubbing brands in London, such as Scandalism (for electro-disco and bass), Bedrock (for house) and, of course, Bugged Out themselves. But it's also a new hotspot for filthy dubstep and drum 'n' bass bangers, as the club teams up with parties and labels like Basslaced, Planet Mu and Wheel & Deal for the weekly (and value for money) XOYO Presents.

It's into the Hackney abyss that the party scene is really taking off, where basement dives line the streets and a true sense of unbridled and anti-commercial hedonism rules.

The Camp's industrial-styled basement, meanwhile, is a favourite for its underground tech, minimal and house nights. The upstairs bar, however, is usually free entry – look out for the especially fun (and tongue-in-cheek) Hipsters Don't Dance, which boasts pure bashment and dancehall vibes for clubbers who most certainly do know how to work it on the dancefloor.

Similar wayward antics can be found on the eastern side of Shoreditch. The Book Club (7684 8618, www.wearetbc.com) is a lovely two-floor social club with cocktails and DJs spinning chilled out tunes on the first level, with raucous basement party antics below. The Electro-Swing Club is a huge hit here for its inventive mix of vintage swing and big band beats laced with electro, breaks and even drum 'n' bass, while east London's burgeoning disco-house scene is represented by regular party One Bad Habit and its raft of guest DJs including exciting label Futureboogie and old-school house don Robert Owens. And all for under a tenner!

But it's up Kingsland Road and into the Hackney abyss that the party scene is really taking off, where basement dives line the streets and a true sense of unbridled and anti-commercial hedonism rules. Take for example the Shacklewell Arms (7249 0810, www.shacklewellarms.com) (emphasis on the shack part…). It's a longtime Dalston dive and pub, now owned by the people behind the Lock Tavern, yet it has retained its original decor – dodgy tropical-themed murals, signs for 'the dancehall' inside – and edgy programming. Music falls on the experimental side of electronic, with parties such as Feeding Time, Beach Creep and Lanzarote keeping the chin-stroking locals enthralled, but they've the odd mixed and gay night (Homoelectric and Hot Boy Dancing Spot) and girly electro-disco rave-up (Lovesick and Club Motherfucker) in the mix too.

Equally as new and exciting is the Nest (www.ilovethenest.com). The basement club (they all are around here) is in what was Bardens Boudoir, the original Dalston indie venue, but has taken the hallowed space's sound in a fresher direction. Its weekly Saturday party Lemonade is the physical equivalent of Annie Mac's Radio 1 show, crammed with cool electro, disco, house and rock 'n' rave tunes, while its in-house Friday nighter attracts the cream of the DJ crop from across the electronic spectrum, with names like Rustie, Gesaffelstein and Modestep stepping up.

Over the road, the Alibi (7249 2733, www.the alibilondon.co.uk) is an underground labyrinth of mirrors, booths and dancefloors, loved for its nightly free entry and roll call of achingly hip bassline-driven nights such as Wifey, Yeah Maybe and Get Me!. Next door is where it all started, though: Dalston Superstore (7254 2273, www.dalstonsuperstore.com) spearheaded Dalston's creative renaissance in 2009 and still pulls huge crowds into its intense and pitch-black dancefloor. Upstairs, alternative drag cabaret stars line the bar and whip revellers into shape with their sharp one-liners, while downstairs goes for a typically east London mix of classic and cutting-edge music – mainly house – which could be anything from vogueing stompers (at the bi-monthly Paris Acid Ball) to acid (at monthly session Society).

Further afield, the polysexual fashion elite assemble for no-frills nights at Stoke Newington speakeasy Vogue Fabrics (www.voguefabrics dalston.com), or cram into brand new venue the Waiting Room (175 Stoke Newington High

Street, no phone/web), which is where N16 locals go for a cheap night out in an intimate setting.

North

Trendy boozers have well and truly taken over north London. They're filled with top-quality DJs and bands, serve pub-price drinks and have low entry fees. No wonder they're so popular. The Westbury in Kilburn (7625 7500, www. westburybar.com) and the Old Queen's Head in Islington (7354 9993, www.theoldqueens head.com) are such heaving places. The former favours urban flavours on the decks – think hip hop, R&B and UK garage – with turntablists such as DJ Yoda and Krafty Kuts passing through, plus regular beats bash Southern Hospitality. At the latter pub-club, you'll find indie-er fare, where offbeat music website the Quietus, and Goldierocks' rockin' radio show, the Selector, have monthly parties.

Camden, although stagnating in a swamp of trilby-toting Hawley Arms hangabouts, still has a few diamonds up its sleeve. Namely the Lock Tavern (7482 7163, www.lock-tavern.co.uk), which, despite its diminutive size, packs in the cool kids at the weekends. Its all-day Sunday shindigs are a rite of passage for any seasoned clubber and are nearly always free to get in. Or, down towards Mornington Crescent, swing past the high street's latest fixture, the Blues Kitchen (7387 5277, www.theblueskitchen.com), for late-night '50s and '60s treats – or, for more modern sounds, the all-new Wheelbarrow pub (www.wheelbarrowlondon.com) next door.

Over at King's Cross, the legendary trio of superclubs – the Key, the Cross and Canvas – may be long gone, but the brand new University of the Arts campus has thrust a new wave of creative youngsters into the area. Entrance to longstanding fixture the Big Chill House is still less than a fiver at the weekend, while whiskey-lined watering hole the Lexington (7837 5371, www.thelexington.co.uk), which puts on the coolest bands from America, is free-£15. Multi-floored York Way club EGG (7871 7111, www.egglondon.net) is still a draw for its fierce and very late-night techno beats, though it's only cheap to get in early on in the night. For a more offbeat night, try shop-cum-café-cum-club Drink, Shop & Do (7278 4335, www.drinkshopdo.com), which draws both cocktail-guzzling City girls and quirky, crafty types.

West

For clubbers, West London centres around the Notting Hill Arts Club (7460 4459, www.notting hillartsclub.com). Its brilliant programming features endless multimedia dance parties, from hip hop to tropical electronica. Seb Chew and Leo Greenslade's Thursday nighter YoYo is a must: its DJs mash together some of the best R&B, '80s boogie, hip hop, ragga and Bmore beats around live sets from tipped-for-the-top acts and secret performances from some of the biggest – everyone from Lily Allen to Odd Future has taken the stage here. During the rest of the week, parties work it to a world music and old-school funky beat – Bristolian ska and reggae veteran DJ Derek, now in his seventies, still holds a monthly residency, while Alan McGee's famed indie shindig Death Disco is free entry every Wednesday. It's no longer the only decent clubbing space in west London, either – you'll find cutting-edge house and techno nights at converted photography studio the Loft (77-82 Scrubs Lane, NW10 6QW) in Kensal Rise and, nearby, cheap yet chic gastro-pub-party times at the Paradise (8969 0098, www.theparadise.co.uk).

South

Down south, the increasingly gentrified Brixton is a nightlife mecca. Try the Dogstar (7733 7515, www.anticltd.com), a gold-corniced DJ bar that has always had its finger on the pulse: we recommend Audiosushi every Saturday with its bleeping catherine wheel of electro, house, dubstep, drum 'n' bass, funk, reggae and hip hop block party – all for a maximum £5.

Elsewhere in Brixton, Plan B (7733 0926, www.plan-brixton.co.uk) hones in on quality hip hop every Friday (£5, £3 before 11pm), while, around the corner, Brixton stalwart Jamm (7274 5537, www.brixtonjamm.org) hits the rave mark with excellent, value-for-money programming. Local legends such as Alabama 3 and Basement Jaxx, or some of the capital's best dub-reggae sound systems, are always shaking the speakers at the weekend. For more eclectic and world beats, however, up-and-coming club hubbub Hootananny (7737 7273, www.hootananny brixton.co.uk) is just the ticket, especially its bananas Balkan bash Stranger than Paradise, which is monthly and features bands and even the odd burlesque beauty for your £3 entry fee.

FREE CUBAN SALSA
Tuition from 9pm to 9:30pm with top international guest instructors

JUNGLE FEVER
LAUNCH PARTY ON **14TH APRIL**

THE ULTIMATE SATURDAY NIGHT LATIN EXPERIENCE!

@ Rainforest Cafe, a tropical hideaway in the heart of the West End

LIVE ACTS

With some of Latin America's leading **live musicians, dancers and DJ's** within a remarkable setting, recreating the sights of the Rainforest, tropical rain showers & cascading waterfalls.

2 FLOORS

Main room: Salsa, Merengue, Bachata, Timba & Reggaeton
Brazilian room: Samba, Samba rock, Funk, Forro and the perfect blend of global music with a Brazilian twist!

EAT, DRINK & DANCE!

Club: Saturdays 9pm-2am
Entry: £12 or £8 Guest list - just join our events on Facebook: www.facebook.com/cubaneandosalsaclasses
Dress code: Smart - No Caps or Hoods
VIP area available

A WILD PLACE TO SHOP AND EAT ®

Rainforest Cafe
20 Shaftesbury Ave, London W1D 7EU,
(Nearest tube: Piccadilly Circus)
For table bookings contact: 020 7434 3111
sales@therainforestcafe.co.uk

ORGANIZED BY:

www.cubaneando.com • www.oibrasilshows.com
Tel: 07950184131

Rio Samba Shows

Over in Peckham, it's going off like a rave rocket, too. Counter-cultural warehouse space the Bussey Building (www.thebusseybuilding.com) is a particular draw. As well as hosting studios from local artist collectives, its café, CLF Arts, is a favourite for nights such as Horse Meat Disco, Secretsundaze and Rob Da Bank's Sunday Best Label, as well as for jungle, dub and even soul parties, too.

Central and West End

The central scene has shrivelled, thanks to strict licensing laws and a boom in property development, leaving mostly cheesy gay Soho discos and slick (read: very expensive) members-only and slebby Mayfair clubs.

But for the ultimate in budget discos, the Social (7636 4992, www.thesocial.com) is a must. A party staple for years, it still packs a (cheapo) punch with its popular mid-week nights: Hip Hop Karaoke has wannabe rappers bouncing off the walls every Thursday, and the newer and dancehall-fuelled Madd Raff every Wednesday attracts the capital's best hip-winders. Its all-new assortment of Friday and Saturday nights can be more of a sonic gamble, but Friday Night Disco, from Guilty Pleasure's femme fatale Anna Greenwood, and Players Ball, an ATL-style hip hop night, are sure fire hits.

An equally a winning formula is Madame Jojos (7734 3040, www.madamejojos.com) in Soho. Tuesday night, White Heat, is still where to catch new indie and electronic talent before anyone else, and Friday and Saturday nights keep the lager louts at bay with their discerning yet dancefloor-focused mix of rockabilly, deep funk, soul, mambo, boogaloo and more from seasoned vintage DJs Snowboy, Keb Darge and Andy Smith.

For more retro rhythms, Jukebox Jam at the Alley Cat (7836 1451, www.alleycatbar.co.uk), a basement bar on Soho's infamous Tin Pan Alley, is a haven for vintage R&B, with a fabulously dressed crowd jumpin' and jivin' for a mere £7. Meanwhile, long-running Soho joint St Moritz caters for more of the same every Thursday, when Gaz's Rockin' Blues (www.gazrockin.com) takes over, adding ska, reggae, rocksteady and jive to the mix – as Gaz Mayall has been doing for less than £10 for the last 20 years.

159

Keep up with the cutting edge at the Free Range Graduate Art Fair

The annual Free Range Graduate Art and Design Summer Show has become a serious event in the art world's calendar since its first show eight years ago. Displaying the work of over 3,000 graduate students from some of the UK's leading art colleges, and held each year over 11 acres in Brick Lane's enormous Old Truman Brewery, it's also one of the world's largest art fairs. You'd be hard pressed to buy anything for under a tenner, admittedly, but admission to the vast display of artworks covering a multitude of different media is free and a perfect way to spot the YBAs of the future. The exhibition runs between May and July each year.
www.free-range.org.uk.

160-167

Examine the city's sick past in London's medical museums

Considering London's past record of poverty-ridden slums, overcrowding and successive immigrant influxes, it's no wonder that the city is also blessed with a rich medical history. There are more than 20 locations listed by the London Museums of Health and Medicine website (www.medicalmuseums.org): wherever you turn, the work of early nurses, surgeons, pharmacists, anaesthetists and hospitals is being dissected and displayed.

Kick off your consultation at the atmospheric attic home of the Old Operating Theatre Museum and Herb Garret (9a St Thomas Street, SE1 9RY (7188 2679, www.thegarret.org.uk, £6), tucked behind London Bridge station. Climb the steep spiral staircase to the top of the baroque church of St Thomas's and stumble through the beautifully ramshackle apothecary store to a pre-antiseptic surgical theatre where students once crammed in to watch amputations, gallstone removals and trepanning operations. You can still feel the grooves in the original wooden operating table where unwashed saws once hacked through nervous patients.

For a more clinical approach, head for the Hunterian Museum at the Royal College of Surgeons (35-43 Lincoln's Inn Fields, WC2A 3PE, 7869 6560, www.rcseng.ac.uk/museums,

ld Operating Theatre and Herb Garret

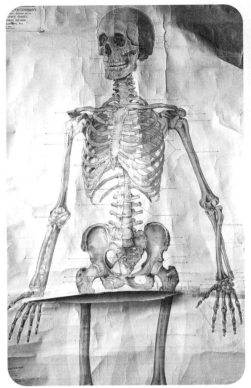

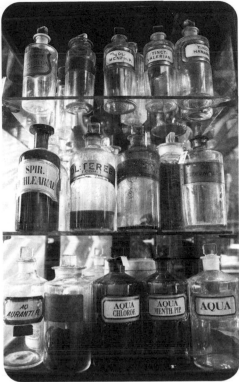

free). Packed with swish, display cases of gruesome specimens and scary surgical instruments, the 400-year-old collection also includes distorted skeletons, before and after photographs of early plastic surgery and video presentations of modern operations. You can even peek at Charles Babbage's brain and Winston Churchill's dentures.

More interested in non-surgical interventions? Pop into the foyer of the Lambeth-based Royal Pharmaceutical Society of Great Britain (1 Lambeth High Street, SE1 7JN, 7572 2211, www.rpsgb.org/museum, free). The tools of the trade on display include pill presses and brand name medicines from the 1700s, lurid green 'poison' bottles and jars for leeches. While you're here, it makes sense to pop into the nearby Florence Nightingale Museum (2 Lambeth Palace Road, SE1 7EW, 7620 0374, £5.80). You'll get a chronological lowdown of the remarkable nurse and campaigner's life along with some interesting mementos, including her stuffed pet owl, Athena.

If your appetite for gore hasn't been sated, there's plenty more. see the laboratory where Alexander Fleming discovered penicillin at St Mary's Hospital (Praed Street, W2 1NY, 3312 6528, www.imperial.nhs.uk, £4 adults £2 reductions); pay homage to Joseph 'elephant man' Merrick at the Royal London Hospital (Whitechapel, E1 1BB, 7377 7608, www.bartsandthelondon.nhs.uk, free); follow the stories of 27,000 hospitalised 'exposed and deserted children' at the Foundling Museum (40 Brunswick Square, WC1N 1AZ, 7841 3600, www.foundlingmuseum.org.uk, £7.50 adults £5 reductions); or try the museum of Bart's Hospital (West Smithfield, EC1A 7BE, 3465 5798, www.bartsandthe london.org.uk, free), founded in 1123 as part of St Bartholomew's priory, where, as well as viewing the surgical wares, you can learn about William Harvey, a physician at the hospital who discovered the circulation of blood in the 15th century. Beware: these collections are almost guaranteed to bring on a nasty case of hypochondria.

168 *Kayak the Regent's Canal*

Despite the proximity of the roaring corridors of City Road and nearby Upper Street, the first thing that strikes you out on Islington Basin is the placid silence. Fully paid-up members of the Regent's Canoe Club (16-34 Graham Street, N1 8JX, www.regentscanoeclub.co.uk) meet two evenings a week, but there are also two-hour introductory nights on the second Monday of each month. After a change of clothes – you'll get wet – it's off for a few warming jars in the nearby Prince of Wales.

169-176

Drink in a pub with a real fire

The height of civilisation and all yours for the price of a pint. We recommend the following:

Anglesea Arms *35 Wingate Road, W6 0UR (8749 1291).*
Crooked Billet *14-15 Crooked Billet, SW19 4RQ (8946 4942, www.thecrookedbilletwimbledon.com).*
Earl Spencer *260-262 Merton Road, SW18 5JL (8870 9244, www.theearlspencer.co.uk).*
Fire Stables *27-29 Church Road, SW19 5DQ (8946 3197, www.firestableswimbledon.co.uk).*
Golden Heart *110 Commercial Street, E1 6LZ (7247 2158).*
Grand Union *45 Woodfield Road, W9 3BA (7286 1886, www.grandunionlondon.co.uk).*
Holly Bush *22 Holly Mount, NW3 6SG (7435 2892, www.fullers.co.uk).*
Three Kings of Clerkenwell *7 Clerkenwell Close, EC1R 0DY (7253 0483).*

177 *Search for the original Chinatown*

Stepping off the DLR at Westferry, where once hundreds of ships' masts towered over fortified docks, there's nothing left on Limehouse Causeway to suggest the maze of alleyways, Chinese cafés and grocers that clustered here from the 1880s to the 1930s. Nothing to suggest the exotic hubbub of real docklands, the whiff of opium smoked openly, the excitement of the *puck apu* numbers racket or the gambling den at Ah Tack's Lodging House – all conjured up by the fiction of Conan-Doyle and Sax 'Fu Manchu' Rohmer. Even Dorian Gray dropped by E14 for his opium.

Well – almost nothing. A tin dragon sculpture at the end of Mandarin Street hints at what used to be, as does Ming Street, now lined with '60s blocks instead of the Confucian temple and local Tong HQ – all of which were part of the slums that were razed in 1934.

Among the ships chandlers and mastmakers, the Merchant Navy Officers' Club and Dock Constables' houses – traces of real docklands, all recycled as flats – Amoy Place was once the epicentre of those 'kind of Limehouse Chinese Laundry Blues'. The old wharves (and new 'gated communities') of riverside Narrow Street were once Fu Manchu's lair – 'the river was his highway, his line of communication along which he moved his mysterious forces'. Now the street houses a Gordon Ramsay pub, the Narrow. The decline in the docks, from the 1930s onwards, meant the dwindling of the Chinese population of the area.

At Commercial Road is the striking British & Foreign Sailors' Hostel (or 'Sailor's Palace'), one window ablaze with the telltale pictograms of the Chinese Association of Tower Hamlets. Opposite, the Star of the East pub 7515 3690 805a Commercial Road, with its original gaslights outside, is a hulking Victorian Gothic take on a Chinese temple. At the end of Canton Street lies the Chinese Sunday School & Chun Yee Society with an old people's drop in centre in the basement. At last, here are people with actual memories of London's original Chinatown.

178 *Pitch and putt near Richmond Park*

Just adjacent to the one-time regal hunting grounds of Richmond Park sit the more modern delights of Palewell Pitch & Putt Golf Course. A gentler and cheaper alternative to the capital's 18-hole options, it's more about honing your skills and enjoying a quick round than thrashing 3-woods and clomping off down the fairway. It boasts pretty surrounds too – the nine holes are spread either side of babbling Beverley Brook – and the greens are well maintained. Coaching sessions are also offered. In short, it's the kind of place you can have a swing without worrying about disdainful eyes.

Palewell Park Pitch & Putt Golf Course *Palewell Park, Richmond-upon-Thames, SW14 8RE (8876 3357, www.pitchnputt.co.uk); £4.80 for 9 holes, clubs £1.10 a pair, balls £1.*

179 *Test Albert Bridge*

'All troops must break step when marching over this bridge', says the sign on the end of Albert Bridge, but you could always plan a meet up with a battalion of friends and see what happens if you don't.

180-187

Tuck into something sweet at the capital's best ice-cream parlours

Fortnum & Mason

David Collins-designed and delightfully dinky, Fortnum's Parlour celebrates the sweet with a coffee-and-cream colour scheme and a menu that takes ice-cream and Middle European pastries seriously. It's not cheap, but it is a treat and the postcard-perfect views over Piccadilly make it a lovely spot for meeting friends. Ice-cream sodas, milkshakes and smoothies are £4.75-£5.75, a flight of three ice-creams £8, Austrian strudel served with whipped cream £5 or vanilla ice-cream £7. The coffees may seem expensive at £3.75 but each comes with a mini ice-cream cone on the side.
181 Piccadilly, W1A 1ER (7734 8040, www.fortnumandmason.com).

Gelateria Danieli

This tiny shop was a hit from the day of opening thanks to its superb own-made ice-cream. Now with several branches in London, Gelateria Danieli offers a daily-changing selection of flavours drawn from over 100 recipes. Chocolate sorbet is the *specialità della casa*, one of several gorgeous dairy-free ices; if health is a concern you'll also find options based on yoghurt. There's virtually no room to stand, let alone sit, so take your selection down to Richmond Green to enjoy. Prices start at £2.25 for a single scoop.
16 Brewers Lane, Richmond, Surrey TW9 1HH (8439 9807, www.gelateriadanieli.com).

Gelateria Valerie

An offshoot of popular chain Pâtisserie Valerie, this eye-popping glass and metal structure strikes a fashionable pose on the King's Road and is, like all the ice-creams, sorbets and yoghurt ices that are made on site, authentically Italian. Eat-in prices start at £3.55 for two scoops of your choice from around 20 flavours; one scoop in a cone to take away is £2.95. Just like in the *gelaterie* of Rome you'll find ice-cream incarnations of popular confectionery and desserts: After Eight, Irish Cream, tiramisu, and crème brûlée – plus nut and fruit flavours. Sundaes (£6.70) are all named after famous artists and laden with whipped cream, though there is a diet option based on vanilla and wild berry yoghurt ice-cream. There's also a branch in Spitalfields.
Duke of York Square, King's Road, SW3 4LY (7730 7978, www.patisserie-valerie.co.uk).

Gelato Mio

Pesca, pompelmo, limone – the Italian labels reflect the heritage of this modish parlour and café in the centre of Holland Park's ritzy parade of shops, though specials may include the likes of green tea ice-cream. Prices start at £2.90 for one scoop; 500ml take-home packs are a tenner. Alternative refreshment comes in the form of *frappes* (Italian milkshakes) and *cremolata* (a Sicilian drink made with ice, seasonal fruit and soda). You'll also find breakfast pastries and Illy coffee.
138 Holland Park Avenue, W11 4UE (7727 4117, www.gelatomio.co.uk).

Gelupo

Run by Jacob Kennedy and his team from the popular Bocca di Lupo restaurant, Gelupo offers own-made gelatos, sorbets and granitas. The flavours, many of them seasonal, transport you to sun-saturated Italy – blood orange, mint stracciatella, ricotta with sour cherry, espresso. Can't decide? Order three in a tub or large cone, or scooped into a sugar-crusted brioche-cum-doughnut. Sit at one of the bar stools in the front or at the park bench in the rear deli section.
7 Archer Street, W1D 7AU (7287 5555, www.gelupo.com).

Marine Ices

Chalk Farm's iconic parlour has been on this site since 1931 but the ice-cream (or rather sorbet) production began back in Gaetano Mansi's original Euston grocery business – because he didn't like to waste fruit. The family hails from Italy's Amalfi Coast so expect classic Italian favourites such as gianduia, marsala and stracciatella. Eat inside and a single scoop costs £2.20; coppe start from £5.60 (Coppa Niki has one scoop of coffee, one of hazelnut, topped with hot fudge sauce). You can have a full meal here too – Italian, of course.

8 Haverstock Hill, NW3 2BL (7482 9003, www.marineices.co.uk).

Oddono's

Outclassing many rivals, Oddono's gelato is not just made on the premises, but made from scratch. By using its own recipes rather than the ready-made mixes common in some cheaper establishments these are some of the best and freshest ice-creams around. The hazelnut, coffee and chocolate (made from a unique Ecuadorian cocoa variety), and the mandarin sorbet, are highly recommended but the range changes frequently – Oddono's has developed over 140 flavours since opening in 2004. Prices start at £2.30 for a single scoop cone or cup.

14 Bute Street, SW7 3EX (7052 0732, www.oddonos.co.uk).

Scoop

Were it not for the queues snaking out of the door on sunny Friday lunchtimes it would be easy to miss this authentic Italian *gelateria* discreetly tucked away in Covent Garden – but to those in the know a shopping trip in the area is incomplete without a tub or waffle cone of its artisan-made ices. The place is wonderfully picky when it comes to the ingredients it uses – which include Piedmontese hazelnuts, Sicilian pistachios and Tuscan pine kernels – flavours that are readily discernible in the ice-creams. Prices start at £3.50 for a small cone or cup and rise to £6.50.

40 Shorts Gardens, WC2H 9AB (7240 7086, www.scoopgelato.com).

188 Have a cheap and cheerful day in Sloane city

Much to the chagrin of the local businesses, Shepherd's Bush-based shopping behemoth the Westfield has poached many of Chelsea's weekend customers. The upside of this, though, is that Saturdays in Sloane land are now a much less hectic proposition.

Start at the lively food market where over 150 speciality food producers sell a mix of hot and cold treats outside upscale food store Partridges (2-5 Duke of York Square, SW3 4LY, 7730 0651, www.partridges.co.uk). This being west London, it's the acme of polite civility and nearly all the stalls offer generous samples – artisan breads (dipped in flavoured olive oil), rare cheeses, decorated cupcakes and spiced meats are usually all there for the tasting. Be sure to head to the Patchwork (0845 123 5010, www.patchwork-pate.co.uk) stall where you can taste a liberal splatter of rustic Cointreau and orange chicken liver pâté against the backdrop of playful tunes from the Dixie Ticklers, a street jazz band that are a King's Road fixture.

Next stop is the much-hyped Saatchi Gallery (Duke of York's HQ, King's Road, SW3 4SQ, www.saatchi-gallery.co.uk), which, despite its free admission, isn't quite the oversubscribed scrum of the likes of Tates Modern and Britain.

Ultra-affluent residents in this area see to it that the local charity shops are well stocked with near mint condition designer garb. Join the bargain hunters at Shawfield Street's well-hidden boutique-style Oxfam (no.123a, SW3 4PL, www.oxfam.org.uk), a short walk up King's Road on the left. Further along, on Old Church Street, sits a well-organised British Red Cross (69-71 Old Church Street, SW3 5BS, www.redcross.org.uk) packed with Ralph Lauren, Marc Jacobs and some vintage Gucci and Chanel. Within eyeshot is the Stockpot (273 King's Road, SW3 5EN, 7823 3175), the Chelsea outpost of Soho's much-loved cut price bistro where a main course and a half bottle of red won't cost you more than a tenner.

Top the day off with a play at the Royal Court Theatre (Sloane Square, London SW1W 8AS, 7565 5000, www.royalcourttheatre.com), where day standing tickets to all shows cost ten pence (only two to four available for each show), and all tickets are £10 on Mondays, available from 9am on the website. Arrive early, and there are comfortable leather sofas and free broadsheets in the downstairs bar.

Saatchi Gallery

189

The somewhat ascetic surroundings of Cecil Sharp House, the home of the English Folk Dance and Song Society (2 Regent's Park Road, NW1 7AY, 7485 2206, www.efdss.org), play host to a variety of folk events. Check online for details of barn dances, ceilidhs and folk-dance classes, banjo and accordion lessons and gigs from a variety of traditional British musicians.

...then explore London's other folk venues

No longer relegated to back
huddled round the fire, f
lively, monthly event
happenings – are p
Here are a few o
folk focus. T
Parkway
note.co
of tr
m

...-room nights
...lk gigs – from
... to intimate one-off
...opping up all over town.
... the many venues with a
...e Green Note in Camden (106
...NW1 7AN, 7485 9899, www.green
...uk) is lively and books its fair share
...aditional artists, along with blues
...usicians and singer-songwriters; there
are Sunday afternoon sessions as well as
five evenings a week.

The Magpie's Nest (www.themagpiesnest.
co.uk) is a folk collective with mid-monthly
Wednesday night gigs at Islington's Old
Queen's Head (44 Essex Road, London, N1
8LN, 7354 9993). Come Down and Meet the
Folks is a session at the Apple Tree (45
Mount Pleasant, W1CX 0AE, 7837 2365,
www.comedownandmeetthefolks.co.uk) on
the second and last Sunday of every month.
The sounds range across folk, roots, blues,
country and Americana.

There's further folky fare at London's weekly
folk clubs, which are dotted around the capital
and scattered through the week. Among the
best are the often irreverent Islington Folk
Club, held on Thursdays (except in the summer)
at 8pm at the Horseshoe in Clerkenwell (24
Clerkenwell Close, EC1R 0AG, 7253 6068,
www.islingtonfolkclub.co.uk) and the Cellar
Upstairs, every Saturday at 8.15pm at Euston's
Exmouth Arms (1 Starcross Street, NW1 2HR,
7281 7700, www.cellarupstairs.org.uk) – the
last word in woolly jumper-wearing folk purism
and showcasing traditional British, Irish and
US artists. Less beardy is the eclectic, more-
or-less monthly The Goose Is Out (www.the
gooseisout.com) in Dulwich.

Finally, there's Walthamstow Folk Club,
every Sunday at 7.30pm at Ye Olde Rose and
Crown Theatre Pub (53 Hoe Street, E17 4SA,
8509 3880 www.walthamstowfolk.co.uk).
Line-ups are engaging and the crowd is
down-to-earth, making this is one of London's
most approachable folk clubs for newbies.

198 *Prove that you're too cool for pool*

The smoke-filled halls may have gone, but
snooker still boasts a deliciously louche image
despite (or perhaps because of?) the immense
skill required to play the game. While almost
anyone can sink a few balls on a pub pool table
and imagine they're a real hustler, the greater
dimensions of snooker's green baize and the
requirement to pot in a specified order pose a
far stiffer challenge. Unlike many venues that
still live down to their back-street reputation,
Acton Snooker Club, with a triangle of red balls
forming its logo above the main entrance, is a
plush place. There are 13 tables, all kept in
exemplary condition.
Acton Snooker Club *Old Oak Common Lane,
W3 7DJ (8743 8284, www.hurricaneroom.co.uk).
£10 annual membership.*

199 *Glimpse a secret Mayfair castle*

Hidden away among the swank hotels and
mansions of Mayfair are the elusive turrets
of Berkeley Castle, built in the 1930s by artist
Frederick Etchells. Inside, the mock-medieval
hunting lodge reflects the leading Modernist's
curious passion for fixtures and fittings recycled
from earlier, tumbledown castles; but the best
we can do is catch a glimpse of the Gothic front
door – through an electric portcullis, up a small
alley on Mount Row between Berkeley Square
and Grosvenor Square. ·

200 *Take in tea and typography on the Strand*

The Twinings shop on the Strand (no.216,
WC2R 1AP, 7353 3511) is London's oldest shop
still to be found in its original location. The
golden lion over the doorway dates from 1787
and refers to the sign outside the original Tom's
Coffee House of 1706 (before street numbers had
been devised). The twin mandarins in the sign
refer to the fact that tea was originally imported
exclusively from China, and 'Twinings' is the
world's oldest logo still in continuous use.

Westminster Abbey

201

Attend evensong at Westminster Abbey...

Attending evensong can be a calming, meditative experience, and it's also a way of seeing glorious Westminster Abbey without paying the rather steep entrance fee. Sung evensong takes place at 5pm on Monday, Tuesday, Thursday and Friday, and at 3pm on Saturday and Sunday.

Westminster Abbey *20 Dean's Yard, SW1P 1PA (7222 5152, www.westminster-abbey.org).*

202

...then explore College Garden

Visit Westminster Abbey's cloisters and wonderful College Garden, surrounded on one side by 14th-century walls and with a great view of the Palace of Westminster's Victoria Tower. The grounds of Westminster Abbey were once used by the monks for growing both medicinal herbs and vegetables and, extraordinarily, have been under continuous cultivation for over 900 years. There is no charge for visiting the garden or the cloister.

College Garden

203

Sing your heart out at Hot Breath Karaoke

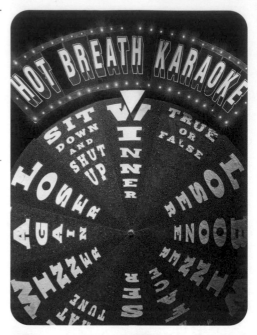

Karaoke is officially a cool pastime these days. At the *Wheel of Fortune*-style party that is Hot Breath Karaoke, wannabes can choose from a whopping 7,000 classic tracks. There are bargain-bin prizes for all who are brave, or misguided, enough to enter and the whole evening is based on throwing your inhibitions to the wind. Check the website for the next event, and start flexing those vocal chords now.

Hot Breath Karaoke
(www.thehouseofhotbreath.com).

204-214

Go to a film festival

London's film festival scene is buzzing. There are dozens of them showcasing every nation, minority, niche or genre you can think of.

Try an indie-fest like Raindance (7287 3833, www.raindance.co.uk, September and October) or trendy Portobello Film Festival (8960 0996, www.portobellofilmfestival.com, September), or the London Bicycle Film Festival (www.bicyclefilmfestival.com/london), part of a growing festival that happens all over the world.

Human Rights Watch International Film Festival (7713 2773, www.hrw.org/iff, March) aims to put a human face on threats to individual freedom and dignity.

Thrusting young festivals screening the output of up-and-coming regions such as eastern Europe and Latin America have left the traditionally dominant film-producing countries of western Europe far behind on the festival scene. The Institut Français has Mosaiques (7871 3515, www.institut-francais.org.uk, May/June), a celebration of cultural diversity. Among the best from eastern Europe is Kinoteka (7440 0241, www.kinoteka.org.uk, March) showcasing Polish films, and there are two Latin American film festivals. Discovering Latin America (7358 3817, www.discoveringlatinamerica.com, November) offers films, docs and shorts that rarely get distribution, while the Latin American Film Festival screens commercial features (www.latinamerican filmfestival.com, November). The London Asian Film Festival (www.tonguesonfire.com) shows independent Indian films of the non-Bollywood variety.

Closer to home are the East End Film Festival (7364 7917, www.eastendfilm festival.com, July), exploring cinema's potential to cross boundaries, and the Rushes Soho Short Film Festival (7851 6207, www.sohoshorts.com) – no entry is over ten minutes and much of the festival is screened via the net in coffee shops and wine bars around Soho.

215 Celebrate Mr Punch's 'birthday'

Every year around 10 May you can catch Punch and Judy 'professors' from all over the country celebrating the moment in 1662 when Samuel Pepys first recorded having seen an Italian Pulcinella (Punch's esteemed ancestor) puppet show on his way back home from the pub. The year 2012 sees Mr Punch's 350th birthday **Covent Garden Puppet Festival** *St Paul's Church Gardens, Bedford Street WC2 (7375 0441). Free.*

216 Check out the art at Broadgate

There's a lot of art crammed into Broadgate; at the time of writing some items were in storage because of redvelopment work, but plenty of pieces remain, such as the enormous Fulcrum by Richard Serra, and Rush Hour by George Segal, cast from real people. Go after dark for the Finsbury Avenue Lit Floor (a striking computer controlled light show). Download an art guide from the website (www.broadgate info.net) and start wandering.

217 Go boating

Spend a sunny summer afternoon messing around in a boat. It costs £10 an hour for adults (£5 for children) to hire a rowing or pedal boat on the Serpentine in Hyde Park (7262 1330, www.royalparks.org.uk). The lake is open for boats from 10am until sunset, from Easter until 31 October. Battersea Park (7262 1330, www.batterseapark.org) also has a fleet of rowing and pedal boats, available in July and August, and at weekends into September as long as the weather holds (£4 adults, £2 children, for half an hour). Finsbury Park boating lake (07905 924282, www.finsburyparkboats.co.uk) is open seven days a week from Easter to October (weather permitting), from noon to 6pm, with extended weekend hours in high summer. All the boats are rowing boats (£6 per boat for 30 minutes).

SAVE UP TO 50% ON THEATRE TICKETS WITH TIME OUT

timeout.com/tickets

218

Discover the ultimate power source at the Royal Institution

Even the most ecologically sound power stations need generators and transformers to transport electricity from source to user and you can see the first incarnations of Michael Faraday's world-changing inventions and the lab where they were built in the basement of the 200-year-old Royal Institution, in what was formerly the Faraday Museum. There's now also a quirky video guide that enlivens other geeky contraptions and shows how other bright RI sparks (14 of whom were Nobel prize winners) discovered ten chemical elements, explained why the sky is blue and engineered the safety lamp that revolutionised miners' working lives. Check out Faraday's digitised notebook and the singing periodic table wall before recharging your batteries at the swanky Time and Space cocktail bar.

Royal Institution of Great Britain *21 Albemarle Street, W1S 4BS (7409 2992, www.rigb.org). Free.*

219

Be a philosopher at Café Philo

If the level of discourse at the watercooler is getting you down, you can always spend your Saturday mornings exercising the little grey cells by debating the philosophical question *du jour* at the Institut Français' Café Philo. The informal gathering is open to all – and, as was the case in ancient Athens, philosophy degrees are definitely not required. Just roll up at the Institut's classy art deco premises in South Kensington at 10.15am for a prompt 10.30am kick-off. The discussion (which alternates between French and English each week – check which one it is before you go) bounces back and forth between the participants until about noon. Haven't got much to say? No problem. Just sit back and listen – there will be plenty who do.

Institut Français *17 Queensberry Place, SW7 2DT (7871 3515, www.institut-francais.org.uk). Contact Christian Michel (cmichel@cmichel.com) to book a place. £2.*

220

Sink (into a steam room) or swim at Ironmonger Row Baths

Originally a public wash house, Ironmonger Row Baths are still providing a Turkish bath (with steam room, various hot rooms, a plunge pool and marble slabs for massages) for less than a tenner if you go in the mornings (sessions are mixed on some days – check the website for details). As well as all the steam, there's also a 30-metre swimming pool. The pool reopens in late 2012 after refurbishment

Ironmonger Row Baths *Ironmonger Row, EC1V 3QF (7253 4011, www.islington. gov.uk/irb).*

No Non Swimmers Beyond This Point

Ironmonger Row Baths

Deal or No Deal?

Jenni Muir does the maths and finds that some of London's traditionally pricey farmers' markets are good for a bargain after all.

It's 4.30pm on a damp Saturday afternoon at Borough Market, the capital's favourite foodie destination. Trading is scheduled to halt in half an hour, but most visitors are oblivious to this detail as they huddle around stalls picking at samples, line up for hot food and take photos.

Over in the Green Market, where the more itinerant traders set out their wares, a male voice tries to rise above the din: '50 per cent off pâtés.' There's not much on his stall and it's set up at the market's edge where there's no cover from the drizzling skies. He continues his cry, '50 per cent off pâtés,' but while the occasional head turns towards him, most feet don't.

Maybe pâtés aren't in fashion. In any case, there's not much sign of other traders following his lead – until there's a ruckus by one of the bakery stalls where they have brought out some fresh trays and a female voice broadcasts the siren song, 'Two for one on brownies.'

Given these fine specimens are the bakery's most popular product, and (rather controversially, admittedly) priced at £2 each most of the time, two for the price of one is indeed a bargain. Still, it's a while before they start to move; after all, the only time you don't want brownies is when you've spent half a day grazing on all manner of rich foods, cakes, coffees and hot chocolate at a fine food market.

A rival stall realises they, too, are overstocked and offer the same two-for-one discount on loaves of bread. 'It's cheap at half the price,' as the singing street traders from *Oliver!* so memorably reminded us, but two-for-one is not the same as half price. Regardless of the cost, if you decided to take up the offer you would be buying two (or four, or six) loaves of bread. What are you going to do with them – open a branch of Pret a Manger? Even a good quality white loaf will be stale in a couple of days, so unless you have space for the second one in the freezer, most of it could wind up in the bin, not only a waste of money, but a waste of food.

All the way from the other side of the market, male and female voices chant a well-practised duet: 'Any bowl a pound, one pound any bowl.' Deal or no deal? Let's take a look. The stall has several mixing bowls lined up with various combinations of veg – baking potatoes, onions, carrots, cauliflowers and so on, plus the occasional bell pepper (unseasonal, pale in colour and not particularly fresh). It has none of the lush speciality produce that gets chefs so excited on the other stalls; there's no Soil Association logo to indicate the veg is organic, or a sign explaining what local farm they are from. In fact, the stall looks like one you might encounter outside a tube station. Don't be

cold smoke
venison wrap

cured in sweet pick
brine then smoked
over beech chipping
£3.00
served in a tortilla
wrap with mayo, sa

confused by the exalted Borough location: there is nothing gourmet about this stall whatsoever. Still, a regular cauliflower alone would cost over £1 in a big-name supermarket, and baking potatoes 15p-25p each, so £1 for a selection of four or five veg *is* still a good deal.

Modern fine food markets and farmers' markets, on the other hand, have a reputation for being expensive. It's sometimes deserved – after all, these places are meant to showcase the very best artisan produce to be found in the UK, and such foods understandably carry a premium – but it is also possible to do a weekly food shop at a gourmet market at prices that compare very favourably with the best products in supermarkets, if you know what to buy.

To recognise these bargains, simply start taking note of typical prices. Quality bacon and sausages at farmers' markets are usually a good deal. In supermarkets you can expect to pay £3-£4 for 200g of British free range or organic dry cured bacon: exactly the price bracket in which it's sold at various farmers' markets across the capital. At the time of writing, Northfield Farm, a popular Borough Market stall specialising in rare breed meats, sells sausages at £7.25-£7.50 a kilo, while Sainsbury's best sausages range from £6.48 per kilo for its Taste the Difference label, right up to a whopping £14.95 per kilo for Helen Browning's organic quick-cook sausages. Caveat emptor indeed.

When it comes to vegetables, you can confidently expect staple seasonal produce to be 20-35 per cent cheaper at a farmers' market than it is at the superstores. But be aware that wherever you choose to shop you need to beware the cost of trendy speciality veg (Tuscan black cabbage, say, or purple potatoes). It's worth keeping up to date with food fashions so that you know what *not* to buy. As foods become more desirable, retailers and traders find they can get away with charging more and tend to take the opportunity to do so. Lamb shanks and chicken thighs were once considered bargain buys, and pollock was a cheap alternative to cod, but in recent years the cost of all three has risen as their status as speciality food rises.

It also pays to be product-savvy when buying breads – don't splash out on fancy white loaves flavoured with olives, nuts and herbs that will disappear in one sitting when a simple half

of organic sourdough will cost less, last longer and prove more versatile. Similarly, traditional British territorial cheeses such as Wensleydale, Caerphilly and Cheshire can be a gourmet treat when made by a respected farmhouse producer, but tend to cost much less than many of the new British artisan varieties and imported continental cheeses. Why pay £30 a kilo for roquefort or some bizarre-smelling goat's cheese when you could be enjoying fine Colston Basset stilton, Keen's unpasteurised cheddar or Mrs Kirkham's Lancashire for £18 a kilo?

There will always be somewhere in London where you can find dirt-cheap, crappy food that may literally have fallen off the back of a lorry; the trick is to find quality food at bargain prices. Depending on the neighbourhood, street-side stalls can be an excellent source of fresh fruit, vegetables and herbs. Realise, however, that they rarely stock organic or local produce and, when it comes to favourites such as apples, are just as happy as the supermarkets to flog American, Chinese and New Zealand varieties at the height of the British season.

Long-established street markets such as those on Ridley Road in Hackney, Portobello Road in Notting Hill, Chapel Market in Islington, Queen's Market in Newham, and Brixton and Walthamstow Markets are without doubt the best sources of imported fresh produce for ethnic cooking – plantains, yams, chillies, ginger and massive bunches of herbs. Check out their fish stalls too – top quality fresh fish and seafood always costs a lot but prices at these stalls tend to be keen and if you're looking for something inexpensive to eat that day, you could well catch a bargain.

The best advice is to experiment until you find the stalls you trust (becoming a regular, recognisable face does help) or, better still, choose one that lets you select your own produce. The tradition of bunging a dodgy piece or two from behind the stall into customers' bags does still exist on some high street markets, despite the fact that such habits helped drive customers away from market stalls in the first place. But now that Borough and the other farmers' markets have raised the bar for quality and reminded many supermarket-goers of the social pleasures of market shopping, there's no reason why we shouldn't look forward to the reinvigoration of food markets right across the capital.

222 *Discover Two Temple Place*

Two Temple Place opened in October 2011 as a venue to showcase publicly owned art from the UK's regional collections and museums. Previously closed to the public, the building – a late 19th-century neo-Gothic mansion built as an office for William Waldorf Astor – is owned and run by the Bulldog Trust (www.bulldogtrust.org). The interior is ornately decorated with marble fireplaces, patterned floors, stained glass, friezes and carvings. The inaugural exhibition featured highlights from the William Morris Gallery (based in Walthamstow); the second showcases artists in West Cornwall at the end of the 19th century, and runs from 24 January to April 2013). The bad news is that Two Temple Place is only open during exhibitions; the good news is that entry is free.

Two Temple Place *2 Temple Place, WC2R 3BD (7836 3715, www.twotempleplace.org).*

A few of my favourite things

223-229

Dominic Cooke,
Artistic Director,
Royal Court Theatre

A really good place to see quality fringe theatre is the Arcola in Dalston (24 Ashwin Street, E8 3DL, 7503 1646, www.arcola theatre.com). It has a great range of work, from revivals of classics to new plays, often by a diverse range of writers, but what defines it is the fact that the productions are always the work of emerging actors and directors. And it's right in the heart of London's Turkish community, so it's surrounded by really excellent and cheap Turkish restaurants.

On Mondays at the Royal Court (Sloane Square, SW1W 8AS, 7565 5000, www.royalcourttheatre.com), you can get £10 tickets for both the upstairs and downstairs theatres. We get some of the best actors and writers in Britain working here and the production values are very high, so it's very good value for money. Any night of the week you can also get in with a standing ticket for just 10p.

I'm quite big on open spaces so when I have the time I like going for walks. One of my favourites is along the north side of the Thames, from Hammersmith down to Chiswick. You pass some wonderful old buildings along the way, and the views over to Barnes are beautiful, because it's not as developed on that side of the river. The last bit, near Chiswick, has a great stretch of 18th century houses with front gardens going down to the water. It's a wonderful walk to do on a Sunday afternoon and you can follow this with a trip to one of the pubs by the river.

We're so lucky in London compared to cities like New York, because we have so many amazing parks here. Richmond Park (0300 061 2200, www.royalparks. org.uk/parks/richmond_park) is one of the more unusual ones, because it's wild and there are deer roaming free. You really feel like you are in the countryside, miles away from anywhere. It's especially good in May and June, when the rhododendrons are out in the Isabella Plantations.

I'm quite greedy, and luckily West London is full of very diverse restaurants. There's a Syrian place called Abu Zaad (29 Uxbridge Road, W12 8LH, 8749 5107, www.abu zaad.co.uk), near Shepherd's Bush Market tube station where you can get a great value (easily under a tenner) meal with beautiful breads and houmous, which are all made in-house, and fantastic chicken shawarma sandwiches.

Another place in Shepherd's Bush that does really good but unpretentious food is Rajput (144 Goldhawk Road, W12 8HH, 8740 9036, www.rajputrestaurant.com). Unlike so many Indian restaurants where you get gloopy, over-coloured stuff, everything they do is fresh and home-made – and without using colourings. I like the chicken biryani and the lamb rogan josh, but the thing that's really special there is the bindi or cauliflower bhajis, you can really taste the vegetables in them.

If I've been running around London on the weekend, or been to see a matinée, I always drop in to Maison Bertaux (28 Greek Street, W1D 5DD, 7437 6007) in Soho for tea. It's a very French pâtisserie with a real sense of bohemian London meets Paris. It does beautiful homemade cakes and pastries, but the best thing about it is that, unlike other places, they don't chivvy you along, so you can sit there for hours having a pot of tea with a group of friends.

230-239

Spot some street art

What with councils' high-pressure hoses and Banksy's work selling for hundreds of thousands of pounds, you may need to be quick off the mark to catch some of the best graffiti in town.

Shop till you drop

A relatively new Banksy piece, done in 2011, and executed using scaffolding. It depicts a woman clutching a shopping trolley as they both fall through space.
Bruton Place, W1 (www.banksy.co.uk).

In Tesco We Trust

Painted on the wall of an Islington pharmacy in early 2008, this chilling visual satire depicts two young children seemingly pledging allegiance to a Tesco flag being hoisted by a third infant. (The flag has since been defaced.) It's one of a handful of Banksy's works protected by perspex.
Essex Road, N1 (www.banksy.co.uk).

Space Invader

London has been 'invaded' by the renegade tilers behind this global phenomenon several times since 1999 and there are countless examples of their often colourful mosaics stuck high on walls across the capital. All depict pixelated retro space invaders in some form – for example, the huge black and white space invader mosaic that can been seen from the Truman Brewery Courtyard.
Truman Brewery, E1 (www.space-invaders.com).

Scary/Change

Responsible for the bright circus-style giant letters that colour the metal shutters of many east London shops, the hugely popular alphabet artist Eine's bold murals can be found under the bridge outside Cargo on Rivington Street ('Scary'), and on Old Street, near the roundabout ('Change').
Shoreditch, N1 (www.einesigns.co.uk).

Credit Crunch Monster

Ronzo is the creator of Crunchy the Credit Crunch Monster, who can now be found at Grey Eagle Street, overlooking the

Truman Brewery site. There are other pieces of his dotted around Shoreditch, too.
Shoreditch, E1 (www.ronzo.co.uk).

Rat/Rabbit

Roa paints beautiful creatures, and his work appears all over the world, including New York, Paris and Cologne. In London, there are two large pieces along Hackney Road: 'Rat', two storeys tall, is on a building opposite the Joiners Arms; 'Rabbit' is on the side of vintage shop Found (opposite the junction with Ravenscroft Street) and is one storey tall. (There's also semi-obscured squirrel on Club Row, and a large stork on Hanbury Street.)
Hackney Road, E2 (www.roaweb.tumblr.com).

Stik

Stik's work is all over London, although one of the most noticeable examples of his simple but curiously expressive figures is on Cambridge Heath Road, just before you cross the canal travelling north. The website has an up to date map of currently visible pieces.
Cambridge Heath Road, E2 (www.stik.org.uk).

Malarkistani Riots/Cheshire Cat

A large, bright, easily visible piece by Malarky on Redchurch Street. There is also another nice one on Cheshire Street of a Cheshire cat with three eyes and an ice-cream cone.
Shoreditch, E1 (www.malark.blogspot.com).

Yellow flower

Another piece by the stencil-happy ironist Banksy, this large yellow flower plus seated artist is rather altered and defaced (the street's yellow lines once continued up the wall to create the flower) and the image of the artist is now behind perspex, but it still rewards the schlep into Bethnal Green's warrens.
Pollard Street, E2 (www.banksy.co.uk).

Sweet Toof

One of the most recognisable street artists around, Sweet Toof's pink gums and teeth can be seen all over London. Often they appear as additions to other artists' work, for example, to an existing Roa piece on Regent's Canal, at the point where Mare Street crosses it.
Regent's Canal, E8 (www.sweettoof.com).

240-257 *Blow your tenner in the capital's best pub jukeboxes...*

Approach Tavern
Jazz, blues and R&B faves at this updated Bethnal Green boozer. At the time of writing the jukebox was free.
47 Approach Road, E2 9LY (8980 2321).

Boogaloo
A justly famous jukebox, spinning everything from Dusty Springfield to the Pogues; three tunes for a quid.
312 Archway Road, N6 5AT (8340 2928, www.theboogaloo.co.uk).

Bradley's Spanish Bar
London's best vinyl juke, loaded with Hendrix, Presley and the Dead Kennedys (£1 for three plays).
42-44 Hanway Street, W1T 1UT (7636 0359, www.bradleysspanishbar.co.uk).

Crobar
£1 for three hard and heavy tracks from the likes of Lynyrd Skynyrd, Led Zep and a lot of Iron Maiden.
17 Manette Street, W1D 4AS (7439 0831, www.crobar.co.uk).

Dublin Castle
The sweaty rear room venue hosts aspiring guitar bands; the juke in the pub out front is full of indie faves. Five songs for £1.
94 Parkway, NW1 7AN (7485 1773, www.thedublincastle.com).

Endurance
Over 100 tunes to choose from, including the likes of Kings of Leon, Killers and the Stones. Five songs for £1.
90 Berwick Street, W1F 0QB (7437 2944, www.theendurance.co.uk).

Golden Heart
This trad but trendy Truman boozer is a hangout for the arty crowd. Your eyes will be drawn to the penny-chew-coloured jukebox – Three songs for £1.
110 Commercial Street, E1 6LZ (7247 2158).

Hobgoblin
Over 7,000 indie and glam rock tracks, in keeping with the student vibe (ten tracks £2).
272 New Cross Road, SE14 6AA (8692 3193).

Hope & Anchor
Both jukeboxes at this grizzled rock boozer are packed with punk/indie faves. £1 buys three plays, but staff often give out credits.
207 Upper Street, N1 1RL (7354 1312).

King Charles I
A quid buys four songs, covering all corners from reggae and country.
55-57 Northdown Street, N1 9BL (7837 7758).

Mucky Pup
Great name, great jukebox: marvellously mixed-up (Nick Drake, Jesus Lizard, Mastadon) and, best of all, free.
39 Queen's Head Street, N1 8NQ (7226 2572).

Prince George
One of Hackney's finest jukes; ranging from Sinatra to the White Stripes. Five songs, £1.
40 Parkholme Road, E8 3AG (7254 6060).

Reliance
Rock, soul, funk, soul and blues from the 1970s to '90s. All for free.
336 Old Street, EC1V 9DR (7729 6888).

Royal Exchange
Trad and modern Irish plus jazz and '60s-'90s favourites. Three songs for a nugget.
26 Sale Place, W2 1PU (7723 3781).

Three Kings
A selection of 80 vinyl seven-inches that changes each week; £1 for seven songs.
7 Clerkenwell Close, EC1R 0DY (7253 0483).

Shakespeare
A welcoming local where the wide-ranging jukebox plays three tunes for £1.
57 Allen Road, N16 8RY (7254 4190).

The Social
New music from the Heavenly Social label plus regularly changing CDs (free).
5 Little Portland Street, W1W 7JD (7636 4992, www.thesocial.com).

Swimmer at the Grafton Arms
800 CD tracks that rotate every couple of months, from Elbow to Ella Fitzgerald.
13 Eburne Road, N7 6AR (7281 4632).

258

...or go to a free gig in a record store

Instore gigs have become central to a band's marketing plan, so most of the retail giants regularly host free gigs, as do independents such as Rough Trade East (Old Truman Brewery, 91 Brick Lane, E1 6QL, 7392 7790, www.roughtrade.com), which has featured top- class bands and DJs from Beirut and Boys Noize to Crystal Castles and Of Montreal. Check the website for details of performances. You may need to apply in advance for a wristband to gain entry if it's a popular band.

259 *Learn Afro-Brazilian drumming*

Energetic carnival-style funkateers TRIBO are a London-based Afro-Brazilian samba-reggae outfit, originally from Salvador, who run a weekly two-hour workshop for anyone interested in their indigenous percussive arts. It involves learning how to beat a huge samba drum to a set rhythm – not as easy as it sounds, but the emphasis here is very much on finding your groove at your own pace. The classes are casual and welcome all ages and abilities, ultimately working towards students being able to perform in *blocos* (street parades) in London (including Notting Hill Carnival) and in Brazil. TRIBO beginners have even gone on to play with bands back in Salvador. The group is also a regular fixture at the capital's buzzing Latin American clubs, such as Guanabara (Parker Street, WC2B 5PW, 7242 8600, www.guanabara.co.uk) .

TRIBO *Colville Primary School, Lonsdale Road, W11 2DF (07956 652399, www.triboband.com). £9 per person.*

260

Roller disco
All over the capital rollergals and guys are squeezing into lycra leggings, donning fluoro leg warmers and hitting the rink at the Renaissance Rooms (7720 9140, www.rollerdisco.com). Start the weekend early at Thursday's session, which is less crowded and cheaper (£10, or £7.50 if you have your own skates).

261 Spend Sunday with the French

For some guaranteed Gallic flair, pop along at 2pm on a Sunday to the Ciné Lumière's screenings of classy French flicks (tickets £6-£8). Launched by Catherine Deneuve in 1998, this plush cinema puts on a variety of excellent film seasons (including Turkish and Spanish movies) but its Sunday slot is always a French classic from the likes of François Truffaut, Jean Renoir and Jean-Luc Godard.
Ciné Lumière *Institut Francais, 17 Queensberry Place, SW7 2DT (7871 3515, www.institut-francais.org.uk).*

262

Work out at a green gym

Are you keen to improve your fitness but not a fan of indoor exercise? Organised by the British Trust for Conservation Volunteers (01302 388883, www.btcv.org.uk), Green Gym may be just what you're after. A fresh-air alternative to sweaty aerobics classes and soul destroying treadmills, Green Gym groups undertake a variety of tasks to enhance the local environment, such as clearing undergrowth, building an outdoor seat or reinstating a pathway. Research has shown that you can burn almost a third more calories in an hour doing some Green Gym activities than in a step aerobics class. If you fancy giving it a go, there are currently six Green Gym groups in London (Camden, Hampstead, Harringay, Lewisham, Newham, Waltham Forest) – or you could start one yourself. The website has full details.

263

Sail from Tate to Tate

The inspired Tate to Tate boat service leaves from Tate Britain to Bankside Pier (Tate Modern) every 20 minutes during the day, with a stop at Embankment en route (7001 2222, www.thamesclippers.com).

264-270

Be late

Over a few weeks in October, the Mayor's office runs the annual Lates Festival, focusing on a trend that was already happening in many of London's museums. Lates offers a coordinated month of late-night openings and associated 'happenings' – performances, DJs, the all-important cash bar – which are designed to draw culture-phobic 25- to 35-year-olds into institutions such as the Barbican, National Portrait Gallery, V&A and British Museum.

Outside October, a number of attractions have continued the habit, staging regular evening events: Whitechapel Art Gallery and a large number of other East End galleries open late for Time Out First Thursdays (www.firstthursdays.co.uk): the Hayward Gallery is open until 8pm on Thursday and Fridays; on the first Friday of each month Tate Britain opens its doors until 10pm for the always intriguing 'Late at Tate', which entitles you to half-price entry to any current exhibition and a range of other themed events; Tate Modern is also open until 10pm on Fridays and Saturdays. Less arty but more atmospheric are the candlelit evening openings of Dennis Severs' House (*see p234*) and Sir John Soane's Museum (*see p26*).
Lates Festival *7983 4000, www.lates.org.*

271

Observe a Rake's Progress

William Hogarth was an archetypal Londoner but even he needed to escape the teeming streets of the city from which he drew so much inspiration – which is why he had a country retreat in Chiswick. Here you can see his great series of satirical engravings including *A Rake's Progress* and *Marriage à-la-Mode*. Afterwards, make a pilgrimage to his tomb in the graveyard of nearby St Nicholas Church (Church Street, W4 2PH).
Hogarth's House *Hogarth Lane, Great West Road, W4 2QN (8994 6757, www.hounslow.info). Free.*

272-274
Search for bats in London's woods and wetlands

Once London's bats have crawled out of hibernation in late spring, you'll have a number of opportunities to observe these fascinating and endangered mammals close up in the city's wilder locations. Whichever sunset foray you choose (see www.londonbats.org.uk for a list of locations, further information on other walks and bat groups around London), you'll learn about the country's 17 species before heading out (armed with ultrasonic bat detectors) to look for the six that are found in London as they leave their roosts. The detectors translate the echo location signals emitted by bats into sound audible to the human ear, and once you've tuned in you're almost guaranteed a sighting of Britain's smallest bat, the pocket-sized pipistrelle, as it swoops in on its nightly dinner of around 3,000 midges.

Popular bat walks in London take place at lovely Highgate Woods, which were granted to Londoners as an open space by the Lord Mayor in 1886. Here you can bat spot among the oaks and hornbeams of one of the city's most atmospheric parks. These events are free but very popular, so book ahead.

At the London Wetland Centre in Barnes (which has ten confirmed species) there are 30-minute introductory presentations before groups of around ten head out with guides and their bat detectors into the 100-odd acres of the award-winning Site of Special Scientific Interest. There's also chance to spot Britain's biggest bat, the noctule, which can reach speeds of around 30mph. (Contrary to popular belief, they don't dive-bomb you.)

The London Wildlife Trust runs free bat-spotting evenings in various nature reserves – check the website for details of these events. In general, bat walks usually take place at twilight in the summer months and walk dates tend to be sporadic; ring ahead to check times and to book (sessions are often heavily oversubscribed). Even in summer you may have to do a lot of standing around so dress warmly and take a torch. All start times vary with sunset.

Highgate Woods *Muswell Hill Road, N10 3JN (8444 6129, www.cityoflondon.gov.uk/openspaces). Bat watches June-Sept (at least once a month). Free.*
London Wildlife Trust *(7261 0447, www.wildlondon.org.uk)*
WWT London Wetland Centre *Queen Elizabeth's Walk, SW13 9WT (8409 4400, www.wwt.org.uk). Big Batty Walks July-Sept (at least three a month). £10.*

275 *Go up the creek in Deptford*

Once an important industrial tributary of the Thames, for centuries Deptford Creek, with its huge, twice daily seven-metre tidal surge – like an inhalation and exhalation – was an inherent part of Deptford's identity. Even the name Deptford means Deep Ford; a place where people could cross the creek's stony bottom at low tide. But as dockyards, slaughterhouses, tanneries, granaries and tidal mills moved elsewhere in the last century and the river's importance slowly diminished, the tributary sank into neglect and stagnation, gradually becoming a repository for shopping trolleys and other human detritus. That is until 2002, when the Creekside Centre charity decided to clean things up and bring the creek's fragile but unique ecosystem to people's attention.

That's why we're now flailing around in an attempt to don thigh-high waders. It's a chilly Sunday morning in December and although perhaps not the most immediately enticing weekend activity, we're struggling to contain our excitement at the prospect of wading through the exposed mud of 'London's Grand Canyon'. Our infectiously enthusiastic guide is Nick Bertrand, local conservationist and Deptford Creek hero, and it's into a seemingly new dimension that he's about to lead us. Eventually, our group of around ten waddle off, armed with walking poles ('they're your third leg'), leaving behind the centre's wild grounds full of trolley sculptures and artworks assembled from assorted reclaimed creekside materials.

Down on the creek bed, the raucous world of the City, with its buildings hanging high above us, silhouetted darkly by the sun, does indeed seem almost threatening – or perhaps it's just that the river bed quickly becomes more of a comforting, if muddy, cocoon the further we tramp along its course. Over our two-hour tour Nick shows us a stretch not more than about a mile in length, but even on this wintery day there's enough wildlife to see – from kingfishers and herons to chinese mitten crabs, and other squiggly shrimp-like creatures, as well as delicate wild plants. In summer, the place is teeming with butterflies, dragonflies, flounder – the creek is an important breeding ground – prawns, crabs, around 120 species of wildflower, as well as a lot more birds, including cormorants and sometimes even the rare black redstart. You're so low down here that it's easy to get sucked (literally in one case) into the opaque and mysterious world of viscous silt. We poke about like wannabe Swallows and Amazons, delighted not only by a caught mitten crab and the wriggling contents of our white 'pond dipping trays' but also by unidentifiable metal chunks that have perhaps fallen off one of the boats moored (and in some cases still inhabited) in the creek.

But it's worth looking up as well as down. There's a unique perspective to be had from the riverbed – just imagining what would happen to London if those towering flood defence walls were breached makes you dizzy for starters. And those looming constructions even higher above you? Well, Nick's no fan of architects, but there's no denying the ingenuity of Joseph Bazalgette's pumping station; the simple, solid and pragmatic beauty of Mumford's Flour Mill; the graceful sweep of the DLR bridge or the shimmering chutzpah of Herzog and de Meuron's Laban dance centre with its pink, green and blue polycarbonate panels. But there's also a problem here too: Deptford has been slated as one of London's key areas for residential housing development and in the Deptford Creek area alone – about 25 hectares in all – a staggering 3,400 new homes are expected to be built in the next five years. All of which of course means that the creek and its inhabitants – human and animal – are under threat. Go and see it for yourself before the developers have their wicked way with it.

Creekside Centre *14 Creekside SE8 4SA (8692 9922, www.creeksidecentre.org.uk). Low tide walk £10.*

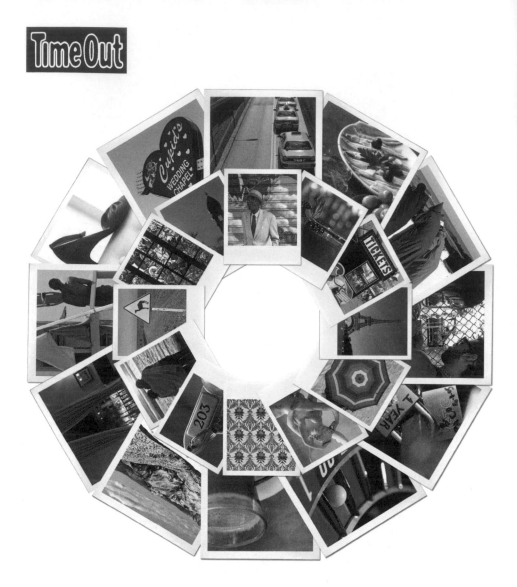

EXPLORE FROM THE INSIDE OUT

Time Out Guides written by local experts

Our city guides are written from a unique insider's perspective
by teams of local writers.

Covering 50 destinations, the range includes the official
London 2012 guide.

visit timeout.com/shop

276

Visit an Arts and Crafts gem

This Georgian house on the Thames conceals a splendid Arts and Crafts interior, with the decoration and furnishings preserved as they were in the lifetime of the owner, printer Emery Walker (1851-1933). There's a combination of Morris & Co textiles, wallpapers and furniture (Walker was a great friend of William Morris), 17th- and 18th-century furniture, and Middle Eastern and North African textiles and ceramics. The house – run by a small charitable trust – opens for small groups of visitors (eight at a time) from April to September.

Emery Walker House *7 Hammersmith Terrace, W6 9TS (www.emerywalker.org.uk).*

277

Catch blooms all year round

Kew Gardens may cost more than a tenner, but horticultural diehards on a budget can take solace from the fact that the Isabella Plantation, tucked away in the south-west corner of Richmond Park, is completely free. An enchanting ornamental woodland garden, dotted with clearings, ponds and streams, it was established in the 1950s and today there's always something in bloom – or at least colourful – among the collection of exotic plants and trees. It's also a good place to see birds: resident species include redpoll, bullfinch, woodpecker, sparrowhawk and tawny owl.
www.royalparks.org.uk.

Isabella Plantation

Take a stand

Alan Rutter guides you through the dos and don'ts of stage performance.

'My hands were shaking so much that I couldn't hold the piece of paper I was reading from. I had to take the microphone off its stand, put the paper on the floor, and then kneel down to do my poem. I was that nervous.'

Niall O'Sullivan is describing the first time he ever performed a poem live to an audience, at an open mic night at the Poetry Café in Covent Garden, back in 1997. Given the traumatic nature of that experience, you'd be forgiven for assuming that he promptly vowed never to put himself through it again – but he's now a successful poet, reading across Europe, and he's taken over as compere at the night that caused him so much pain: Poetry Unplugged.

O'Sullivan is just one of a number of big names who have braved the microphone at Unplugged, which has been running for 11 years. Established poets such as Tim Wells (founding editor of the *Rising* series of poetry magazines) and Tim Turnbull (winner of the inaugural Edinburgh Book Festival Slam) both came through Poetry Unplugged. Scroobius Pip (*see p43*) was a regular before he hit the big time with Dan Le Sac, and troubled troubadour Pete Doherty has performed there several times.

'We're completely democratic,' explains O'Sullivan. 'Anybody can turn up and put their name down between six and seven o'clock, and everybody gets five minutes to perform. There's no vetting of material, and no restrictions on content or style. I occasionally get established performers asking if they can do a featured slot, but I tell them that they'll have to put their name down like everyone else.'

The inclusive nature of the night ensures a mixed bill of performers. 'We get everyone – old women on the "poem about my cat" circuit, hip-hop MCs who are looking to do something a bit more lyrical, ranters… the whole gamut. Usually around half the audience are there to perform as well.'

There are no shortcuts to getting over the nerves. 'Some people are slick from the word go – they've got it all scripted out, and they read it from memory. Other people need the words in front of them, and some do get the

Green Note

jitters. The best thing to do is just to throw yourself into it – the crowd will always be welcoming. It is worth checking you're comfortable with the five minute time-limit, and maybe building in a minute for margin of error.'

And leave any high-minded preconceptions about poetry at the door. 'Some people come along expecting it to be an elitist thing – that we'll be a bunch of grammar-Nazis, or that it will be highbrow, precious or cliquey. It's not like that at all – and as compere, if I see things going in that direction, I'll try to step in.'

However, there *are* a couple of points of etiquette worth bearing in mind. 'If you bring an entourage of mates to watch you, remember to be mindful of the other performers. And it's considered bad form to "read and run" – do your slot and then leave without listening

to everyone else. The only thing I'll really say no to, though, is somebody turning up with an acoustic guitar. I don't want the night to drift into a showcase for singer-songwriters.'

Fortunately that category of peformer is well-catered for elsewhere, however. There is a plethora of acoustic music open mics across London – although, given that they're not exactly cash-cows for the organisers, they do tend to appear and disappear quite rapidly. You'll find them in small spaces – typically a room above a pub – and they tend to fill the quieter gaps in a venue's weekly schedule, often Sunday, Monday and Tuesday nights.

The Green Note is a cosy vegetarian café-bar in Camden Town. It has hosted an open mic since September 2007, and the music ranges across folk, blues, roots, world, jazz. The session now takes place on the last Tuesday

CellarDoor

of the month, with sign-up from 7pm, and open mic virgins are definitely welcome.

There are other acoustic open mics with a similarly welcoming vibe. Down in south London, the Half Moon Pub in Herne Hill is a stalwart for acoustic acts – as well as the odd spoken word performer. Up north, eARmusic has a number of open mic nights: there's one every Sunday at the Camden Head, and one on Tuesdays at the Abbey; both are free. The eARmusic website (www.earmusic. com) is an excellent place to get up-to-date information on open mics across London. Over in Mile End, the fashionably retro Victoria draws a good crowd for its open mic night (on alternate Wednesdays).

Some sessions cater for more than singer-songwriters. The open mic session at Soho's 12 Bar Club happens on the last Sunday of the month (unless the venue is booked for a private party), and is run by nearby Enterprise Studios. 'A lot of the bands that play the open mic rehearse at the studios, so we've got a fairly good idea of what standard the acts are,' says Lee Jones at the Enterprise. 'But there's no actual vetting of talent. We'll generally have five bands who book their spot in advance and play 25 minutes each, plus as many singer-songwriters as we get on the night.'

If you're going to play an open mic, it's definitely worth checking out the facilities in advance – and one advantage of venues such as the 12 Bar Club is the fact that they provide a fair amount of equipment. 'We've got a full back line, including mics, high-watt amps and a drum kit,' says Jones. 'Which means all you need to bring are your instruments and yourselves.'

These kind of events are also a good place to meet like-minded performers and possibly even share costs and any profits. 'Most of the acts are doing it for the experience, and they might get together with some other performers to do a gig together. It also means there's less risk of having death metal and jazz on the same bill.'

If you're keen to play with other performers, but haven't got a band, you could always head for a jam session instead. The Ain't Nothin But the Blues Bar on Kingly Street in Soho runs a jam night on Mondays until 1am. The standard is high and slots are popular – to get a definite chance of being involved, get your name down before 8.30pm or 9pm at the latest. Or if you want to sing but you're entirely incapable of playing a musical instrument you can take part in Rockaoke at the Roundhouse in Chalk

Farm on Monday and Wednesday nights – pick a song, and sing live with the backing of one of the bands who play regularly at the venue. To keep the evening from tumbling into a Spinal Tap-esque shambles, you'll need to register in advance (with your choice of song), and it will be much appreciated if you at least learn the lyrics before you turn up. Another more serious option to karaoke comes in the form of Trash Tuesday nights at the tiny cabaret basement CellarDoor. If you're a solo vocalist you can head along to Champagne Charlie's session for cabaret, musical theatre and jazz singers – all you have to do is take your sheet music and plenty of support.

Whatever flavour of performance you're into, open mics offer a unique opportunity for beginners to get over the hurdle of playing in front of an audience. 'For some people it's the first time they've ever played in front of another person, which can be really scary,' says Watts at the Green Note. 'My biggest advice is just to relax. Remember: even top performers were in that position once upon a time.'

Open mic nights

Ain't Nothin' But The Blues Bar
Venue: 20 Kingly Street, W1B 5PZ (7287 0514, www.aintnothinbut. oo.uk). 8pm 1am Mon. Entry free. Contact: www.myspace.com/monday bluesjam.

Trash Tuesday
Venue: CellarDoor, Zero Aldwych, WC2R 0HT (7240 8848, www.cellar door.biz). 9pm-1am Tue. Entry free. Contact: open@cellardoor.biz.

eARmusic Open Mic
Venue: Abbey, 124 Kentish Town Road, NW1 9QB (7267 9449, www.abbey-tavern.com). 7.30pm-midnight Tue. Sign-up from 7pm. Book ahead to guarantee a performer's slot. Entry free. Contact: 07732 396468, www.earmusic.co.uk.

Green Note
Venue: 106 Parkway, NW1 7AN (7485 9899, www.greennote.co.uk). 7pm Tue. Entry free. Contact: www.myspace.com/ greennoteopenmic.

Half Moon Open Mic
Venue: 10 Half Moon Lane, SE24 9HU (7274 2733, www.halfmoonpub.co.uk).

8pm-midnight Tue. Sign-up from 7.30pm. Entry free. Contact: www.myspace.com/ needleandthreaddotorg.

Poetry Unplugged
Venue: Poetry Café, 22 Betterton Street, Covent Garden, WC2H 9BX (7420 9887, www.poetrysociety.org.uk). 7.30-11pm Tue. Sign-up 6-7pm. Entry £6 (£5 reductions) for participants and audience. Contact: 7420 9887.

Rockaoke
Venue: the Roadhouse, 35 the Piazza, Covent Garden, WC2E 8BE (7240 6001, www.roadhouse.co.uk). 5.30pm-3am Mon, Wed. Booking ahead essential if you want to perform. Entry free before 10pm, £5 after. Contact: 7240 6001.

12 Bar Club
Venue: Denmark Street, WC2H 8NL (7240 2622, www.12barclub.com). 5pm-midnight last Sun of mth. Sign-up from 4pm. Entry free. Contact: 7240 2622.

Victoria
Venue: 110 Grove Road, E3 5TH (8980 6609, www.thevictoriae3.com). 7pm-midnight alternate Wed. Sign-up from 7pm. Entry free. Contact: 8980 6609.

287 *Remember lost luvvies at the Actors' Church*

St Paul's Covent Garden is justly known as the Actors' Church. Thespians commemorated on its walls range from those lost in obscurity – step forward Percy Press, one-time Punch and Judy man – to those destined for immortality: that'd be Charlie Chaplin, then. Perhaps most charming are the numerous sublunary figures. William Henry Pratt, for example, better known as Boris Karloff, and universally famous as the real flesh behind unforgettable monsters – Frankenstein, being one of them. Take a bow too, Hattie Jacques, archetypal matron in the interminable series of Carry On films. The Jacques memorial is so plain you wonder if the inscriber felt that any embellishment would seem an impertinence in the face of such a big comic persona. And surely no more romantic tribute is paid anywhere in the city than that to Vivien Leigh. Her plaque is simply inscribed with words from Shakespeare's *Antony and Cleopatra*: 'Now boast thee, death, in thy possession lies a lass unparallel'd.' When we visit, however, our first homage is always paid to the memory of the mysterious 'Pantopuck the Puppetman', one AR Philpott, a master puppeteer whose work included films such as *The Dark Crystal*, *Labyrinth* and *Star Wars*. We choose to imagine his spirit wooing the excellently named Hollywood actress Edna Best, remembered not far away as 'The Constant Nymph'.

St Paul's Church *Bedford Street, WC2E 9ED (7836 5221, www.actorschurch.org). Free.*

288 Go old-school...

Ragged schools, providing tuition, food and clothing for destitute children, were an early experiment in public education, and this one was London's largest; Dr Barnardo taught here in Mile End. Kids love the mocked-up classroom, where formal lessons – complete with slates – are staged. There's also a Victorian kitchen, displays on local history and industry, and popular holiday activities. **Ragged School Museum** *46-50 Copperfield Road, E3 4RR (8980 6405, www.raggedschoolmuseum. org.uk). Free.*

289 ...or 'Suffer the little children' at the Foundling Museum

England's first hospital for abandoned children was established by Thomas Coram in 1739 and was home to 27,000 children until its closure in 1953. The museum tells the story of these children (the exhibit of humble tokens left by the mothers who had to give up their babies is especially poignant) and the adults who campaigned for them, such as Thomas Gainsborough, William Hogarth and George Frederic Handel. Hogarth's support and gifts of paintings enabled the hospital to establish itself as Britain's first public art gallery and a selection of Handel's manuscripts are displayed on the top floor. **Foundling Museum** *40 Brunswick Square, WC1N 1AZ (7841 3600, www.foundlingmuseum.org.uk). £7.50, £5 concessions.*

290
Get a Wren's-eye-view of St Paul's

Over the 33 years that it took to transform an optimistic architectural plan into St Paul's Cathedral, Sir Christopher Wren resided over the river on Bankside at Cardinal Cap Alley in order to give him the best possible perspective on his work. It's a view you can take in yourself from the ceramic plaque that now marks the spot.

291-295
Take a whistle-stop tour of Roman London

It's now almost 25 years since Museum of London archaeologists discovered the epicentre of Londinium, and ten years since the 2,000-year-old Roman amphitheatre was opened to the public underneath the Guildhall Yard. Admission into the savage realm of slaves, gladiators and wild animals is via the Guildhall Gallery (Guildhall Yard, EC2Y 5HN, 7332 3700, www.guildhallartgallery.cityoflondon.gov.uk, free). It's an amazing chance to step back into the city's bloody past, which even trumps the previous chart-topping subterranean Roman thrill – admiring the pavement and villa remains in the undercroft of St Bride's Church (Fleet Street, EC4Y 8AU, 7427 0133, guided tours £6), hidden treasures that had been lost before bombs struck during the Blitz.

The fortifications of London Wall were constructed and continually developed between 200 and 410AD, when the Romans upped and left for home. Its six gates are still easy to find in the *A-to-Z*, with the best surviving stretches at Tower Hill (along with a statue of Emperor Trajan) and on the Barbican Estate, where one of the regular lookout towers, or bastions, survives next to the church of St Giles-without-Cripplegate.

Nearby, the grounds of the Museum of London (150 London Wall, EC2Y 5HN, 7001 9844, www.museumoflondon.org.uk) boast a 13th-century tower built on top of London Wall and a Roman fort gate beneath pavement level (unfortunately only rarely open for public viewing). Inside, the museum houses 47,000 Roman objects uncovered by building work over the centuries, including the wonderful marble sculptures of gods from the Temple of Mithras (Minerva, Venus combing her hair, the Egyptian god Serapis, and, of course, the bull-fighting Mithras himself) as well as ceramics, coins, metalwork, mosaics – and leather bikinis. Discovered in 1954, the foundations of the Temple of Mithras – the soldier's temple, later rededicated to wine god Bacchus – are, at the time of writing, temporarily in storage.

YOUR GUIDE TO ARTS, ENTERTAINMENT AND CULTURE IN THE WORLD'S MOST EXCITING PLACES

timeout.com

296-299

Find yourself a cure for... anything!

Focus your intelligence with the warmth of the lin zhi mushroom (ganoderma). Try mo yao resin (myrrh) to activate blood circulation. Ju hua (chrysanthemum) flowers dispel wind-heat, and are a common treatment for flu symptoms, and you can eliminate 'food stagnation and bloating' with the sweet, pungent seeds of the lai fu (radish) plant. Alternatively, ventilate your lungs with the roots and rhizomes of the aster plant or supplement your yang and give your kidneys a boost with the stripped bark of the hardy du zhong rubber tree (eucommia). London has hundreds of Traditional Chinese Medicine (TCM) practitioners: from those promising to 'Help You With Acne, Hair Loss, Gynecology! Losing Weight In One Months!' to more authoritative sounding places.

At the beautifully presented, traditional clinic Hong Yuen (22 Rupert Street, W1D 6DG, 7439 2408) they are 'very low key', according to its owner. 'No advertising. No propaganda.' What better recommendation than a centre that allows results to generate custom via word of mouth?

The Institute of Chinese Medicine (44-46 Chandos Place, WC2N 4HS, 7836 5220, www.instituteofchinesemedicine.org) is one of several rival institutes that have attempted to form an affiliation of practitioners. It commands respect as a supplier of herbs to many of London's other practices, and runs its own highly rated treatment centres.

Benny May of the Acumedic Centre (101-105 Camden High Street, NW1 7JN, 7388 5783, www.acumedic.com) is something of a leader in the traditional Chinese medicine community. He started out writing technical books and as a supplier to other practices, but is long established at this treatment centre.

SEN (47 Albemarle Street, W1S 4JW, 7495 0493, www.senhealth.com) has an accent on east-west fusion and accessibility. Look past the beautiful Sen brand packaging for consultations on chronic illness, herbal and acupuncture treatments and massage and acupressure full-body healing.

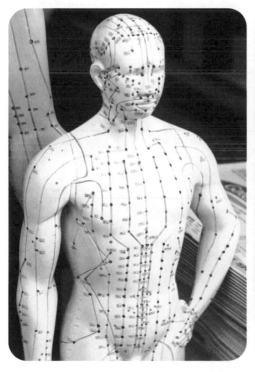

300 *Muck out at Spitalfields City Farm*

Given the smells and the sounds – it's all quack-quack, oink-oink, bah-bah round here – emanating from Spitalfields City Farm, you'd be surprised to learn that you're less than a mile from the Square Mile. Set up in 1978 on a disused railway goods depot just off Brick Lane, the farm has been a favourite with local Tower Hamlets families ever since. Kids and parents come down for workshops on healthy eating, sustainability and animal welfare, as well as to learn where milk and eggs come from. For children aged eight to 13 there's an after-school club on Thursdays and a Young Farmers Club on Saturdays, as well as courses during the holidays (all are free; phone to book). Unsurprisingly, though, the main attraction is meeting the animals – typical city farm friendly beasts, made cocky from the vast amount of attention showered on them from visiting children. Favourites include donkeys, (that can be ridden in spring and summer, at events), strokeable mice and rabbits, two pigs, Watson & Holmes, and Tilly, a cheeky – and chunky – Shetland Pony. Check the website for details of the volunteer programme if you fancy mucking in – or out.

Spitalfields City Farm *Buxton Street, E1 5HJ (7247 8762, www.spitalfieldscityfarm.org).*

301-309

...then check out the others

Deen City Farm *off Windsor Avenue, SW19 2RR (8543 5300, www.deencityfarm.co.uk).*
Freightliners City Farm *Paradise Park, Sheringham Road, N7 8PF (7609 0467, www.freightlinersfarm.org.uk).*
Hackney City Farm *1A Goldsmiths Row, E2 8QA (7729 6381, www.hackneycityfarm.co.uk).*
Kentish Town City Farm *1 Cressfield Close, off Grafton Road, NW5 4BN (7916 5421, www.ktcityfarm.org.uk).*
Mudchute City Farm *Pier Street, E14 3HP (7515 5901, www.mudchute.org).*
Newham City Farm *Stansfeld Road, E16 3RD (7474 4960, www.newham.com).*
Stepney City Farm *Stepney Way, junction with Stepney High Street, E1 3DG (7790 8204, www.stepneycityfarm.org).*
Surrey Docks Farm *Rotherhithe Street, SE16 5EY (7231 1010, www.surreydocksfarm.org).*
Vauxhall City Farm *165 Tyers Street, SE11 5HS (7582 4204, www.vauxhallcityfarm.org).*

310-319 *Have cocktails*

It's hard to find exquisite cocktails when you're on a budget, so here are a few top watering holes where your tipple will set you back less than a tenner.

Café Kick

As you might have guessed, football is the name of the game at this Clerkenwell hotspot. Table football is the main draw – you can reserve one of the three table football tables – and soccer paraphernalia adorns the walls. The feel is retro meets Lisbon, and tapas, sandwiches and charcuterie can be washed down with great Kick cocktails – mojitos, caipirinhas, martinis and margaritas (£6.95, and only £4.85 between 4pm and 7pm).
43 Exmouth Market, EC1R 4QL (7837 8077, www.cafekick.co.uk).

Callooh Callay

A funky, cosmopolitan, evening-only cocktail bar, where most cocktails are less than a tenner; the Rivington 65 (£9) contains Tanqueray gin with fresh pink grapefruit juice and own-made chamomile syrup topped with prosecco. The main bar room has low, purple seating and a long bar counter. Staff are savvy and DJs spin at weekends.
65 Rivington Street, EC2A 3AY (7739 4781, www.calloohcallaybar.com).

Christopher's Martini Bar

Christopher's has a super-sized list of martinis and cocktails. The choice includes a sloe gin martini (£8.50), a classic martini (from £8), a mai tai and a passionfruit and ginger caipirinha (both £8.50). The maroon-striped booths, globe lights and swivel bar chairs add to the Big Apple feel.
18 Wellington Street, WC2E 7DD (7240 4222, www.christophersgrill.com).

Dollar

Another Yankee Doodle Dandee, Dollar is also cashing in on the trend. Outside, the gaudy red neon sign says 'Grills & Martinis' – inside, the vibe is more *Sex and the City*. The signature cocktail is the Porn Star martini (£8.95) – Cariel vanilla vodka and passion fruit.
2 Exmouth Market, EC1R 4PX (7278 0077, www.dollargrills.com).

Floridita

Named after the famous Hemingway haunt in Havana, this glitzy bar has a suitably Cuban cocktail list: most concoctions (priced around £8.50) blend Havana Club Anejo Blanco expertly shaken with fresh mint, fresh lime, sugars and various dashes by a vivacious barman. The Hemingway Special also contains fresh grapefruit and Maraschino; the Presidente has sweet Vermouth and orange Curaçao; and

the New York Flip – one of 14 *nuevo cubano* choices – vintage port shaken with egg yolk.
100 Wardour Street W1F OTN (7314 4000, www.floriditalondon.com).

Hawksmoor

The bar here at the original Hawksmoor didn't used to be much to look at, but in 2012 it got all glammed up. Nevertheless, the drinks are still the most important factor, and the celebrated bar staff remain London's cocktail intellectuals. They know their stuff, and the menu makes for entertaining reading too. Silver Bullet (£8.50), with gin, Kummel and lemon juice, a head-clearing concoction, is apparently Prince Philip's favourite cocktail, while under the heading 'disco drinks' you'll find Dr Funk Swizzle (also £8.50), containing rum, falernum, lime, own-made grenadine, Angostura Bitters and a dash of absinthe.
157 Commercial Street, E1 6BJ (7247 7392, www.thehawksmoor.com).

Happiness Forgets

This cosy cocktail cavern is small, subterranean and clearly slung together on a shoestring. But never mind all that, because it's really nice, with down-to-earth decor, extremely well-crafted cocktails, switched-on staff and good music. Simple, really. The 11-strong cocktail list changes every fortnight, and is devised by Alastair Burgess, formerly of Milk & Honey and New York's Pegu bar. Examples include the Perfect Storm (dark rum, plum brandy, ginger, honey and lemon) and the Louis Balfour (scotch, port, picon bitters and honey (both are £7.50).
8-9 Hoxton Square, N1 6NU (7613 0325, www.happinessforgets.com).

1 Lombard Street

Another converted bank in the heart of the City, this swanky Michelin-starred restaurant boasts a bright and suitably posh glass-domed circular bar, but a round of cocktails won't leave you in the red. Classic cocktails, such as a caipirina and a pina colada, cost £9.50, as do after dinner tinctures such as the Black Russian (vodka, coffee liquor and Coca Cola) and the Grasshopper (crème de menthe, crème de cacao and cream). Best buy is the negroni, at £8.50 – this is the City, after all.
1 Lombard Street, EC3V 9AA (7929 6611, www.1lombardstreet.com).

Calloh Callay

Shochu Lounge

Part *Shogun*, part 21st-century cosmopolitan chic, Shochu Lounge is the basement bar of Roka, the contemporary Japanese restaurant. It's named after a Japanese vodka-like spirit made from rice, barley and buckwheat, which forms the basis for its divine cocktails. These include the Noshino martini (shochu with cucumber, £8.60) and the Hei sour (jasmine shochu, lemon, almond syrup and ylang ylang – fragrance in a glass). More recent additions include the Glass Maze (lychee shochu, lychee juice and ylang ylang) and the Ki-la Rose (schochu, rose petal vodka, lemon, cranberry and cucumber).
Basement, 37 Charlotte Street, W1T 1RR (7580 9666, www.shochulounge.com).

Worship Street Whistling Shop

This cellar room is darkly Dickensian, full of cosy corners and leather armchairs. In the back is a windowed laboratory crammed with equipment modern and antiquated, used to create the wondrously described ingredients that constitute the cocktails (high pressure hydrosol, clorophyll bitters and so on). These are original and stimulating drinks that rarely exceed the £10 mark – the house gin fizz costs £8.50. And staff are great – it would be easy to come across po-faced or pretentious with such a studied approach to drink-making, but they're staunchly friendly and helpful all night.
63 Worship Street EC2A 2DU (7247 0015, www.whistlingshop.com).

320

Thames Dragons (www.thamesdragons.com) train crews to row in lung-bursting races, usually over 500 metres and occasionally longer distances such as this 22-mile annual Great River Race marathon. The first training sessions are free, although there are membership subscriptions if you then decide to join the club.

321-323
...or let others take the strain

Hang on a minute: glass of Pimms in hand? Balmy spring weather? Total absence of aching limbs? Maybe watching Oxbridge types grunt their way through the Boat Race is more your cup of tea? If so, join 250,000 fellow revellers along the riverbank for the next installment of the 150-year-old Boat Race (www.theboat race.org, late March or early April). See the two 'eights' power past from viewpoints at the start (Putney Bridge, Putney Embankment or Bishops Park), by the bridges at Hammersmith or Barnes, or at the finish (Dukes Meadows and Chiswick Bridge), perhaps taking advantage of big screens (usually in Bishops Park and Furnival Gardens) to watch the rest of the race.

If watching two crews of burly ringers isn't to your taste, the Doggett Coat & Badge Race (www.watermenshall.org) is much more sparsely supported, but far more historic. Contested since 1715 by young watermen (once a Thames-borne equivalent of the modern-day cabby), the race is rowed each July in traditional 'gigs' over four miles and five furlongs (nearly five miles) from London Bridge to Chelsea.

Or you could try the Great River Race (8398 9057, www.greatriverrace.co.uk). Every September, 300 traditional rowed boats from all over the world – and a variety of historical epochs – race a frightening 22 miles from Millwall Riverside to Richmond's Ham House. Hungerford Bridge, the Millennium Bridge and Tower Bridge are all good viewpoints.

324
See a performance at the Scoop

The Scoop at More London (www.more london.com/scoop.html), to use its full name, is a sunken open-air amphitheatre seating 800 people on the South Bank (in front of City Hall) that runs a programme of free films, concerts, plays and other events from May to October each year; one evening each Christmas it's also a magical setting for carols and storytelling.

325
See a bit of New England in Old England

The Grosvenor Chapel on South Audley Street is widely known as the American Church in Mayfair. Virtually unaltered since its construction in 1731, with its Tuscan portico, square tower and steeple, it now looks as though it could have been airlifted in from New England: that's how popular the look subsequently became in the States. The secluded gardens between the chapel and the Roman Catholic Church of the Immaculate Conception on Farm Street is full of benches dedicated to Americans, and became a favourite dead-letter drop during the Cold War.

Grosvenor Chapel *24 South Audley Street, W1K 2PA (7499 1684, www.grosvenor chapel.org.uk).*

326
Go to the Proms

True to its original democratic principles, you can still attend Promenade concerts for around a fiver. Of the 70-odd performances held at the Royal Albert Hall during the Proms season (www.bbc.co.uk/proms, mid July to early September), most offer same-day cheap tickets – up to 1,400 standing tickets are released 30 minutes before each performance. You have a choice of standing (or sitting on the floor) in the Arena pit in the middle or standing in the gallery running round the top of the hall. Queues form early and snake around the block for the popular shows, but for many you will rarely have to wait more than half an hour to see world-class classical music performances. Forget the slightly frightening bombast of the Last Night (you're unlikely to get a tickets under a tenner for this anyway) – there's so much more worth queuing for.

327

Check out Maltby Street

On the streets around these railway arches in SE1, a small clutch of food and drink specialists holds court from 9am to 2pm on Saturdays. Well-known names include Monmouth Coffee in arch 34 on Maltby Street, and St John Bakery in arch 72 on Druid Street (causing quite a stir with its custard doughnuts), but there are plenty of smaller scale suppliers here too. We love Topolski (selling produce from Poland, including wonderful sausages and pickles), which shares an arch (no.104 Druid Street) with a couple of cheese importers, among others. This area is also home to Kernal Brewery (1 Rope Walk), which always draws a crowd.
Maltby Street *www.maltbystreet.com.*

328

Go bargain hunting, or seal the deal, at the Wills-Moody Jumble Sale

Hugely popular with in-the-know students, this well-established indie gem happens on the first Sunday of the month (1-8pm) at the Lexington (96-98 Pentonville Road, N1 9JB. Either pitch up and sell your own casts-offs or priceless retro gems or spend the day rummaging around for second-hand offerings such as Britpop-era band tees, rare vinyl, vintage comics and hand-made jewellery. Of course, this being a rock 'n' roll jumble sale, there's also a dirt cheap bar and racy but not too intrusive – it is a Sunday, after all – rock tunes on the stereo.
www.willsmoody.com.

Maltby Street

329-333
Rock out on Denmark Street

Perhaps only Abbey Road is more significant to
the story of London's rich rock 'n' roll heritage
than this tiny West End thoroughfare that
connects Charing Cross Road with St Giles
High Street. It's thought there are over 10,000
instruments for sale at the stores here, and you
can usually try before you buy. Regent Sounds
(4 Denmark Street, WC2H 8LP, 7379 6111), now
specialising in Fender electrics, was once
a recording studio where the Rolling Stones
recorded their first album; London Sax (21
Denmark Street, WC2H 8NA, 7836 7872,
www.sax.co.uk) has many, many models of
saxophone; and Hank's Guitar Shop (24
Denmark Street, WC2H 8NJ, 7379 1139,
www.hanksguitarshop.com) can fulfil all your
acoustic needs. For sheet music, try Argents
(19 Denmark Street, WC2H 8NA, 7379 3384).

Alternatively, if you're suffering from stage
fright, just check out the museum-like shop
windows, with their displays of curious vintage
and collector pieces, or visit during the Tin Pan
Alley Festival (usually in late summer; www.
tinpanalleyfestival.co.uk), when the street closes
to make way for an indie street party with music
from emerging and established rock bands.

334 *Find the word on the street in Notting Hill*

Paved with gold? Pah! How coarse! West
London's streets are paved with something
infinitely more profound (and probably more
useful in these black economic times) – poetry.
Thanks to a local artist and life-long resident
Maria Vlotides, Notting Hill now boasts seven
specially designed manhole covers. Each is
engraved with a lyrical ditty from other local
writers including Margaret Drabble (who
describes the Coronet Cinema as a place of
'diamonds, dreams and tears'), PD James,
Sebastian Faulks and John Heath-Stubbs.
All are based near Notting Hill Gate; start at
Daunt Books (112-114 Holland Park Avenue,
W11 4UA) and stroll around to see if you
can find the rest.

335
Watch hockey for free

Unlike the premier division games of most other
team sports, professional hockey is usually free
to watch – though you might be quietly nudged
into buying a programme for £1. Games are
played at weekends: check out the likes of the
Hampstead & Westminster, Old Loughtonians
and Surbiton. For details of who to see and
where to see them, check the website.
www.englandhockey.co.uk.

336-345
Search for beautiful trees

London still has hundreds of magnificent trees
despite disease and redevelopment. Here are
our top ten: for detailed information on how
to get to them, see www.treesforcities.org.
Ash (*Fraxinus excelsior*) in Old St Pancras
Churchyard, King's Cross, NW1.
Fig (*Ficus carica*) in Amwell Street, EC1. Free food.
Holm oak (*Quercus ilex*) Fulham Palace
Gardens, SW6. A 500-year-old evergreen oak.
Huntingdon elm (*Ulmus x hollandica*) on
Marylebone High Street, W1. The last elm
surviving in Westminster.
Hybrid strawberry tree (*Arbutus x
andrachnoides*) in Battersea Park, SW11.
Indian bean tree (*Catalpa bignonioides*)
in the yard outside St James's Church,
Piccadilly, SW1.
London plane (*Platanus x hispanica*) in Berkeley
Square, W1. The quintessential street tree.
Queen Elizabeth's oak (*Quercus robur*) in
Greenwich Park, SE10. The remains of this
ancient oak, where Henry VIII wooed Anne
Boleyn and young Bess played, are fenced off
and marked by a plaque. A new sapling has
been planted in its place.
Royal oak (*Quercus robur*) in Richmond Park,
TW10. This tree is 700-800 years old.
Yew (*Taxus baccata*) in St Andrew's Church,
Totteridge, N20. Over 500 years old.

Hybrid strawberry tree

Going underground

Hankering for the glamorous – and grimy – world of latter-day espionage, Time Out's agent Robin Saikia goes undercover.

If you stand outside Tate Britain on Millbank and look across the Thames, you can't miss Vauxhall Cross, the striking headquarters of MI6, the British secret service. But for all the moody green cladding and bullet-proof glass, and despite its guest appearances in a couple of recent Bond films, this is a resolutely practical and functional building. As such, it may be something of a disappointment for the espionage fan in search of mystery, deception, eccentricity, romance and sleaze.

However, these attributes are all to be found in greater or lesser degrees in former secret service headquarters: 54 Broadway, SW1, with its brass plaque proclaiming 'Minimax Fire Extinguisher Company'; 21 Queen Anne's Gate, SW1, lair of Captain Sir Mansfield Smith-Cumming, the first 'C', with his swordstick, wooden leg, false moustaches and phoney German accent; Bush House, WC2, HQ of Claude Dansey, 'Uncle Claude' or 'Colonel Z' to his few friends and many enemies; originator of 'Z Organisation', an alternative MI6 of his own devising; Curzon Street House, W1, the quarters (it was rumoured) of hundreds of specially trained carrier pigeons – and home to the 'Registry', an ever-expanding filing system including the details of over two million people, hidden behind windows so encrusted with grime that they could doubtless have resisted a massive explosion.

Those were the days – and if Vauxhall Cross has any glamour at all it is surely a corporate, ostentatious glamour, not remotely redolent of the covert blackmail, silk stockings and cyanide of yesteryear. For mementoes of those, one has to go north of the Thames: Dolphin Square in Pimlico, SW1, an eminently respectable development of some 1,250 flats built in the mid 1930s, delivers a good measure of intrigue, sleaze and secret service history. There are 13 blocks in the square, each named after a naval hero – Drake House, Collingwood House, Hood House and so on. There is an agreeable bar, a good restaurant and pleasant gardens. Former residents include Princess Anne, Harold Wilson, William Hague and Peter Finch, as well as a steady stream of more or less blameless judges, politicians, writers and journalists. But there were dark horses too. Call girl Christine Keeler (a sub-tenant of Dolphin Square) caused a national scandal

when it was revealed in 1961 that she had had affairs with both the Conservative politician John Profumo, Secretary of State for War, and Yevgeny Ivanov, a Soviet naval officer.

But despite the nation's outrage, these were trifling indiscretions in comparison with the antics of John Vassall, resident of Hood House in the late 1950s. Vassall, a naval attaché in the British Embassy in Moscow, was lured to a homosexual party organised by the KGB and photographed in what he later conceded was 'a complicated array of sexual activities with a number of different men'. The KGB blackmailed him into working for them, though many claimed that Vassall, poorly paid and yearning for the high life, needed little coercion. He subsequently sold secret documents to the Russians, smuggling them out of the Admiralty in a copy of *The Times*, squandering the proceeds on expensive suits from Savile Row, rare antiques and exotic holidays. The Square's respectable spy – an important figure in the history of British espionage – was Maxwell Knight, who, from 1925, ran Section B5(b) of MI5 from his flat in Hood House. The purpose of B5(b) – 'Knight's Black Agents' to those in the know – was to infiltrate subversive groups, which under Knight's leadership it did with some success. (Knight also pursued a successful career as 'Uncle Max', broadcasting nature programmes for children for the BBC.)

A well-run hotel is the perfect spot to strike a Faustian bargain, and hotels will probably always be popular meeting places for secret agents. Brown's Hotel (Albemarle Street, W1S 4BP) was an occasional and very elegant secret service rendezvous, notably for the interrogation by Peter Wright of the scientist Alastair Watson, suspected in the 1960s of passing technical information to the Soviets. As Roy Berkeley observes in his excellent book *A Spy's London* '…the Soviets took their people to the basement of the Lubyanka, while the British took their people to Brown's'.

Wladislaw Sikorski, the Polish Prime Minister and Commander-in-Chief of Polish forces in World War II, set up his headquarters at the Rubens Hotel (39 Buckingham Palace Road, London, SW1W 0PS) in 1940. From here the Polish Resistance operated an extensive spy network until Sikorski's death in 1943.

The Mount Royal Hotel (now the Thistle Marble Arch, Bryanston Street, W1H 7EH),

was a meeting place for Russian double agent Oleg Penkovsky and agents from MI6 and the CIA. Penkovsky passed on invaluable secrets to his new colleagues in British and US intelligence, detailing the extent of the Soviet nuclear arsenal. In 1962, as a result of a tip-off from the British agent George Blake, he was arrested by the KGB. It is said that he was tied to a board with piano wire before being fed feet first into the oven of Moscow Crematorium.

The former Ebury Court Hotel (now Tophams Hotel, 28 Ebury Street, SW1W 0LU) was a known meeting place for the secret service and the Special Operations Executive (SOE) during World War II and it is still an agreeable place to meet for a quiet drink. Its unassuming wartime manageress, Yvonne Rudellat, was recruited into SOE and subsequently became a heroine of the French Resistance, successfully running a network in France. She was eventually captured by the Germans and died in a concentration camp.

St Ermin's Hotel (2 Caxton Street, SW1H 0QW) was another wartime outpost. Here, potential recruits were routinely interviewed in the subdued glamour of the restaurant, successful candidates (among them Noël Coward) being spirited up to the fifth and sixth floors, which in those days had been completely requisitioned by MI6. It was here that Kim Philby was interviewed and recruited into the secret service by Guy Burgess – a deal they sealed with a weekend of heavy drinking prior to an early start in Section D (for 'Destruction' – stirring up active resistance to the enemy) in the summer of 1940.

MI9, the World War II escape and 'exfiltration' department, set up shop on the second floor of the old Great Central Hotel (now the Landmark Hotel, 222 Marylebone Road, NW1 6JQ), having outgrown its former ad hoc HQ in room 424 of the Metropole Hotel (no longer in existence) in Northumberland Avenue. An underrated and too little known wing of the secret service, MI9's principal task was to help Allied servicemen stranded or imprisoned in enemy territory to escape or find their way back home. Footsoldiers such as Airey Neave masterminded the repatriation of troops and agents after disasters such as Operation Market Garden at Arnhem, while resourceful agents like the theatrical conjuror Jasper Maskelyne and the former pilot

Christopher Clayton Hutton developed a series of useful gadgets and devices – tools concealed in cricket bats, maps in gramophone records, compasses in buttons and so forth.

These survival innovations are not to be confused with the rather more sinister devices developed at 35 Portland Place, W1, by SOE: exploding rats, exploding pencils, exploding animal droppings, collapsible crossbows, suicide pills, a .22 calibre cigarette gun, garrottes and a tear gas fountain pen. (Gadgets of this sort are the stock in trade of spies of all allegiances. Later, during the Cold War, the KGB developed the 'Kiss of Death', a lipstick tube containing a 4.5mm single-shot pistol that was used by both female agents and by the notorious KGB 'ravens', gay men on entrapment missions.)

Throughout World War II, SOE progressively requisitioned whole blocks in Baker Street, to the extent that members would refer to themselves and the section simply as 'Baker Street'. No.64 became the operational HQ in October 1940. No.83, Norgeby House, had a plaque proclaiming it as the 'Inter-Services Research Bureau', but in reality the whole of 'F Section' ('F' for France) was run here by Colonel Maurice Buckmaster. F Section was split into cells, some large, some consisting of a single agent or a small team. Their codenames and personnel are resonant to this day: 'Wrestler', run by Pearl Witherington, the 'best shot in the service'; 'Salesman', with Violette Szabo, nicknamed 'la p'tite Anglaise'; 'Physician', a larger team that included Yvonne Rudellat, formerly of the Ebury Court Hotel and the beautiful Indian agent Noor Inayat Khan, the first female radio operator sent to France by SOE.

Agents needed a wide range of skills to survive in the field, everything from lockpicking to noiseless assassination, and these were taught at Michael House, 82 Baker Street. The second-floor flat in Orchard Court, Portman Square, with its famous black onyx and marble bathroom, was a briefing and debriefing station for SOE recruits. Officers would check that agents looked and behaved in a suitably Gallic fashion before despatching them on a tour of duty with the French Resistance. Chiltern Court was HQ to the Scandinavian section of SOE, while 221

Baker Street housed the clothing and disguise section, where tailors would work round the clock making 'authentic' continental clothing for agents.

'The KGB developed a 'Kiss of Death' lipstick containing a 4.5mm single shot pistol that was used by agents on entrapment missions.'

Buckingham Palace may seem an odd landmark to include – but it is there, after all, that art historian Anthony Blunt continued to fulfil his duties as Surveyor of the King's (and subsequently the Queen's) Pictures, long after he had confessed in 1964 to Arthur Martin of MI5 that he was a Soviet agent. Blunt was a member of the Cambridge Spy Ring – a group working for the Russians that had met at Cambridge University and included fellow KGB agents Guy Burgess, Donald Maclean and Kim Philby. Blunt was spared exposure and imprisonment in exchange for a full confession. Until his retirement as its director in 1974, Blunt also had the run of the Courtauld Institute of Art, then housed at 20 Portman Square. It was only in 1979, after the publication of Andrew Boyle's book *Climate of Treason*, that he was finally publicly disgraced (though he was never prosecuted). Named as a traitor by Margaret Thatcher in 1979, Blunt was stripped of his knighthood and, memorably, booed out of a cinema in Notting Hill Gate. Ever the cosmopolitan scholar-boulevardier, and seemingly unfazed by these very English setbacks, he quietly set about completing a definitive book on the Italian painter Pietro da Cortona without so much as a twang of piano wire to trouble him.

362 Get into korfball

Korfball, a mix between netball and basketball, was invented in 1901 in Holland. Which is perhaps surprising, given the '90s-fad-sounding name and the impressively progressive basic premise: fat, thin, tall, short, male or female; the only thing that matters is your ability to cooperate with your team mates. Twelve teams – each comprised of four men and four women – compete in London's regional league, and they all welcome beginners; see the website for more information.
www.londonkorfball.co.uk.

363 Be careful you don't get nicked in Trafalgar Square

The smallest police station in London is to be found hidden away in a lamp pillar in the south-east corner of Trafalgar Square. If you didn't know, you might take it for an ice-cream kiosk; but, no, it's really a one-man, auxiliary police station.

364 Watch nature among brutalist concrete

Ducks? Check. Reeds? Check. You're at the London Wetland Centre, right? Wrong, wrong, wrong. The Barbican Centre (Silk Street, EC2Y 8DS, 7638 8891, www.barbican.org.uk) is known by those who loathe it as a concrete monstrosity, but city-lovers know to linger by its lake and ponds, the water and waterfowl all the more delightful for the unlikely setting. Take a coffee to one of the outdoor tables and gaze out over the main lake, taking in the fountains, the waterfall (at the eastern end), St Giles's church (Milton's last resting place, directly opposite the café) and, yes, nature: waterlilies in summer, mallards, moorhens and their offspring in spring, even the occasional heron. You can pop out here during the interval – it's just as lovely at night – and there are more landscaped water gardens if you arrive at the Barbican on the Highwalkway from Barbican station. Even more transporting is the steamy Conservatory (open 11am-5.30pm Sun, unless there's a private event), a lush jungle of tropical plants and carp ponds. You won't believe you're still in the centre of town.

Barbican Centre

365-371 *Check out the city's best streets for window-shopping.*

As long as you're happy looking rather than buying, there's fun to be had on London's shopping streets.

In the last few years, concept stores, independents and pop-ups have reinvigorated the London shopping scene. Nowhere is this more apparent than in Redchurch Street, E2, still grimy in parts but often hailed as London's trendiest street. Here you'll find established but niche brands such as Aesop (no.5a),the botanical beauty shop from the Aussie skincare brand, and Aubin & Wills concept store (nos.64-66), as well as grungy thrift shop Sick (no.105) and decadent interiors outlet Maison Trois Garçons (no.45). A world away in atmosphere, but equally fashion conscious, is posh Mount Street, W1, home to master butcher Allens of Mayfair (no.117) and cigar supplier Sautter (no.106) but also increasingly the likes of Marc Jacobs (nos. 24-25), perfumer Annick Goutal (no.109) and Christian Louboutin (no.17). Ledbury Road, W11, also makes for upmarket gawping: here fashion boutiques such as Matches (nos.60-64) and Aimé (no.32) are joined by lifestyle boutique Wolf & Badger (no.46) and modish B&T Antiques (no.47).

More villagely in feel is Lamb's Conduit Street, WC1. This partially pedestrianised stretch holds a nicely diverse bunch of shops, from the People's Supermarket (nos.72-78) at one end to the French House (no.50) homewares store at the other. In between are individual fashion outlets such as Folk (nos.49 and 53), not to mention delightful Persephone Books (no.59). Equally charming is Camden Passage, N1. Once the haunt of antiques dealers, it's now more mixed, with upmarket knitting shop Loop (no.15) rubbing shoulders with womenswear designer Susy Harper (no.35) and Paul A Young Fine Chocolates (no.33). We're also very fond of Smug (no.13), which sells a covetable range of homewares.

Broadway Market, E8, has the added attraction of a swathe of stalls. Saturday is when the market is in full swing, but shops such as deli L'Eau à la Bouche (nos.35-37), accessories treasure trove Black Truffle (no.4) and Broadway Books (no.6) are open all week. Finally, Pitfield Street, N1, is short but interesting – stubbornly grotty for years, without a decent shop or café to its name, it now features some fantastic shops including a designer tattoo parlour Nine Nails Tattoos (no.25) and a smart interiors store with a café, Pitfield London (nos.31-35) – with more to follow no doubt.

A few of my favourite things

372-378

Leslie Grantham, actor

One of my favourite places in London is the Horniman Museum (100 London Road, SE23 3PQ, 8699 1872, www.horniman.ac.uk). Horniman was a tea merchant who collected all sorts of amazing objects on his travels, from huge totem poles from America to silks from China and sundials from around the world. The museum is only 15 minutes from the centre of London and it's free.

I've filmed a lot around the Docklands area and have become quite interested in its history. The Museum of London Docklands (West India Quay, E14 4AL, 7001 9844, www.museumindocklands. org.uk) tells you the whole story of the place from Roman times; it's also great to just stroll around the docks and see how all the various warehouses have been converted.

At St Mary Overie Dock in Southwark you can go and see a replica of Sir Francis Drake's ship, the *Golden Hinde* (Cathedral Street, SE1 9DE, 7403 0123, www.golden hinde.com). They have recreated what life was like on board a ship in his day, which is fascinating. It's the sort of thing they taught us about back when I was at school, and it's great to go and see it come to life. For £7 you get a guided tour and you can even hire the place out for parties.

I think one of the best things to do in London is go for a walk down the Thames from Docklands to Twickenham. You can stop off on the way for a drink and a bite to eat in one of the riverside pubs, and then when you get there, visit the Twickenham Museum (25 The Embankment, TW1 3DU, 8408 0070, www.twickenham-museum.org.uk). It covers the history of the local area of Twickenham, Hampton and Teddington, but it also has a lot about the history of the river itself.

You won't see many Wombles on Wimbledon Common (SW19 5NR, 8788 7655, www.wpcc.org.uk), but it's a great place to go to watch the world go by. There's a lovely tea shop on the edge of the common called the Windmill (Windmill Road, SW19 5NQ, 8788 2910, www.windmilltearooms.com), where you can park up and have a coffee or something to eat and watch people riding past on their horses.

Lots of kids I know love going to Leicester Square when there's a big movie premiere on to do some star-spotting. Loads of films have their premieres there, from the Bond films to Harry Potter. You can get a cup of hot chocolate from one of the cafés nearby and stand by the barriers as all the luvvies go in, and the earlier you get there, the closer you can get.

Whenever I used to go on TV shows like *Noel's House Party,* I'd always see the same people in the audience and that's because they'd be on a BBC mailing list. You can contact the BBC and ask for tickets to be in the audience for your favourite show (0370 901 1227, www.bbc.co.uk/ tickets, free). Going inside a TV studio and actually seeing how programmes are made is fascinating.

379

Take the long view in Richmond Park

You can put this 'thing to do' on the back burner if you like; the view is not likely to change any time soon because it is protected by law. That means nothing can be built that obstructs the ten-mile sightline from the top of King Henry VIII's mound in Richmond Park (the Tudor monarch used to hunt in these parts) all the way to St Paul's Cathedral in the City to the east. After you've taken in the vista make your way to the Isabella Plantation (*see p97*).

Richmond Park, *TW10 (7161 9721, www.royalparks.gov.uk/Richmond-Park.aspx.*

Richmond Park

380

Read history into stained glass at St Margaret's

The parish church of the House of Commons since 1614, St Margaret's is well worth a visit for its stained glass windows alone. As old in foundation as Westminster Abbey, the building there today dates largely from the 16th century. Highlights include the east window, which is 15th-century Flemish and was paid for by Catherine of Aragon. It depicts the Crucifixion scene, flanked by St George and St Catherine of Alexandria. Underneath is the sickly Prince Arthur, elder brother of Henry VIII and Catherine of Aragon's first betrothed. The west window is by the eminent Victorian Arts and Crafts window makers Clayton and Bell, and shows Sir Walter Raleigh (in the middle), who was executed only a few yards away, in Old Palace Yard. The south aisle windows are by John Piper and were added in 1966.

St Margaret's *20 Dean's Yard, Westminster Abbey, SW1P 3PA (7222 5152, www.westminster-abbey.org).*

381-384
Go for a walk in a wood

Epping Forest
The big one. Nearly 6,000 acres of woodland, interspersed with heaths, lakes and rides. The wood formed after the last Ice Age and is mainly oak, beech and hornbeam. Watch out for the massive branches of previously pollarded trees, left to grow since the passing of the Epping Forest Act in 1878. A good starting point for walks is the area around Queen Elizabeth's Hunting Lodge, which is now a museum.
Queen Elizabeth's Hunting Lodge, Ranger's Road, E4 7QH.

Highgate Wood/Queen's Wood
Highgate and, on the other side of Muswell Hill Road, Queen's Woods are remnants of the ancient forest of Middlesex, which once covered most of north London and the county of Middlesex. The smaller Queen's Wood has the more diverse ecology, with its predominant oak and hornbeam canopy and strangely named 'wild service tree'
a marker for the age of the woodland. Highgate Wood also has a café, a playground and playing fields.
Muswell Hill Road, N10.

Holland Park
Although Holland Park is one of London's grand formal parks, there is a surprisingly extensive wood in its northern half. Set off down one of the shaded paths and within a minute the sounds of the city will become muffled and then all but disappear.
Abbotsbury Road, W11.

Shooters Hill Woodlands
Oxleas, Jack and Shepherdleas woods – remnants of the post-glaciation wildwood that once stretched over the whole country – cover Shooters Hill with a mixture of oak, sweet chestnut and hazel, plus the tell-tale maple-like leaves of the 'wild service tree'. The rare palmate newt lives in ponds in the woods.
Shooters Hill, SE9.

See the future, now
In mid September each year design junkies descend on the London Design Festival (www.londondesignfestival.com), which showcases the best of the capital's creative designers, artists and fashion makers. Held at various locations across town, the fun usually centres on Brick Lane's Truman Brewery, and the programme features a couple of hundred commercial and cultural events.

386
Get into the Tower for free – but don't be late
The ticket price puts a normal visit to the Tower of London beyond the scope of this book, but – if you're organised – you can see something the hordes of paying tourists won't be able to see... and without paying a penny. Dating back seven centuries, the Ceremony of the Keys happens at exactly 9.53pm each evening, when the Yeoman Warders begin the process of locking the Tower's entrances. They have failed to do so on the dot only once since the Ceremony began, when shockwaves from nearby Blitz bombs tumbled the party to the ground, causing a delay of several minutes. (The Yeoman Warders were sufficiently ashamed of this failure to write an apology to King George VI.)

The ticketed public assembles at the West Gate at 9pm, through which they enter the outer wall and follow the ceremony around each gate. When it's all over, at about 10pm, the Last Post sounds. This little piece of repeated history is understandably popular, of course, so you'll need to apply for tickets (offering two possible dates) at least two months in advance. For full details, see www.hrp.org.uk/toweroflondon/whatson/ceremonyofthekeys.aspx. Tower Hamlets residents are, however, unusually blessed: they can get into the Tower of London for just £1, without applying in advance for anything. And they get to see the Crown Jewels and inside all the various towers. Just take proof of residence and a library card with you when you go to the ticket office.

387-394

Savour the capital's finest kebabs...

London may be beset with dodgy doner houses, but it is also blessed with some of the finest kebabs this side of Istanbul. Here are some of our favourites.

Abu Zaad

This Syrian restaurant in Shepherd's Bush has reasonably priced Damascene food ranging from meat-heavy kebabs to vegetarian-friendly mezze and, being Syrian, the odd spicy kebab and lots of oven-baking in yoghurt. Try the kebab bil tahina – a traditional dish of spicy lamb topped with yoghurt and rich tahina.
29 Uxbridge Road, W12 8LH (8749 5107, www.abuzaad.co.uk).

Kebab Kid

This little takeaway is a cut above the rest, with no greasy doners of fatty minced lamb, just proper shawarmas (chicken or lamb) of prime cuts of meat (from Smithfield Market), or shish kebabs cooked on skewers to order. We also like the crunchy shredded salad, and the (optional) smear of own-made taramasalata. A medium shawarma costs £5.70.
90 New Kings Road, SW6 4LU (7731 0427).

Mangal 1 Ocakbasi

Come to the original branch of Turkish Mangal in Dalston for heaps of prime meat at low prices – and its BYO policy. There's no printed menu; you choose skewers of meat from the glass display counter and they're grilled in front of you. Shish (marinated lamb chunks), beyti (spicy minced lamb) and pirzola (lamb chops) are all exemplary and served in generous portions with a huge mound of salad and warm leavened bread (from £9.50 eat in).
10 Arcola Street, E8 2DJ (7275 8981, www.mangal1.com).

Patogh

This tight-packed Iranian café off Edgware Road offers wonderful flatbreads with minced lamb or chicken wrapped around skewers, then chargrilled (from £6). Most mains are served on grim metal plates, but somehow it all adds to the authentic experience. The salads include whole fresh fronds of mint and tarragon, which really make the flavours sing.
8 Crawford Place, W1H 5NE (7262 4015).

19 Numara Bos Cirrik I

It's appropriate that the dominating feature of this ocakbasi is the embossed copper extractor hood at the right-hand end of the counter: the place is all about that smoking charcoal grill. The main event is the meat: shish, adana and chicken kebabs, spare ribs, beyti and köfte - perfectly charred without being burnt, and all saltily, juicily magnificent. The extras are done right too – expect a great feed for pleasingly little cash.
34 Stoke Newington Road N16 7XJ (7249 0400www.cirrik1.co.uk).

Ranoush Juice

The original branch of this Lebanese café chain is a great pitstop for either an easy lunch or post-partying sustenance. The Lebanese mezze of houmous, chicken livers, sujuk sausages and so forth are all excellent, but the *pièces de résistance* are the two formidable shawarmas (chicken and lamb) rotating at the front of the shop. Juicy slices are deftly shorn off by the staff and scooped into the waiting arrangement of bread (£4).
43 Edgware Road, W2 2JR (7723 5929, www.maroush.com).

Sitaaray

This Bollywood-themed restaurant is camper than a Rajasthani caravan, yet its cooking is surprisingly sophisticated. We particularly like mint-marinated, chargrilled tiny lamb

chops and the unusual variation on shami kebabs studded with sweetcorn but tasting of fenugreek. Vegetarians are also well catered for, even if kebabs are the star attraction. *167 Drury Lane, WC2B 5PG (7269 6422, www.sitaaray.com).*

Tayyabs

This Pakistani canteen in Whitechapel has consistently been popular: there's almost always a queue. Among the starters are chicken or mutton tikkas, lamb chops, seekh kebabs and shami kebabs – all of which are seriously low-priced (starting at £1) and beautifully cooked. *83-89 Fieldgate Street, E1 1JU (7247 9543, www.tayyabs.co.uk).*

395 *...or make your own*

Many butchers sell meat ready prepared to kebab; try M Moen & Sons in Clapham (24 The Pavement, SW4 0JA, 7622 1624, www.moen.co.uk) or Macken Brothers in Chiswick (44 Turnham Green Terrace, W4 1QP, 8994 2646, www.mackenbros.co.uk).

Ranoush Juice

396

Take table tennis to another level

Every second Tuesday, ping pong takes over two floors of the Rich Mix cultural centre in Bethnal Green. Throw yourself into various challenges and madcap games, such as the Pongathon Mini Bat Challenge with the world's smallest bats, and Beat the Pongbot, which offers the chance to play against a robot. There's also visual art, prizes and DJs. The best bit? Entry is free.

Pongathon *Rich Mix, 35-47 Bethnal Green Road, E1 6LA (www.pongathon.com).*

397

Remember the watergate scandal

Between the bottom of Buckingham Street and Embankment Gardens stands a weathered stone gate – once the watergate belonging to the great 17th-century York House, which stood between here and the Strand. It isn't now immediately recognisable as a watergate that once led from a grand garden down to the Thames – primarily because it's fully 150 yards from the river, thanks to Joseph Bazalgette's 1864 construction of the Embankment.

Today, clues to York House's ownership still lie in the surrounding streets. George Street, Villiers Street, Duke Street (now gone) and the absurdly named Of Alley (now York Place, Formerly Of Alley) in the immediate vicinity of Buckingham Street, together serve to remind us of George Villiers, Duke of Buckingham. Sexy George swanned into London in 1614, and quickly became the court favourite of King James I, who referred to him as 'sweet child and wife': rumour and intrigue followed him for the rest of his life, but if nothing else it was a canny short-cut to having a whole corner of London named after you.

398 *Reflect on a crime of passion over a pint*

Today, the Magdala pub in Hampstead (2a South Hill Park, NW3 2SB, 7435 2503, www.the-magdala.com) is a sedate spot with huge leaded and stained-glass windows and is also home to the monthly Alpine comedy club. However, back in 1955, this is where Ruth Ellis, the last woman to be hanged in Britain, shot estranged lover David Blakely on Easter Day, and two weathered bullet holes on the outside front wall (plus framed press cuttings) mark the event. While supping a pint of Sharp's Doom Bar or Greene King IPA you can eavesdrop on the various walking/murder tour guides' commentaries and reflect on Ellis's admission that 'it is obvious when I shot him I intended to kill him'.

399 *Sing along with a five-piece funk band*

Ever dreamt of standing in front of a crowd of adoring fans while belting out your favourite funk classic, with the support of a professional backing band? Well, now's your chance. SoulBrew Karaoke takes place on the last Friday of the month at the Queen of Hoxton in Shoreditch. There are more than 100 soul and disco classics to choose from – from Amy Winehouse to James Brown, Kool & the Gang to Beyoncé. Our advice – stay sober until after you've sung.

SoulBrew Karaoke *Queen of Hoxton, 1-5 Curtain Road, EC2A 3JX (7422 0958, www.queenof hoxton.com). Tickets £5.*

400 *Get caffeinated at a coffee festival*

The London Coffee Festival (www.london coffeefestival.com) is a three-day event that celebrates the city's vibrant coffee culture, with artisanal coffee for sale and to sample, barista demonstrations, food treats and live music. Tickets for Saturday and Sunday are valid for brunch, lunch or teatime sessions. Tickets cost £9.50 in advance.

401 *Learn Brazilian dance at Guanabara*

Salsa is a bit '90s and tango's a little too technical – if you want to learn to dance Latin-style, go Brazilian. One of the capital's best Brazilian bars, Guanabara (Parker Street, W2CB 9PW, 7242 8600, www.guanabara.co.uk), runs free dance classes (Mon, Wed, Sun); try samba, forró and even Brazilian ballroom dancing, gafieira. Classes take place before the place fills up with regulars, which means that when the lesson ends you can practise your moves on the dancefloor with those who really know their stuff. Alternatively, hit the bar for a caipirinha.

402

Check out the street furniture in SE...

In Peckham's Bellenden Road, street bollards are designed by Anthony Gormley, pavements and bus stops by Zandra Rhodes and local artist Tom Phillips created the curlicue lamp posts and wall mosaics. Restored Georgian and Victorian terraces, upmarket bistros, boutique fashion and book stores all add to the burgeoning café culture.

403 Drink sherry

That's everything from the light tangy Puerto Fino through to intense fruity PX sherries such as the 1975 Don Pedro Ximenez Gran Reserva. If you can't stretch to the top-notch four-course Saturday sherry lunch at Moro (34-36 Exmouth Market, EC1R 4QE, 7833 8336, www.moro.co.uk), then sip an old favourite such as manzanilla (£3.50/glass) at the bar and snack on the excellent tapas dishes instead, or visit offshoot tapas bar Morito (32 Exmouth Market, EC1R 4QE, 7278 7007). Another small, no-bookings tapas bar is José (104 Bermondsey Street, SE1 3UB, 7403 4902, www.josepizarro.com), where the list of sherries is longer than the tapas menu. Tiny Bar Pepito (3 Varnishers Yard, N1 9DF, 7841 7331, www.camino.uk.com) is dedicated to sherry – to sample the breadth of flavours, try a flight of sherries for £8. The bright, stylish surroundings at Fino (33 Charlotte Street, W1T 1RR, 7813 8010) are another fine spot to sample a list of around 20 sherries; most start at £5 a glass.

404-405
Examine the new blue plaques

Famous residents newly celebrated include novelist Graham Greene – he wrote *Brighton Rock* at 14 Clapham Common North Side, SW4 – and florist Constance Spry, who had her shop at 64 South Audley Street, W1, from 1934-1960.

406 Watch out for Appearing Rooms

Danish artist Jeppe Hein's water sculpture *Appearing Rooms* has proved so popular (especially with children) that it returns to the South Bank every summer. The rows of fountains, in grid formation, are liable to squirt unpredictably – trapping you in one of the square 'rooms', unless, of course, you're up for a soaking. Find it in front of the Royal Festival Hall, SE1.

407 Board Hammerton's ferry

This tiny boat, taking just 12 foot passengers (and the odd bicycle), operates daily from Marble Hill House to Ham House (and vice versa) from March to the end of October. It's the sole survivor of the numerous ferries that plied this stretch of the river for hundreds of years. Times have changed: the boat has an electric motor these days, and the fare – a penny when it was started in 1908 by one Walter Hammerton – is now £1 for adults, 50p for children (plus 50p for adult bikes).
www.hammertonsferry.co.uk

408 Don't touch anything in the Islington Museum

In the Islington Museum you'll find a bust of communist leader Lenin (who published his radical *Iskra* at nearby 37a Clerkenwell Green). Originally gracing the Russian Embassy, it was later moved to Finsbury Town Hall but, following repeated vandalism, it's found a safer, and perhaps more appreciative, audience here. Once you've finished doffing your cap to Lenin, check out the museum's curiously ironic relic: the books from Islington's libraries that were famously defaced by playwright Joe Orton and his lover Kenneth Halliwell. What a difference a few decades make: back in 1962, the pair were jailed for six months for their ill-advised doodling.
Islington Museum *245 St John Street, EC1V 4NB (7527 2837, www.islington.gov.uk/leisure/heritage/heritage_museum/). Free.*

409 Experience the heavy hand of the law

Members of the public can watch British justice in action at the Central Criminal Court (open 10am-1pm, 2-5pm Mon-Fri), so long as they leave any bags, cameras, dictaphones, mobile phones or food at home (there are no storage facilities provided at the court). The front door details forthcoming trials.
Central Criminal Court *Old Bailey, EC4M 7EH (7248 3277, www.cityoflondon.gov.uk). Free.*

A few of my favourite things

410-415

Johnny Vaughan, TV and radio presenter

In my opinion, nothing beats a good, simple British boozer. The Beehive in Clapham Junction (197 St John's Hill, SW11 1TH, 7207 1267) is like an English themed pub from the '70s and it's just brilliant – juke box, fruit machine, nice landlord, no food served and children not welcome. Fantastic. The clientele tend to be one man and his dog, or blokes doing the *Evening Standard* crossword. If you show up there with a mate it's like you're being flash. It's where I slope off to read a paper if I'm on my own.

A trip to Lollipop (201 St John's Hill, SW11 1TH, 7585 1588) is another nice bit of nostalgia-lite. It's a really old-school sweet shop, with all your Merry Maids, Cola Cubes and Tom Thumb Drops. None of this jelly babies in plastic – everything's packed in white and red striped paper bags. They might not be penny sweets anymore but it's still cheap. Every adult who goes in there starts reminiscing about Bulls Eyes or some other obscure childhood sweet, and you get people arguing about important subjects like Opal Fruits becoming Starburst.

Whenever the Carters Steam Fair (01628 822221, www.carterssteamfair.co.uk) is in town we always visit that. It's basically how a funfair should be, with merry-go-rounds, carousels, old-fashioned dodgems, stalls – and because it's run by real enthusiasts everything is so well looked after and beautiful. You walk around and sort of imagine World War II soldiers going there for a last night out before going back to war. It's class.

I'd advise anyone who hasn't done it to take the Woolwich Ferry (8853 9400, www.greenwich.gov.uk/Greenwich/Travel). It's just a car ferry which crosses the Thames, but it's free and the river is quite wide at that point so it makes for a nice little cruise. Often you can pay quite a lot to go on river boat tours and they take so long and are so boring but this one just does the job.

I've been going to Maroush (21 Edgware Road, W2 2JE, 7723 0773, www.maroush.com) for years. Two of you can eat for under £20 and the food is delicious. They do a chicken or lamb shawarma with garlic sauce and huge chillies which comes rolled up really tight in pitta bread – and we all know the power of pitta to make anything taste good. And their mixed fruit cocktail is all you'll need to sort you out if you have a hangover.

If you're going to museums or galleries you've got to avoid places where it's all about the gift shop, otherwise you just end up blowing your budget even if it's free entry. I think the Imperial War Museum (Lambeth Road, SE1 6HZ, 7416 5320, www.iwm.org.uk) is great. It's really good for kids to see things like tanks close up, which they've previously only played with in miniature. And they have the Victoria Cross room which is so moving – when we think we're going through bad times it provides a reminder of the people who faced something a bit bigger than our own struggles.

416 *Make the world more beautiful...*

In late 2004 gardening radical and Elephant & Castle resident Richard Reynolds set up his own underground movement, inviting others to join him 'to fight the filth in public spaces with forks and flowers'. The idea is to overhaul neglected areas of greenery; a particular favourite is roundabouts – often unattractive spaces, yet seen by hundreds of people every day. You can check out which digs are planned – and suggest your own on the website, www.guerrilla gardening.org, which also has news of similar popular gardening initiatives, talks and communities overseas.

417 ...or take a short cut and visit a garden that is already beautiful

During Open Squares weekend (held in the middle of June, see www.opensquares.org), wrought iron gates are swung back and city oases, usually hidden behind high laurel hedges, are opened to the public. There are around 200 gardens and squares to choose from and they come in all shapes, colours and sizes: there are the impressively grand set pieces – Belgrave Square, SW1, is an enormous four-acre garden with an enviable collection of statuary, and a tennis court – and there are the hidden City jewels such as the Salters' Garden (Salters' Hall, 4 Fore Street, EC2Y 5DE, pictured), redesigned as a knot garden by David Hicks in 1995 to mark the 600th anniversary of the Worshipful Company of Salters. That impressive pedigree is in evidence in the medieval city wall that forms the garden's southern boundary.

Take it to the bridges

Wealth, death and a lot of bad language, Charlie Godfrey-Faussett talks us through traversing the Thames.

It was thanks to Hadrian that Londinium, with its timber bridge over the river, was able to consolidate its prestige a century after being sacked and burned by Boudicca. And without London's bridges it's quite possible that we'd still be waiting for a waterman to ferry us across to the other side of the river in his boat – though we probably wouldn't have to wait very long. In Elizabethan times, when there was still only one bridge in London, there were some 40,000 watermen working the river (to put that in perspective, there are around 20,000 licensed black cabs in the city today). A famously feisty and foul-mouthed bunch (a law was once passed attempting to moderate their backchat), when more bridges were proposed in the 17th century, it was the watermen (along with the City of London) who successfully opposed the idea. Let's give thanks, then, that you can now walk across the Thames free of charge, keeping your feet dry and your thoughts clean, on no less than nine different bridges in the two miles or so between the Tower of London and the Houses of Parliament.

A pleasant stroll through Tower Gardens leads round the medieval walls of the Tower of London and up some steps on to Tower Bridge Approach. And what an approach it is: this preposterous neo-Gothic construction, the first bridge ever built downstream of London Bridge, has become even more iconic than the fortress it was supposed to complement. And what's more, it actually works. With its lifting 'bascules' and pedestrian skywalks, it looks more like the entrance to an elfin wonderland than a bridge. But perhaps the real reason it's so popular is that it has buildings on it – harking back to Old London Bridge, which was packed with houses – and you can hire the Bridge Master's Dining Room in the south abutment for a day, or an evening, of private dining.

Thanks to one of those feats of continuity that the City of London does so well, the Bridge House Estates, founded in 1097 by King William Rufus for levying taxes for the repair of London's only bridge, are still paying for the upkeep of the five City bridges today. They grew considerably in importance during

the Middle Ages, after the new stone bridge became the City's lifeline, and were given a Royal Charter in 1282. They now manage some £700 million worth of assets and, as the City Bridge Trust, also give £15 million to charitable causes in London each year. They also paid for Tower Bridge, which opened with much pomp and ceremony in 1894.

At the south end of the bridge, head down the steps and turn right on to the riverside Queen's Walk. It passes the glass kidney of City Hall, the gleaming office blocks of MoreLondon and HMS *Belfast* – which is moored at the end

of Battle Bridge Lane, apparently named after the supposed site of Boudicca's final rout by the Romans. Further along, a plaque on the embankment wall marks the site of Old London Bridge, its first stone laid in 1176. It was replaced in 1831 by a new one designed by the indefatigable Scottish engineer John Rennie (who also built the first Waterloo and Southwark bridges). His London Bridge was famously sold to McCulloch Oil in 1968 and rebuilt in Lake Havasu City, Arizona. The new London Bridge, finished in 1973, with its three arches, is hardly a beauty but it's still well worth crossing for the view of Tower Bridge downstream – and for the beeline it makes into the City, towards the imposing offices of the Guardian Royal Exchange Assurance Group (1921). On the left, Cannon Street station's brick towers, and its iron railway bridge, were constructed in 1865 and are early works of John Wolfe Barry, who later saw Tower Bridge through to completion (he was the son of Sir Charles Barry, who designed the Houses of Parliament).

> **'There were some 40,000 watermen working the river – to put that in perspective, there are around 20,000 licensed black cabs in the city today.'**

At the north end of London Bridge, by the Egyptian art deco Adelaide House, take the steps down to the riverside on the right. Carrying on upstream from here, great views of Southwark cathedral open up across the river from Watermen's Walk (a name loaded with cruel irony, given that they would surely have preferred you to take a ride in their boats). On the north side of the river, Watermark Place, with its swish wooden gantries and euro-chic dining options, is set to open in the place of Mondial House, the stylish 1970s bomb-proof telephone exchange that once stood here. Expect fine views over the water to Pickford's Wharf, Winchester Wharf, the old Thameside Inn, and the replica of Sir Francis Drake's world-circling little *Golden Hinde* in its dock.

Just before you pass under Cannon Street station, note the plaque unveiled in 2005 'to celebrate 60 years of peace between the peoples of Britain and Germany, and to commemorate 600 years during which some 400 Hanseatic merchants inhabited peacefully in the City

of London from the 13th to 19th centuries, in the German self-governing enclave on this site known as the Steelyard'. Steelyard Passage, running under the bridge and lit by dinky blue lights dotted on the ground, leads to a refreshing stopover in the shape of the Banker on Cousin Lane. Its funny little outdoor deck, right on the river, looks across to the more famous (and busy) Anchor on Bankside, but this one gets all the sun in the afternoon. Fortify yourself before continuing along Walbrook Wharf past Cory Environmental's Transfer Station, where the City of London's garbage is containerised before being floated out of town on big barges to the Mucking Marshes (thankfully a remarkably odourless operation these days).

The approach to Southwark Bridge is up Fruiterer's Passage (check out the Fruiterers' crest on the wall showing Adam and Eve in the garden, proving what a serious matter fruit and veg can be). Southwark Bridge, built between 1913 and 1921, and designed by Sir Ernest George, mentor to Edwin Lutyens, has a beautiful old gold, eau-de-nil and cream colour scheme and lovely lamps that are especially atmospheric when there's a mist hanging over the river at night. Crossing south over the bridge – apparently aligned with the older Blackfriars Bridge upstream to minimise tidal turbulence – you're confronted by the spinnaker façade of Riverside House, home of media regulator Ofcom. Heading right along Bankside at the end of the bridge, you pass the reconstructed Globe Theatre, its thatched roof now authentically mossy.

However, St Paul's Cathedral and Tate Modern are the big events here – and the Millennium Bridge connects the two. Also in the care of the Bridge House Estates, the first new pedestrian bridge over the river for a century is a shining wonder to walk across. Famously wobbly on first opening, the cunning design of its flattened out suspension cables means that there are great views to the left and right and it's a memorable approach straight across towards the great dome of St Paul's.

Don't get distracted by the cathedral, though: you've got more bridges to cross. From the north end of the Millennium Bridge drop hard left on to riverside Paul's Walk. Outside the entrance to the City of London School is a polar sundial, the time indicated by the shadow of its oxhead gnomon (a gnomon is a sundial's 'needle', in this case positioned in the centre of the sundial and vaguely resembling an oxhead). Paul's Walk continues along the river past flower-filled tubs, wooden pergolas and benches backed up against the brick wall of the Blackfriars Bridge Underpass. Pass beneath Blackfriars Railway Bridge (another of John Wolfe Barry's works, with Henri Brunel, son of Isambard, opened in 1886), which stands next to the shadow of its former self – the massive supports of the London, Dover and Chatham railway bridge of 1862 jutting purposelessly out of the water.

The original Blackfriars Bridge was put up in 1769 (then only the third in London) and the watermen were duly compensated. It was then replaced by 1869 and opened by Queen Victoria, at that time so unpopular she was hissed by the crowd at the opening ceremony (a statue of her stands at the northern end of the bridge, notwithstanding). Dickens described the bridge as 'one of the handsomest in London ... the general outline is bold and the ensemble rich, if perhaps a trifle gaudy, especially when the gilding, of which there is an unusual proportion, has been freshly renewed.' In honour of this being the river's tidal turning point – the point at which fresh and saline water meet – you'll notice that the bridge's piers are decorated with stone seagulls and seabirds on the downstream, seaward side, and kingfishers, herons and other freshwater birds on the upstream side. It also has a surprisingly low Venetian gothic balustrade: could it be coincidence that it was from this bridge that the Italian banker Roberto Calvi, known as the Pope's banker, was found hanging in 1982?

At the other end of the bridge avert your eyes from the ugly Sea Containers House before passing the successful OXO Tower Wharf redevelopment into the attractive, tree-lined and laid-back approach to Waterloo Bridge. Before long, however, the great blocks of the National Theatre announce a different, concrete world – sterner and more practical, perhaps, but certainly, in the case of the bridge at least, more beautiful. Not only are the views from the bridge itself inspiring – wedged as it is on a sharp bend in the river – but with it the architect, Sir Giles Gilbert Scott, surely produced his finest work. Bearing its name

proudly on its side, like a ship, its five leaping spans, supported by massive concrete box girders, manage to appear wonderfully light. It was completed during World War II, in 1942, and much of the construction work was carried out by women. It is the people's bridge.

'Waterloo Bridge, bearing its name proudly on its side like a ship, was completed during World War II.'

After a break at the terrace café in Somerset House on the northern side, Victoria Embankment Gardens are well worth strolling through on the way to your penultimate bridge. The footbridges on either side of Hungerford Bridge were opened in 2003, making them the newest bridges on the river. Take the left-hand Golden Jubilee footbridge to see the City; take the right-hand one to see Westminster.

Now you're in the busiest and most popular bit of the South Bank, home to the London Eye and County Hall, but you can avoid the crowds (nearly) by going through the tunnel beneath the Coade stone South Bank lion, then taking the southern pavement of Westminster Bridge towards the Houses of Parliament. The first bridge on this site was constructed in 1750, after overcoming the usual long-held objections from the watermen and the City. Wordsworth immortalised it with his reflections from it on the city at dawn but this one replaced Wordsworth's in 1862. It was designed by Thomas Page with input from Sir Charles Barry, architect of the Houses of Parliament, and possibly the reason why it complements them so neatly. Follow the bridge to its west end on the north bank and you'll find a striking statue of Boudicca. If she – or the watermen – had had their way, there might never have been any London bridges at all.

427-430

Hear church choirs

There are many glorious church choirs in London and all of them can be heard for little more than the cost of a bus fare or whatever donation you feel inclined to leave in the plate. The choirs of Westminster Abbey (www.westminster-abbey.org), St Paul's Cathedral (www.stpauls.co.uk), Westminster Cathedral (www.westminstercathedral.org.uk) and the Brompton Oratory (www.brompton oratory.com) are all well known (visit their websites for details), but there are also several less prominent churches that offer a great opportunity for musical uplift.

One such is the Parish Church of St George (Hanover Square, W1S 1FX, 7629 0874, www. stgeorgeshanoversquare.org), an elegant Queen Anne church. There is animated carving on the reredos from the workshop of Grinling Gibbons and the 16th-century Flemish glass in the east window has a uniquely smoky beauty. Famous for high society weddings, St George's was the venue of choice for Eliza's upwardly mobile dustman father, Alfred Doolittle, in *My Fair Lady*. The choir sings every Sunday morning at the Parish Eucharist.

At the end of one of North London's most lovely residential streets, Church Row, you'll find a grand church and graveyard, dating back to 986. The Parish Church of St John-at-Hampstead (Church Row, NW3 6UU, 7794 5808, www.hampsteadparishchurch.org.uk) has a strong musical heritage originally created by its great organist and choirmaster, the late Martindale Sidwell. That heritage is upheld by the present director of music, Lee Ward, and generously supported by the urbane and enthusiastic Hampstead congregation. There is a sung Parish Eucharist and Choral Evensong every Sunday (4.30pm in winter, 6pm in summer, check website for details).

St Mary's Church (Bourne Street, SW1W 8JJ, 7730 2423, www.stmarythevirgin.org.uk) is an offbeat haven in the heart of Belgravia. The church is Anglo-Catholic, and you are therefore just as likely to hear a polyphonic *Salve Regina* by Juan de Aranda as you are Anglican music by the likes of Stanford and Parry sung by the 'invisible' choir on high in the west end gallery.

The Parish Church of St Mary the Virgin (Elsworthy Road, NW3 3DJ, 7722 3238, www.smvph.org.uk) near Swiss Cottage offers a sung Eucharist every Sunday morning and Evensong once a month. St Mary's figures prominently in the Anglican choral tradition and its vicar in Edwardian times, Percy Dearmer, collaborated with Ralph Vaughan Williams on the New English Hymnal. Dearmer was as much renowned for his sense of sartorial style as he was for his interest in music, favouring a cassock, gown and velvet cap during day-to-day parish rounds. 'To hell with the Pope!' shouted a rude little boy on seeing Dearmer in this outfit. 'Are you aware,' replied Dearmer, 'that this is the precise costume in which Latimer went to the stake?'

431

Hide away at Greenwich Peninsula Ecology Park

At the Greenwich Peninsula Ecology Park you can delight in being in a way-out wet place bouncing with life and beauty – just a stone's throw from the O2 centre. If it's astonishing enough that a park like this should exist here, given the area's industrial history, it's even more amazing that the animals living here are not put off by the encroaching city. But then the park was always intended as an urban project, providing a new wetland habitat and enabling scientists to find out more about urban ecology. Abundant wildlife – frogs, toads, newts, beetles, brightly coloured dragonflies and damselflies, butterflies and wild flowers – throngs the inner and outer lakes. You can go on evening bat walks (*see p93*) and there are also specially designed hides from which you can check out the various resident and visiting bird species in more detail. Check the website for more details of the different monthly and seasonal events.

Greenwich Peninsula Ecology Park
The Ecology Park Gatehouse, Thames Path, John Harrison Way, SE10 0QZ (8293 1904, www.urbanecology.org.uk).

432
Spend a Sunday morning on Columbia Road

One of London's most visually appealing markets, Columbia Road overflows with bucketfuls of flowers on a Sunday morning – and rings with the patter of chirpy Essex barrowboys. The market opens at 8am – early birds can get breakfast when they arrive. Start at the Ezra Street end of the market, next to the Royal Oak gastropub (73 Columbia Road, 7729 2220, www.royaloaklondon.com). Here the delightful little square is a great place to eat delicious treats and listen to the buskers. Grab coffee and a bagel at ivy-covered, farmhouse-kitchen-style Jones Dairy Café (23 Ezra Street, 7739 5372, www.jonesdairy.co.uk), or stock up on artisanal cheeses and fresh bread in the café's provisions store. A mooch around the Courtyard, also on Ezra Street, will provide drooling opportunities with the restored furniture of B Southgate (4 The Courtyard, 07905 960792, www.bsouthgate.co.uk) and the art in Columbia Road Gallery (7 The Courtyard, 07812 196257, www.columbiaroadgallery.com).

Back on Columbia Road itself, check out the shops that run either side of the flower traders. This end is best for gawping at art, with Elphick's (no.160, 7033 7891, www.elphicks shop.com), Nelly Duff (no.156, www.nellyduff.com) and Start Space (no.150, 7729 0049, www.startspace.co.uk). Fun shops include friendly accessories boutique L'Orangerie (no.162, 8983 7873) – chunky bead necklaces, straw sun-visors and fat glass rings are among the cheaper items, old-fashioned sweetshop Suck & Chew (no.130, 8983 3504) and retro kitchenware shop Treacle (nos.110-112, 7729 5657, www.treacleworld.com), where you could invest in a cupcake. Columbia Road institution Milagros (no.61, 7613 0876, 7613 0876, www.milagros.co.uk) offers Mexican curiosities and trinkets, including single tiles for 70p, while Supernice (no.106, 7613 3890, www.supernice.co.uk) sells Thomas Paul melamine plates and trays that start from £6. Ready for lunch? Try Brawn at no.49 (7729 5692, www.brawn.co).

433-442 Splash out on chocolate

Forget those cheap bars at supermarket checkout counters: spend £10 on chocolate from the capital's finest chocolatiers.

Demarquette Fine Chocolates

Despite a French-Chinese background, savvy chocolatier Marc Demarquette hasn't let the trend towards British produce pass him by, adding Surrey blackcurrant, Kentish pear and Yorkshire rhubarb, among other fruits, to his range of exquisitely made chocolates. Still, it's his infusion combinations (Tunisian Bharat; Nile cumin; Japanese cherry blossom) that distinguish this premium-priced operation. Connoisseurs of single origin bars should look out for the chocolates made from 'wild cocoa' grown in the Bolivian Amazon.
285 Fulham Road, SW10 9PZ (7351 5467, www.demarquette.com).

L'Artisan du Chocolat

L'Artisan du Chocolat, London's most experimental chocolate shop, is a good bet for spectacular ganaches, truffles, mints and candied fruits. Irish-born proprietor Gerard Coleman makes all of his trademark tobacco 'couture chocolate' (smoky, silky and intense) by hand. He has also created many other delicious innovations, among them the best-selling liquid salt caramels.
89 Lower Sloane Street, SW1W 8DA (7824 8365, www.artisanduchocolat.com).

Maison du Chocolat

Robert Linxe's Parisian choc palace is a browser's paradise: spacious and slick, with giant glass windows, the store sells seasonal individual cakes – perhaps a chocolate, mango and ginger Maiko in summer, or a Rigoletto caramel mousse-filled cake for winter.
45-46 Piccadilly, W1J 0DS (7287 8500, www.lamaisonduchocolat.com).

Melt

Watch the chocolates being made in the pristine white open kitchen at the rear of this pretty Notting Hill boutique. Melt's bars are all made by hand and come in inspired flavours such as milk chocolate with raspberry and black pepper, or sesame. Love bars (silky milk chocolate with creamy filling) have a secret pocket in the pack for your own private message. The takeaway hot chocolate is dark and delicious.
54 Ledbury Road, W11 2AA (7727 5030, www.meltchocolates.com).

Montezuma's Chocolates

In contrast to the precious attitude of some of their competitors, Montezuma's has a lighthearted attitude towards chocolate, and their variety of giant chocolate buttons, animal shapes and dipped fruits make quirky, colourful presents. Much of the range is organic and Fairtrade and they also offer a service where you can create your own one-kilo bar.
51 Brushfield Street, E1 6AA (7539 9208, www.montezumas.co.uk).

Paul A Young Fine Chocolates

A gorgeous boutique with almost everything – chocolates, cakes, ice-cream – made in the downstairs kitchen and finished in front of customers. Young is a pâtissier as well as chocolatier and has an astute chef's palate for combining flavours. In summer, try Pimm's cocktail truffles featuring cucumber, strawberry and mint flavours, and white chocolate blondies made with raspberries and blueberries.
33 Camden Passage, N1 8EA (7424 5750, www.payoung.net).

Prestat

Another British business that has long since proved itself alongside the chocolate masters of Brussels, Prestat's 'Appointment to the Queen' status is echoed in glorious packaging – pretty boxes in regal purples and ruby reds, embellished with gold crowns and elegant script. The store's strongest product is its plump, round, velvety truffles.
14 Princes Arcade, SW1Y 6DS (7492 3372, www.prestat.co.uk).

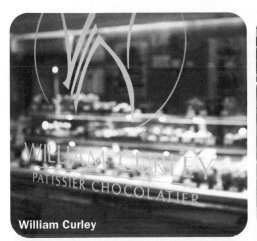

William Curley

Rococo

Chantal Cody's Rococo has a fondness for unusual flavours (cardamom, chilli pepper or orange and geranium bars, say), but combines this with some nostalgic ones: English rose and violet creams, plus fresh cream truffles, for example. It has also been a pioneer in the UK when it comes to ethical practices. Try the Grenada 71% bar, made on the same estate the cocoa is grown on.

321 King's Road, SW3 5EP (7352 5857, www.rococochocolates.com).

Theobroma Cacao

Phil Neal hand-makes the chocolates spread over the counter and adjacent dresser of this cosy Chiswick shop. There are large truffles, fruit-flavoured whips in chocolate cups and good marzipan options but our favourites are the cocoa-dusted chocolate 'sticks', rich enough to serve as dessert in themselves. Look for the discreetly boxed chocolates featuring Kama Sutra positions.

43 Turnham Green Terrace, W4 1RG (8996 0431, www.theobroma-cacao.co.uk).

William Curley

This charming pâtisserie is the brainchild of husband and wife duo William and Suzue Curley. The couple opened their Richmond shop a number of years ago, to rave reviews. It sells an exquisite range of cakes and chocolates including a tropical *entremet*, orange and praline cake and sea-salt caramel chocolate.

10 Paved Court, Richmond TW9 1LZ (8332 3002, www.williamcurley.co.uk).

443 *Relive the jet set days at Croydon Airport Museum*

If the words 'terminal building' invariably summon 'terminal boredom' to mind, you'll find an antidote in the free visitors' centre at Croydon Airport. Defunct since 1959, this vestige of empire relives the early days of aviation: a time when getting airborne and staying there was no mean feat, when air traffic control was a thing of the future, and when the expression 'jet set' was invented to imply impossibly glamorous luxury. The beautifully crafted art deco terminal building was constructed on two World War I airfields, and this was the main commercial airport for London until Heathrow opened in 1953. In its heyday the great aviators all came here – Charles Lindbergh touched down in 1927 shortly after his solo trans-Atlantic flight,

and Amy Johnson flew from Croydon to Australia – and, incredibly, back again.

All the surprising romance of Croydon's lost past is celebrated at the visitors' centre in the old control tower, where the world's first air traffic control system (1921) has been recreated with original equipment. You can see Amy Johnson's flight bag and even dress up as a passenger from the 1930s. There's a De Havilland Tiger Moth in the preserved booking hall and a Heron outside the door. All it lacks is Hercule Poirot, en route to solve a high-class murder in Paris. Never let it be said that romance is dead in Croydon.
Croydon Airport Visitors' Centre *Airport House, Purley Way, Croydon CR0 0XZ (8669 1196, www.croydonairport.org.uk).*

444-448 *Pedal...*

The odd argument with drivers aside, the capital can be a great place to cycle through – and it's free! We especially like the following routes.

...through the City at night

This five-mile jaunt is best left for the weekends, when the hordes of suited workers have gone home and the place is shrouded by an eerie calm. It's the ideal time to drink in the stagily magnificent architecture – from Richard Rogers's ultra modern Lloyd's building to the Acropolis-like Royal Exchange – especially at night, when it's all aglow and the lack of traffic allows you to pause in front of buildings without dismounting. Start at Bishopsgate, continue on to Leadenhall Street, St Mary Axe, Cornhill, Threadneedle Street, Poultry and Cheapside, before ending at St Paul's.

...to the shops

Head to Holborn, Farringdon and Islington for a spot of window shopping and bargain browsing. Start at Bayley Street and take in Russell Square and Guilford Street, before heading up Calthorpe Street into Farringdon, Rosebery Avenue, Upper Street and Camden Passage. Highlights, in order of appearance, include the lovely Russell Square Gardens, Lambs Conduit Street – with its idiosyncratic independent outlets including Persephone Books and the People's Supermarket – and Exmouth Market with its eccentric clothes shops. After zipping past Sadler's Wells you'll reach Camden Passage near Angel, a cobbled lane with everything from high-end jewellers to heavily laden vintage shops.

...around the south-east

This is a workout for serious cyclists that meanders through 13 miles of gorgeous river views and renovated docks. The route takes in two quirky river crossings as well as great maritime institutions, dockside industries and plenty of parkland. Begin at Greenwich and head to village-like Charlton and Woolwich, where you'll cross the river by ferry. Then it's on to car-free Canary Wharf and Island Gardens, where you can get the lift down to the Greenwich foot tunnel (you have to dismount here) and head back south under the river to the station and where you started. Unless, of course, you're tempted to do the whole thing again.

...by Battersea

This pleasant 12-mile waft along the Thames to Kew starts at Westminster Pier (you can return by ferry). Take the road behind the Houses of Parliament and continue along to Millbank, past Tate Britain and Vauxhall Bridge; soon Battersea Power Station pops up on the other side. Further on, just before Battersea Bridge, there's a little colony of houseboats on the river. (The path is privately owned for some stretches here so you may have to dismount.) The ferry back to Westminster leaves from Kew Pier and takes about an hour and a half (7930 2062, www.wpsa.co.uk). If it's busy, you might not be able to take your bike, but you can always catch the train from Kew Bridge Station to Waterloo.

...from east to west

This nine-mile schlep starts with the trendy grit of London Fields in Hackney, before heading north west towards Islington, where at Canonbury Park, you may be shocked to discover that some Londoners have gardens the size of your street. Next, it's over Upper Street through leafy Barnsbury and down to Camden, pristine Regent's Park and on to the grand streets surrounding St John's Wood. After Lord's cricket ground, head downhill to Maida Vale before scooting round swish Sutherland Avenue and along the foliage-shaded canal to Portobello Road. Where it's time for a sit-down and a cup of tea.

449 Get into the Inns of Court

Meandering in a broad zig-zag from Holborn down through Chancery Lane to Blackfriars and the Embankment, the Inns of Court are the four self-contained precincts where barristers traditionally train and practise – an oasis of academic calm in the middle of the city. Like hushed and venerable Oxbridge campuses with their Grade I-listed medieval chapels, Tudor-style libraries, quads and lawns dominated by majestic plane trees, it's no wonder so few Londoners realise that they are open to the public.

The Inns – Lincoln's Inn, Gray's Inn, Inner Temple, Middle Temple – trace their history back to the 14th century, when the old manor house belonging to Sir Reginald de Grey, Chief Justice of Chester, was converted into a 'hostelry' for law students fleeing the disarray of King Edward's court (hence Inns). They then spread to incorporate land owned by the medieval Christian military order of the Knights Templar (hence Temples). While the Inns no longer accommodate students, judges are still entitled to stay overnight in advantageously apportioned apartments, though they rarely do in practice (it's 'a security nightmare', according to those in the know).

In true Dickensian style, the first thing you'll notice when you visit are the off-putting signs announcing the removal of anyone 'constituting a nuisance'. (The best of these is at the entrance to Staple Inn, just by Chancery Lane station, which expressly forbids the presence of 'old clothesmen' and 'rude children'.) Anyone bold enough to venture further, however, will find paved courtyards dominated by tinkling fountains and impressive swards such as Gray's Inn Gardens or the rolling fields of Lincoln's Inn.

As well as being well and truly pickled in history, the Inns of Court are unsurprisingly no strangers to celluloid either: the huge Tudor Hall dominating Lincoln's Inn (a 19th-century facsimile of the 15th-century original) was one of the settings for Bleak House, the latest period drama (after Wilde, Pride & Prejudice, and also, of course, Harry Potter and the Order of the Phoenix) to use the Inns as a backdrop for Ye Olde London. In fact the place is so popular with location finders that the road around Lincoln's Inn Fields can often be blocked up with camera crews. When it isn't, however, we urge you to stop on one of the generously sized benches and watch the gas lamps being lit as dusk falls (see p41). Squint just enough to blur out the modern appurtenances – the Audis in the parking slots, the synthetic colours of the cyclist's lycra – and you can imagine yourself in a palimpsest of the modern, frenetic city that lies outside the gates; a London that's more tranquil, more civilised and, somehow, more mysterious.

If you want to visit the redoubtable Halls, with their august stained glass and old-buffer wood panelling (and, in the case of Middle Temple Hall, genuine minstrels' gallery), you'll need to be organised (or riding on a barrister's coat-tails). You must group-book ahead, and even then you're strictly forbidden to disturb the Inns' most sacred ritual: dining. But the Inns also have their own places of worship – and these are generally open to the public (11am to noon and 1pm to 4pm, outside of special services). The Inner Temple Church is built on the site of a 12th-century Knights Templar church and graveyard. Here you'll come across effigies of crusty old knights, as well as Nicola Hicks' sculpture of a pair of knights on a scrawny horse that sits on a plinth in the adjacent square. If you turn up on Fridays you can catch the current 'Master' of the church, Robin Griffith-Jones, lecturing weekly to tourists on the inadequacies of Dan Brown's da Vinci 'research'.

Conspiracy theories and Dickensian locations aside, however, there's plenty to keep you occupied here. The Inns have a singular ambience; and a simple stroll along the cobbled lanes – through archways and into secret gardens – is reward enough for most, especially on a crisp sunny day.

450 *Start skateboarding*

Although skateboarding in the some parts of the city may incur a fine if you get caught, it's fair to say that the capital's skateboarders have never had it so good as far as legitimate or semi-legitimate skate spots are concerned. Up north there are the streety bowls in the southern corner of Finsbury Park, N4, and Cantelowes skatepark (www.cantelowesskatepark.co.uk) halfway up Camden Road, NW1. There's a new concrete skatepark in Clissold Park, Stoke Newington, N16. In west London you'll find the oddly named skatepark siblings Meanwhile One (a series of interconnecting concrete bowls next to the Regent's Canal at Westbourne Park tube) and Meanwhile Two (a small, smooth, covered concrete street course with a 1970s freestyle ramp under the Westway at Royal Oak tube). There's also the large, covered Bay66 skatepark near Ladbroke Grove (Bay 65-66 Acklam Road, W10 5YU, 8969 4669, www.baysixty6.com).

Just behind Brixton Academy in south London is the expansive and recently resurfaced Stockwell skatepark (Stockwell Park Road, SW9), while out east there's the tight concrete Mudchute skatepark, near Mudchute DLR (the corner of Westbury Road and Spindrift Avenue), and Mile End skatepark (in Mile End Park), which is free and really popular. More central is the imaginatively designed White's Grounds concrete skatepark underneath the railway arches off Tooley Street, SE5, next to Tower Bridge. More centrally, Shoreditch's skaters have two grindblocks in Shoreditch Park, N1.

But no discussion of skateboarding in the city would be complete without mention of the hallowed blocks, banks and steps of the South Bank, SE1, which, after a campaign to preserve its status as UK skating's spiritual home, is as busy as ever.

For the latest places to skate, the Slam City Skates shop (16 Neal's Yard, WC2H 9DP, 7240 0928, www.slamcity.com) has a tourist-friendly map of London skateparks. Ask nicely and they'll also give you the lowdown on up and coming spots.

Stockwell skatepark

451-460

Go in search of heroes and kings

Tick off some of London's quirkiest and most fascinating statues, starting at Trinity Church Square in SE1. Here stands a weather-worn full-length statue, probably dating from the 14th century, usually identified as King Alfred. The only statue of the great English hero in London, it was moved here from medieval Westminster Hall in 1824.

The oldest outdoor sculpture in London must surely be the 3,600-year-old carving of Egyptian warrior goddess Sekhmet, which has guarded the door of Sotheby's Art Auctioneers (34-35 New Bond Street, W1) since the firm's move here in 1917. The black basalt bust was the subject of 'Sotheboy' Bruce Chatwin's first published piece of work, in 1966.

In Victoria Embankment Gardens, WC2, you'll find a memorial to composer Arthur Sullivan (the tuneful half of Gilbert and Sullivan). This bust was carved by the Welsh sculptor William Goscombe John and depicts a scantily draped embodiment of

Music fainting on Sullivan's pedestal, having apparently just let slip the score of the *Yeoman of the Guard* from her hand.

Hyde Park is home to a huge bronze statue of Greek hero Achilles wielding his short sword and buckler behind the Duke of Wellington's former home Apsley House (149 Piccadilly, W1J 7NT, 7499 5676, www.english-heritage.org.uk). Made from captured French cannons and paid for by 'the women of England' in gratitude to the Duke, it was erected in 1822 – the first nude public statue in Britain. The fig leaf added later to protect the Greek hero's modesty has been removed twice – most recently in 1961.

Best viewed from the top deck of a bus, John Bunyan looks down from a niche above the door of Baptist House, Covent Garden (6 Southampton Row, WC1). The full-length statue of the great non-conformist preacher is underscored by the first lines from his most famous work, *Pilgrim's Progress*: 'As I walked through the wilderness of this world, I lighted upon a certain place, where was a den, and I laid me down in that place to sleep, and as I slept I dreamed a dream.' It's hard to imagine that happening on Southampton Row today.

A bust of Virginia Woolf, apparently a copy of the only one ever taken from life, was erected in Tavistock Square. It was unveiled in June 2004 by 'the last member of the Bloomsbury Group', Anne Olivier Popham Bell, wife of Quentin Bell, Virginia's nephew. Anne was a member of the Monuments, Fine Arts and Archives section (MFAA) during World War II. The 'Monuments Men', as they were known, a group of 345 people from 13 different countries, are credited with locating and eventually returning some five million artworks looted by the Nazis. The gardens also contain a cherry tree planted in 1967 to commemorate the victims of Hiroshima – and a beautifully contemplative statue of Mahatma Gandhi.

Mary, Queen of Scots surveys Fleet Street from the first floor of a building now called Mary Queen of Scots House (143-144 Fleet Street, EC4). The statue was erected in the 1880s by the MP for Caithness, Sir John George Tollemache Sinclair. Sir John released various recordings on Columbia, Gramophone and Odeon in 1906, including his recitation of the 'Adieu of Mary, Queen of Scots', an English translation of the French poem by the revolutionary Napoleonic poet Béranger.

Shakespeare can be found leaning out of the first floor window of a corner pub on Carnaby Street, W1, casting a quizzical (if poorly modelled) eye on the swinging street scene below. Ashen-faced, looking like a clown, and wearing blue-striped pyjamas and a ruff, he appears to be staying in the Shakespeare's Head pub behind Liberty, which was once owned by the Shakespeare brothers, supposedly distant relatives of the playwright. The figure has been in place since just before World War I and lost a hand to a bomb in World War II.

Sir Winston Churchill and Franklin D Roosevelt are relaxing in conversation on a park bench on New Bond Street, W1. The bronze, entitled *Allies*, was modelled by Lawrence Holofcener and was unveiled by Princess Margaret in 1995, to commemorate a half century of peace. The sculpture shows little evidence of Roosevelt's famous distrust, bordering on dislike, of Churchill, though he did once concede to the drunken PM that 'it is fun being in the same decade as you'.

Ponder the mystery of Pages Walk tank...

Take a left off the Old Kent Road in south London on to Mandela Way, just after the Tower Bridge Road roundabout, and you are quickly confronted with an enormous 32-ton Russian T-34 tank that someone has seen fit to park in a garden at the end of Pages Walk. Rumour has it that a doting father bought this Soviet relic for his seven-year-old son's birthday. The years may have passed but the gift never palled and is still there for all to see (one year it was painted pink, now it's back to black and white camouflage). Apparently, the council once tried to have it removed but failed because the overgrown land it sits on also belongs to the tank's owner. He may not have forgiven them: according to local legend, its gun points towards Southwark Council's offices.

...or head along to the Imperial War Museum

Housed in the old lunatic asylum known as Bedlam (the Bethlehem Royal Hospital) just down the road from Pages Walk in Lambeth is another more impressive collection of military hardware. Focussing on the history of conflict from World War I to the present day, the Imperial War Museum has a vast tank, antique guns, aircraft and artillery parked in its main entrance hall – and a gratifying wealth of information about them too.

Imperial War Museum *Lambeth Road, SE1 6HZ (7416 5320, www.iwm.org.uk). Free.*

463

Try pole dancing

Pole dancing is arguably more sport than sleaze these days. Try for yourself at the London Academy of Pole Dancing taster lessons (£7).
London Academy of Poledancing *(8520 1985, www.laphq.co.uk).*

464

Marvel at Strawberry Hill
This 'little Gothic castle'
(8744 1241, *www.strawberry
hillhouse.org.uk*) looks more
splendid than ever after a
£9 million restoration. It
was home to, and created
by, Horace Walpole, father
of the Gothic novel.

A few of my favourite things

465-470

Patrick Wolf, musician

I like learning about medieval London – the London of before the Fire – and the Clink Prison (1 Clink Street, SE1 9DG, 7402 0900, www.clink.co.uk, £7) is such a beautiful, interesting museum. It's located in the city's oldest jail, and it tells the history of punishment and policing... violinists would be put in the stocks for playing in the street because the authorities thought fiddling was the devil's music. And you can try on a chastity belt here as well!

I'm going to sound like a right crustie here, but a great food tip is to go around Borough Market (SE1 1TL, 7407 1002, www.boroughmarket.org.uk) and eat all the samples. You can have your whole lunch there for free. They see me coming every week, 'Oh god, it's him again!' The hot Polish sausage is the best.

Just across from Spitalfields market, you can listen to the choir at Christ Church Spitalfields (Commercial Street, E1 6LY, www.spitalfieldsvenue.org, 7377 6793). They have a free recital one Friday a month at 1.10pm.

Another great place to hear free classical music is Covent Garden. A lot of the buskers playing there are from professional orchestras, because orchestras really don't pay very well, so you can hear world-class musicians as you wander around. I used to busk there every week when I was 17.

When I feel depressed, instead of going to counselling, I go to the National Portrait Gallery (St Martin's Place, WC2H 0HE, 7306 0055, www.npg.org.uk). I think that you can really find your own identity within portraits of other people. For me, it's like a biography museum. My favourite is a portrait of a woman called Lady Ottoline Morrell, a wartime aristocrat. She started off very rich and then descended into madness. There was a story that she used to keep flies in the net of her hat because she thought that they were her friends. In Augustus John's portrait of her, her head's held high with her big hat on, and you can sort of feel the flies.

I grew up around Northcote Road in Wandsworth and there are about 11 charity shops in one stretch – the kind where nothing has been priced and there's just a pile of old clothes that you have to rummage through. That's how I used to dress myself when I was 11 and wanted to look like Jarvis Cocker. My best buy was a Burberry trench coat for £2, but I'd buy all my synths down there too.

471

Visit Chatsworth Road market

Clapton's Chatsworth Road has a long history. In the 1930s it had up to 200 stalls peddling their wares up to five days a week. After the war, the market dwindled and finally petered out in 1990 leaving Chatsworth Road slightly bereft. In November 2010, a band of locals and traders aimed to bring back the bustle and campaigned to get the market back on its feet. After two successful test runs, Chatsworth returned regularly (11am-4pm Sun), with more than 40 stalls selling gourmet foods, vintage bric-a-brac, crafts, cakes and preserves, clothing, jewellery – and more than its fair share of hipsters. (A handful of the traders also have stalls at Broadway Market.) There's also plenty of fresh produce available at the Sunday Morning Market – a few steps away at Rushmore Primary School (www.sunday morningmarket.blogspot.com) – where you'll find fruit and veg, posh breads, homemade cakes and more bric-a-brac.

Chatsworth Road market *Chatsworth Road, E5 0LH (www.chatsworthroade5.co.uk).*

472

Head for Belgravia

With its grand white houses, secluded gardens and elegant squares, Belgravia is another world – and a fantastically rich one at that. You'd need a small fortune to own even a kitchenette in these rarified surroundings but going for a walk is free – though it may cost you your soul in envy. Start outside the Thomas Cubitt pub (44 Elizabeth Street, SW1W 9PA, 7730 6060, www.thethomascubitt.co.uk), dedicated to the memory of the master builder who constructed most of this district in the 1820s. Cubitt was supposedly the first to introduce tea breaks for labourers, so celebrate his humanity with a pint, before heading north west along the street to Eaton Square, one of London's most expensive addresses. Notable residents have included Neville Chamberlain at no.37, Sean Connery at no.6 and Vivien Leigh at no.54. But to really get a sense of how the other half lives, head for no.100, London residence of Gerald Grosvenor, sixth Duke of Westminster and owner of the freehold on most of the square and surrounding district. The area is named after him too – given that he's Viscount Belgrave, as well as a Duke.

From this elegant abode, it's a short stumble up Belgrave Place to fabulous Belgrave Square, one of London's grandest Victorian squares. As well as a sprinkling of swish embassies (the German, Turkish, Portuguese and Norwegian among them) there are statues of great explorers (Christopher Columbus, Prince Henry the Navigator), the Liberator of South America (Simón Bolívar) and the first Marquess of Westminster, who was grandfather of the first Duke of Westminster and another key figure in the development of this area.

Make your final salute to the follies of the rich in the south corner of the square. This mansion – known in the early 20th century as Downshire House – was the London home of Lord James Pirrie. It was here that, one evening in July 1907, the managing director of the White Star Line came to dinner and planned the production of three new ships, the largest in the world. One of them was, of course, the *Titanic*.

473 *Celebrate midsummer the way the French do*

On a midsummer's day (21 June), music – classical, jazz, hip hop – reverberates from street corners right across France. London's version of Fête de la Musique may not have the geographical scope of its forebear, but it's certainly got depth. Since its launch by the Institut Français, what was Exhibition Road Music Day now takes place on a day in June as past of a larger event called Supersonix (www.exhibitionroad.com/supersonix), and has drawn in most of the heavyweight local cultural institutions (the Goethe-Institut, Imperial College, the Natural History Museum, the Royal College of Music, the Serpentine Gallery, the Ismaili Centre, the Victoria & Albert Museum) and now occupies Hyde Park, using a sound stage opposite the Royal Albert Hall. Expect anything from experimental electronica to Sufi chants on this day of midsummer musical madness.

474-483

De- (and re-)clutter your house at a car boot sale

There's no question that car boot sales are more fun than the depersonalised world of eBay – yes, you lose the thrill of swooping in with a last-second winning bid, but you gain ridiculous sales patter, the opportunity to off-load your unwanted junk, bargains aplenty and the chance to just potter around laughing at the tat. Here are our suggestions for the best places to find cut-price loot. Note that the entry fee is listed for buyers; the cost for sellers varies, but you can expect to pay between £10 and £15 for a pitch.

Battersea

The Battersea Tech College transforms itself into a lively trading hub each Sunday. It attracts a mix of house-clearance vultures as well as well-heeled local residents having a de-junk.

Battersea Park School, 401 Battersea Park Road (entrance in Dagnall Street), SW11 5AP (07941 383 588, www.battersea boot.com). Open 1.30-5pm Sun. Entry 50p.

Cuffley

Well over 100 pitches sell a varied selection of secondhand and antique items every Sunday in this north London suburb.

Just north of Potters Bar, at the junction of Cattlegate Road and Northaw Road, Cuffley, EN6 (01707 873 360). Open Apr-Oct from 7am Sun, bank holiday Mon. Entry 50p.

Epsom

This site outside Espom, half an hour from Waterloo by train to Ewell West station, is the daddy of bank holiday car boot sales. Expect a great mix of new and second-hand gear from its 700 pitches.

Hook Road Arena, at the junction of Hook Road and Chessington Road, Epsom, Surrey KT19 8QG (07788 132 977). Open from 7.30am Sun, bank holiday Mon. Entry 50p (£1 before 7.30am); children free.

Hatfield

There are loads of bargains to be found at this impressive sale. It's strictly second-hand.

Birchwood Leisure Centre, Longmead, Hatfield, Herts AL10 0AN (01992 468 619, www.countryside promotions.co.uk). Open Apr-Oct from noon Sun. Entry free.

Holloway

This small sale on the Holloway Road is worth a rummage. It attracts a mix of sellers – from regulars peddling DVDs, electrical goods and fake perfume to local homeowners looking to profit from a one-off clearout.

Opposite Odeon Cinema, Holloway Road, N7 6LJ (01992 717 198). Open from 8am Sat; from 10am Sun. Entry free.

Kilburn

Kilburn's big car boot sale has a wide variety of new and second-hand stock from sellers from all over north and west London.

St Augustine's Church of England Primary School, Kilburn Park Road, NW6 5SN (8440 0170, www.thelondoncarbootco.co.uk). Open from 11am Sat. Entry 50p (£3 before 11am).

North Weald/Harlow

New and second-hand gear is sold from over 150 pitches at this popular Essex sale.

Bluemans Field, on the A414 to North Weald, near

Talbot Roundabout, Essex (01992 468 619, www.countrysidepromotions.co.uk). Open May-Sept from 10.30am Sat. Entry £3 (£2 from 11am; free after noon).

Orpington

The stock at this well-established sale is high in both quantity and quality thanks in part to the affluent location. You'll find mainly second-hand goods at the 75 pitches.

Hewitts Farm, Court Road, Orpington, Kent BR6 7QL (01959 532 003). Open from 9am Sun. Entry free.

Wimbledon Stadium

This is a big, spread-out boot sale with a good mix of sellers peddling all manner of unexpected second-hand goods. It's especially good for bargains on furniture and crockery.

Wimbledon Stadium, Plough Lane, SW17 0BL (07785706506). Open from 6.30am Sat, 7am Sun. Entry £1 (£5 before 8.30am; £2 before 10am).

Wood Green

The 65 pitches at this small and focused boot sale sell an interesting mix of new and second-hand goods.

New River Sports Centre, White Hart Lane, N22 5QW (01992 468 619, www.countryside promotions.co.uk). Open from 6am Fri. Entry free.

Crash course

After gatecrashing her way around the capital, Serena Kutchinsky imparts some useful advice.

The best things in life may be free, but that doesn't necessarily make them easy. You don't always have to work hard to unlock London's freebie potential, but if your lust for the party lifestyle is bigger than your bank balance (and assuming you don't have celebrity parents and you're not an *X Factor* finalist) you will need to become an expert in the art of the blag. So what does it take to live it up for free in London? Apart from a degree of shamelessness, nerves of steel and some forward planning, of course. Having devised a gruelling 'crashing schedule with a friend – complete with multiple costume changes and myriad props – we put my blagging skills to the test over the course of a long weekend.

After a few frantic phone calls and a decent bout of research, we were ready to hit the party scene. Any good gatecrasher knows that the weekend starts on Thursday night, and we decided to kick things off on a cultural high note, venturing into the heart of the East End art scene for an evening of gallery hopping, high-brow mingling and, more to the point, gratis boozing. Our first port of call was the area around Bethnal Green's Vyner Street, scene of multiple exhibition openings on the first Thursday of each month.

Dressed in my best art-school threads (blaggers, take note: heels are a no-no on cobbled East End streets) and with a sizeable bag slung over my shoulder (useful for stockpiling free beers), I approached the Vilma Gold gallery (7729 9888, www.vilmagold.com) on Minerva Road. Imperceptible, apart from the hipster crowd smirting (that's smoking and flirting) outside, Vilma Gold is the epitome of warehouse chic: concrete floors, video art illuminating blank white walls and two large buckets brimming with ice and beer. Bingo!

Aware of the need to look like we belonged – and to gain crucial information on which gallery to visit next – we engaged two young dandies in conversation. We'd done some research on the featured artists and, after wowing them with our art speak, were ready to move on to Fred (8981 2987, www.fred-london.com), an enticingly hard-to-find gallery at the back of what looks like a car park. As well as some outlandish, cartoon-style

drawings, we were happy to find not just wine but interesting looking cocktails on offer. After a few more drinks with my new best friends ('key players on the curator scene', they assured us), it was time to tackle the after-party. Given that artists generally have limited (if any) funds, this usually consists of piling into the nearest pub – in this case the Victory, also on Vyner Street. But by midnight I'd exhausted my stash of smuggled beer and was ready to depart, happy in the knowledge of a mission accomplished: I'd had a great evening, met new people, not spent a penny – and even learnt a bit about art.

Several hours and a few Nurofen later, we were just about ready for Friday night's challenge. The plan was to blag our way into a sell-out gig posing as makers of a forthcoming documentary about the nation's hottest new bands. Sticking to the plot, we'd chosen the hyped Foals gig at the Brixton Academy (211 Stockwell Road, SW9 9SL, 7771 3000, www.o2academybrixton.co.uk), a hip band whose distinctive dance-punk was making serious waves. (If you're a novice blagger, it's wise to pick a mid-range band for your first attempt; security is more relaxed and success will give you the confidence you need to move on to bigger and better blags.)

After a hectic afternoon spent convincing the promoter to let us film, we rocked up at the venue a few hours before doors opened dressed in regulation leather jackets, jeans, trainers and sunglasses. Thankfully a huge camera is not a necessity these days: lots of filming is done on tiny digital models. We headed straight for the stage door, located the band's manager and moments later – after proudly clipping our 'Access All Areas' passes to our jackets – we were in.

Backstage is not exactly glamorous at the Academy, but it was still heaving with groupies and assorted hangers-on. The band even popped open a bottle of pre-gig bubbly. Invites to the after-party at nearby Plan B (418 Brixton Road, SW9 7AY, 7737 7372, www.plan-brixton.co.uk) were handed out and we headed off to do some more 'filming' in the pit at the front of the stage, basking in the warm glow of a successfully handled gatecrash.

Saturday night was always going to be the big one. We started early with a free makeover courtesy of Selfridges (0800 123 400, www.selfridges.com). A bit of advance research was required to work out which counters have waiting lists and which ones expect you to buy products afterwards. Playing

it safe, we went for Bobbi Brown, where there was plenty of availability and lots of products for under a tenner. Despite looking slightly like a cross between the Pussycat Dolls and Blondie, we were nevertheless impressed with the results. Our first evening stop was a lively Thai buffet in Soho where both of us were regulars. We'd rung up and booked a table for a few mates, stressing the fact it was an important occasion (my 25th birthday, of course). As soon as we walked in, the manager swooped on us letting the whole place know it was my birthday. Several free shots of a strong Thai whisky followed, plus a rather embarrassing rendition of 'Happy Birthday' from the entire restaurant. Feeling in danger of whisky overload, we quickly paid our super-cheap bill and headed off into the Soho night.

Our next stop was meant to be swanky members' bar, 5 Cavendish Square (7079 5000, www.no5ltd.com), into which mere mortals are allowed in for free on Saturdays before 11pm. However, here we got derailed. First there was the hen party in a pink limo, who caught sight of my massive birthday badge and insisted we

climb in for a glass of bubbly. And then, hooked on the idea of the improvised challenge, we decided that 'crashing our way into Candy Bar, at that point Soho's most famous lesbian bar, was a good plan. Apparently, a few famous 'drag kings' were hosting a club night and there were some celebrities inside. Unable to believe our luck, we pulled out the record bag we'd been carting around. I walked confidently up to the butch bouncer and informed her I was there to play a fill-in DJ set.

Everything was going swimmingly until the manager appeared. 'So,' she said, peering down at me, 'you're here to play with DJ Wicked?' 'That's right,' I said, playing it cool. 'He asked me to help out at the last minute.' Her look of irritation turned to one of total outrage as she slowly repeated my words, 'He did, did he? What kind of bar do you think this is? DJ Wicked is a woman.' Red-faced and stuttering, clutching the record bag to my chest for protection, I knew the game was up and we legged it.

Reaching the climax of our blagathon, our final destination was hip club night Secretsundaze (www.secretsundaze.net), a mecca for East End trendies, music bods and fashionistas. Bundling into the back of a cab, we engaged in a hasty costume change. Pulling on burlesque-style black bob wigs, futuristic techno clothing and a few carefully placed tattoos, we were ready to roll. The plan was simple: I would impersonate world-famous DJ Miss Kittin (I've been told I look a bit like her anyway) and a mate would pose as my assistant. We would pull up at the club, strut out of the cab with hefty-looking record bags, introduce ourselves and walk straight into the club. Give or take the odd accent slip from me, we played our respective parts to perfection. Not only did it work, but I even had to give the bouncer my autograph. Safely inside, we ditched the wigs, checked the now empty bags into the cloakroom and danced the night away.

Free fun is there for the taking in London – you just have to know where to look and what to say when you get there. We might not have managed to score any goodie bags, but we'd had a few seriously fun-packed nights: we'd partied everywhere from art galleries to cool clubs, paid for very little and lived dangerously on our blagging wits.

485

Go down to the docks for the river view on London history

Nowhere in the capital gives you a better sense of the importance of the Thames to the evolution of London than this museum. Set in a 200-year-old warehouse (itself a Grade I-listed survivor of the city's extensive trading history), this isn't a place that ducks the big subjects: witness the thought-provoking 'London, Sugar and Slavery', examining the city's involvement in the transatlantic slave trade, and the hard-hitting 'Docklands at War' section. Over several storeys, models, videos, artefacts and reconstructions tell the story of the river from Roman times through to the commercial redevelopment of the docks in the 1980s and 1990s. The impressive exhibits include a full-scale, walk-through mock-up of a working quay and of a 'Sailortown' back alley.

Museum of London Docklands *No.1 Warehouse, West India Quay, Hertsmere Road, E14 4AL (0870 444 3851, www.museumindocklands.org.uk).*

486-488

Split your sides without breaking the bank

London is a superb place to see live comedy – even when you want enough money left over from £10 to buy yourself a drink. The quality can be a little hit and miss, but you can take a risk when there's no entrance fee. A minor warning: many clubs invite donations at the end of the night. Don't feel bad if you can't make a contribution, but if you've enjoyed the show, why not pay what you think it was worth?

Set Up… Punchline takes place at Archangel (11-13 Kensington High Street, W8 5NP, 7228 7733). On Monday nights, this friendly club showcases mostly new material from established comics, plus newcomers working on their first five or ten minutes of material. Free and Funny in Angel is held every Thursday at the Camden Head (2 Camden Walk, N1 8DY, 7485 4019, www.camdenhead.com), and proves that

Thursdays are indeed the new Fridays. The bills here usually include a top headliner, up-and-coming talent and a few acts trying stand-up for the very first time.

Finally, Downstairs at the King's Head (2 Crouch End Hill, N8 8AA, 8340 1028, www.downstairsatthekingshead.com) was a club was started by Pete Grahame in 1981, when the alternative comedy scene was just beginning. It remains a favourite with big-name comedians for trying out new material, but has always showcased new talent too: the long-running Thursday 'try-out night' (£4) – where up to 16 new acts take the mic each week – kick-started the careers of Mark Lamarr and Eddie Izzard. Even a Saturday night here only sets you back £10; Tuesdays and Sundays are even cheaper. For more free comedy, see www.timeout.com.

489-495
Hound Holmes and Watson through the London streets

It's got to be one of London's most agreeable cheap thrills, emerging from the Baker Street Tube only to bump into a certain long-striding, meerschaum-sucking, deerstalker-sporting figure drumming up business for his detective agency... his gentleman's lodgings... OK, the eponymous museum at 'The World's Most Famous Address' (221b Baker Street, NW1 6XE, 7935 8866, www.sherlock-holmes.co.uk, £6). The whole point about Sir Arthur Conan Doyle's appropriation of 221b Baker Street was that the address didn't exist at that time, but never mind, the study here is now a loving recreation and a splendid photo-op for fans of Victoriana: the bedrooms are scattered with appropriate personal effects, make-believe papers and other paraphernalia, while waxwork tableaux depict scenes from the stories.

Near Baker Street, 2 Devonshire Place (the site of Conan Doyle's medical practice) and 9 Queen Anne Street (where Dr Watson roomed) are essential destinations for fans, and, if you can find a Hansom cab and a foggy night, it's still possible to recreate the route of Holmes – and the murderous Moriarty – from *The Memoirs of Sherlock Holmes*: 'As I passed the corner which leads from Bentinck Street on to the Welbeck Street crossing, a two-horse van furiously driven whizzed round and was on me like a flash. I sprang for the footpath and saved myself by the fraction of a second... I kept to the pavement after that, Watson, but as I walked down Vere Street a brick came down from the roof of one of the houses and was shattered to fragments at my feet...'.

Further south, a walk along the Strand can take in 12 Burleigh Street, once the offices of the *Strand Magazine* and where many of the stories were first published. Then there's the site of the original Scotland Yard and the Sherlock Holmes pub (10-11 Northumberland Street, WC2N 5DA, 7930 2644) – formerly the Northumberland Hotel, which appears in *The Hound of the Baskervilles*. Upstairs, a waxwork Holmes awaits, but the main attraction is another replica of Holmes and Watson's sitting room and study.

496

Spot the fake houses

Strolling past the grand stuccoed terraces in Bayswater's Leinster Gardens, you might notice the windows of nos.23 and 24 look a little strange. That's because they're trompe l'oeil works of plaster and paint. Walk round the back, to Porchester Terrace, and you can see the great iron struts that support the film-set façade of these fake houses – and you might catch a District Line tube thundering through the 'garden' below.

497
Brush up on anarcho-syndicalism

Hidden down Angel Alley, just off Whitechapel High Street by the art gallery, you'll find the headquarters of Freedom Press and Bookshop, England's oldest anarchist publishers. Pass the mural of prominent anarcho rabble rousers and head up the stairs into a cosy den of books and pamphlets that cover history without government, sex without rules and struggle without end. They also sell cool posters and T-shirts.

Freedom Press & Bookshop *Angel Alley, 84b Whitechapel High Street, E1 7QX (7247 9249, www.freedompress.org.uk).*

498
Shoot a few hoops

London 2012 is giving a real boost to basketball in the capital, with more players getting involved at all levels, and the National Basketball Association now making regular trips across the Atlantic from the States to showcase the sport's biggest names. If you want to play competitively yourself, www.basketballinlondon.co.uk is a useful resource and has details of the London Metropolitan League.

499
Jump on board the Deptford Project

Housed in converted 1960s South East Trains rolling stock, the Deptford Project is not your typical eaterie and the menu is considerably better than you'd find on most trains. Inside, a brightly painted table spans the length of the carriage, and cheery decking out front adds to the laid-back, arty vibe. The café is part of a regeneration plan for the area that includes a creative industries market and various art galleries and pop-up installations – the website details future plans. The food on offer here is unpretentious and comforting, ranging from muffins and free-range eggs (laid by the Project's own chickens) for breakfast to light lunchtime salads and hot dishes. A bright spark in a newly rejuvenated neighbourhood.

Deptford Project *121-123 Deptford High Street, SE8 4NS (07545 593 279, www.thedeptfordproject.com).*

500

See the birthplace of a very special relationship

Scientist, diplomat, philosopher, inventor and Founding Father of the United States, Benjamin Franklin lived behind the doors of this grand, Grade I-listed Craven Street house between 1757 and 1775. As much of his time here was spent brokering peace between Britain and America on the eve of the American Revolution, it is considered to be the site of London's first de facto US embassy; the birthplace, then, of our enduring transatlantic love-in. It is also Franklin's only home to have survived. The 45-minute tours give a strong sense of the scale of the man's myriad achievements, as well as the times in which he lived.

Benjamin Franklin House *36 Craven Street, WC2N 5NF (7839 2006, www.benjamin franklinhouse.org). £7.*

501 *Make chess mates in Holland Park*

Most days in Holland Park, chess enthusiasts gather for friendly competition. All ages and abilities are welcome; just turn up at the park's open-air café – with or without your chess set – and ask to join in. Play takes place between 2pm and 9pm in summer, and 2pm and 5pm in winter (when it's really cold players move inside the café). Kids will also love the park's giant chess set, which is free to use every day. *www.hollandparkchess.com.*

502 *Join London's Rath Yatra*

Spiritual bliss is the promise of this spectacular annual Carnival of Chariots (www.ratha yatra.co.uk), a day-long parade organised by the capital's supernal street noiseniks the International Society for Krishna Consciousness. In celebration of the Hindu god Krishna's return to his home, three brightly decorated wooden chariots bearing waving, toga-clad Hindu deities ('who come out of the temple to freely distribute their loving glances to anyone and everyone') are carried by hand (quite a feat in itself) by the chanting faithful from Hyde Park to Trafalgar Square. Here, among the street performers and stalls selling crafts and books, a free vegetarian *prasadam* (a gracious gift) is available to all.

503 *Get naked – and rich*

If you're an exhibitionist, the tendency will pay off at the Bare Facts workshop, designed for aspiring life models. You won't make Jordan-scale money (the fee is £12.50 an hour), but there are worse things you could do with your time… You'll be assessed for basic aptitude and blush factor, and – if you are deemed to be up to scratch (most are) – you can join as a life model, then watch the cash roll in. You get to test your inhibitions on Wednesday evenings at the life-drawing classes held at the Islington Arts Factory (2 Parkhurst Road, N7 0SF, 7607 0561, www.islingtonartsfactory.org); should you wish to draw rather than doff your pants, classes cost £10 a session.

504 *Take in the views from Severndroog*

Hidden away high in Oxleas Wood in Eltham is the 18th-century folly, Severndroog Castle (www.severndroogcastle.org.uk). It's usually closed to the public, but you can sometimes visit during Open House weekend (*see p21*). From the top, on a clear day, there are views out over seven counties.

505-514
Eat more for less

Cyrus Shahrad, editor of Time Out's Cheap Eats guide, spills the beans on his super-cheap favourites.

Assa

The food at Korean restaurant Assa is as authentic as it is delicious. A set lunch of bibimbap (£6.50 noon-3pm, £7.50 after 3pm) comprises a hot bowl of rice with assorted vegetables, an unexpected helping of minced beef and a raw egg yolk, the flavours melding deliciously as the contents cook in the container. A range of hotpots caters to couples sharing – try the rich chilli kick of the bubbling broth of beef and kimchee (fermented, seasoned vegetables).

53 St Giles High Street, WC2H 8LH (7240 8256).

Yalla Yalla

Baozi Inn

The decor – Beijing, circa 1952 – favours kitsch over culture, but the street snacks served here are the real deal. The eponymous baozi (steamed bread filled with pork or vegetables) are typical of northern China and can be accompanied by a bowl of slightly sweet millet porridge to make up an inexpensive meal. Otherwise, try the spicy dan dan noodles, which are handmade on the premises daily.

25 Newport Court, WC2H 7JS (7287 6877).

Benito's Hat

London's Tex-Mex eateries are ten a peso, but this one, its bright lime walls overlooking sturdy wooden tables, serves some of the best burritos in town – £6.10 without guacamole (£6.80 buys chicken or pork with guacamole). A hearty meal in themselves, the soft, floury tortillas come loaded with slow-cooked pork (or chicken or beef), fiery salsa brava, refried or black beans and avocado.

56 Goodge Street, W1T 4NB (7637 3732, www.benitos-hat.com).

Bonnington Café

This vegetarian restaurant is community-run and uncommonly friendly. Local cooks take turns at the helm each night, so the cuisine – and therefore the standard – varies wildly. The prices, however, are consistent, and low: £10 for two courses (a main and either a starter or a pudding). Mains might include penne panna, packed with porcini mushrooms, or comforting tomato nut roast, accompanied by a dressed bean salad. Help yourself to crockery and cutlery, and note that Thursday is vegan night.

11 Vauxhall Grove, SW8 1TD (no phone, www.bonningtoncafe.co.uk).

Comptoir Libanais

This Lebanese café, serving fresh dishes with zingy citrus and herb flavours, is remarkably affordable. The small meze plate (£7.95) allows you to try several of the warm and cold dips and salads; there are tagines (£7.95) too. Take note, though: it closes at 8pm.

65 Wigmore Street, W1U 1PZ (020 7935 1110, www.lecomptoir.co.uk).

Hummus Bros

The formula at this canteen-style café/takeaway is to serve creamy, flavoursome houmous as a base for a selection of toppings, which you scoop up with warm, fluffy pitta bread (£3.50-£7.70). Choose from fresh-tasting, zingy guacamole, stewed mushrooms, slow-cooked beef and fava beans, and round it all off with a brownie, baklava or malabi (a milk-based dessert with date honey).

88 Wardour Street, W1F OTH (7734 1311, www.hbros.co.uk).

Little Bay

The menu at this funky modern European restaurant takes in burgers, duck breast, plenty of fish and, in the vegetarian dishes, a lot of goat's cheese. The chips, fried in goose fat, are terrific. There are frequent promotions, so check the website for prices.

171 Farringdon Road, EC1R 3AL (7278 1234, www.little-bay.co.uk).

Ooze

Here risotto is the USP, though there are alternatives: tiger prawns with garlic, chilli and trebbiano (a type of grape) to start, say, or pasta of the day. Risottos, both hearty (Italian sausage, taleggio and rosemary, and light, come in at £7.50.

Westfield Level 1, The Balcony, Westfield London, W12 7GE (8749 1904, www.ooze.biz).

Rasa Express

This Keralan curry house is legendary among local office workers. A chicken biryani, say – comes with chapati, a chickpea curry, a mild mung bean curry, a dry lentil side and a sweet rice pudding – for £3.50 or £4.

5 Rathbone Street, W1T 1NQ (7637 0222, www.rasarestaurants.com).

Yalla Yalla

Bijou, charming and with walls decorated with photos of old Beirut, this is an informal spot. Near faultless meze dishes include dense, garlicky houmous, crisp fattoush salad and spicy little sujuk sausages, served in a tomato-based, herby sauce. Grills augment the meze menu.

Green's Court, W1F 0HA (7287 7663, www.yalla-yalla.co.uk).

515-519
Play games in the pub

The Shipwrights Arms (88 Tooley Street, SE1 2TF, 7378 1486) really pushes the boat out with its free Wednesday board games night, run from about 6pm to 11.30pm by the Swiggers Games Club. As well as the usual Monopoly-type offerings, you'll have the opportunity to play the likes of Civilization, Diplomacy, Escape from Colditz, Family Business, History of the World, Settlers of Catan, Antike, Caylus, Louis XIV, Power Grid, Puerto Rico, Shadows over Camelot and Zepter Von Zavandor. If you'd rather stick to the classics, though, there are loads of pubs that can oblige. We particularly like the Three Kings of Clerkenwell (7 Clerkenwell Close, EC1R 0DY, 7253 0483), the Big Chill House (257-259 Pentonville Road, N1 9NL, 7427 2540, www.bigchill.net) and the Flower Pot (128 Wood Street, E17 3HX, 8520 3600), which all have chess, draughts and dominos. The Westbourne (101 Westbourne Villas, W2 5ED, 7221 1332, www.thewestbourne.com) ups the ante with backgammon, Cluedo and Monopoly.

520
Attend the Royal Opera House

Go to the opera – or ballet – for a tenner? Certainly. First off, you can attend the Royal Opera House's excellent weekly series of free lunchtime concerts. Starting at 1pm and always held on the premises (either in the splendidly baroque Crush Room or the Paul Hamlyn Hall), the music ranges from Debussy to Wagner. You must collect your tickets from the box office by 12.40pm, but a limited number can be reserved online a few days in advance. Check the website for the current programme.

Also gratis is the annual Deloitte Ignite festival (www.roh.org.uk/deloitteignite), which began auspiciously in 2008 with a madcap array of art installations, dance performances, concerts and film screening events spread throughout the opera house.

Whatever the programme in the coming years, the opportunity to wander freely about various grand rooms and the outdoor terrace is priceless, even if staff are obliged to search your bag as you enter.

You will have to pay for the traditional tea dances, held on monthly Friday afternoons since 2001 in the airy Paul Hamlyn Hall, but your ticket buys you the opportunity to waltz and cha-cha-cha to the exemplary Royal Opera House Dance Band. No tuition is given (unless one of the friendly dancers takes pity on you), but you do get free tea and biscuits. Be sure to book ahead; for forthcoming dates, see the website.

And, perhaps most surprising of all, you can get into a proper, 24-carat opera for less than £10. Honest. Restricted-view seats start from £3, and while you might be perched rather uncomfortably in the gods, you can console yourself with the thought that some fellow auditors will have paid as much as £195 to see the same glorious show. Tee hee.

Royal Opera House *Bow Street, WC2E 9DD (7304 4000, www.roh.org.uk).*

521
Watch the Great Gorilla Run

This annual charity fundraising event gets runners dressed up as gorillas to pound the pavements in an effort to raise awareness and money for the endangered gorillas of Rwanda. The seven-kilometre circular route begins and ends (amusingly) at Mincing Lane, passing Tate Modern and Tower Bridge, and the 'run' is all about having fun, not who's fastest. Participants are encouraged to customise their outfits, so you'll see anything from power-pramming mums with their little monkeys dressed in furry suits to hirsuite blondes in bikinis – even the route marshals are in fancy dress. If you want to take part, the registration fee is £80 (including a complimentary gorilla suit and fundraising support), but you can always watch for free and donate a voluntary £10 to the cause. For more details, see www.greatgorillas.org/london.

522 *Get bowled over*

Bowling was once synonymous with suburbia: alleys were situated in bland retail parks, the decor comprised blaring arcade machines and sticky floors, and sustenance peaked at the level of chicken nuggets and fluorescent blue 'raspberry' slushies that surely came from no earthly fruit. Even then, the bowling always seemed to take a back seat to birthday parties and boy-girl groups of randy teenagers. No longer. 'Boutique bowling alleys' – darker, less sticky, with bars serving cocktails and no kids – are flourishing in the US. And now, in the wake of Britain's current cultural obsession with retro Americana, Londoners can score strikes in properly cool venues:

Bloomsbury Bowling Lanes (basement of Tavistock Hotel, Bedford Way, WC1H 9EH, 7183 1979 www.bloomsburybowling.com) and the burgeoning All Star Lanes minichain (www.allstarlanes.co.uk), with locations in Bloomsbury (Victoria House, Bloomsbury Place, WC1B 4DA, 7025 2676), Bayswater (Whiteleys, W2 4YQ, 7313 8363) and Brick Lane (Old Truman Brewery, 87 Brick Lane, E1 6QR, 7422 8370). All Star charges per person (£8.75 a game at peak times), while Bloomsbury Bowling Lanes charges per lane (£39 per hour during peak time). Both the venues come with a swanky diner and cocktail bar.

Bloomsbury Bowling Lanes

523-539

Take a Sunday City architecture stroll...

Traffic-light Sundays are perfect for architectural rambles in the City. Construction has gone into overdrive in recent years and there are interesting buildings popping up all over the place. Here's a jaunt round some of the less obvious new buildings (and a few of the older ones), all of them only a short distance from St Paul's Cathedral.

Start at one of the City's most striking new structures: the very pointed City of London Information Centre beside St Paul's (2007, Make Architects), then head down towards the Millennium Bridge approach. At 101 Queen Victoria Street, you'll find Sheppard Robson's elegant, light-filled Salvation Army HQ (2005), with its 'floating' ground floor supported by splayed white-painted legs. Next, go east up Queen Victoria Street and cross over to the dark brick Renaissance-style palazzo of Bracken House (1959, Albert Richardson), sitting on its red sandstone plinth at nos.110-112. Turn left beside it to see the Michael Hopkins 1992 revamp that gutted the building. Outrageous vandalism or fabulous update? You decide, but while you are here, take a look at the old Cannon Street frontage with its wonderful Zodiac clock.

Cross Cannon Street and look back at the flirty concrete arcades of no. 30 (1973-77, Whinney, Son & Austen Hall) – very 1970s, but also suddenly looking very now. Turn north up narrow Bow Lane and then right along Watling Street to the corner of Queen Street. You're now at Peter Foggo's HSBC Building, with its bluish-green chemically created patina and external window grilles. From here, go north up Queen Street, turn left on to Cheapside, right on to Wood Street and stop at Gresham Street. Kohn, Pedersen, Fox's 20 Gresham Street (2008) is on your right, and Norman Foster's wavy-fronted 10 Gresham Street (2003) is on your left. Walk further left to see the cantilevered 'hand-stitched' frontage of Nicholas Grimshaw's 25 Gresham Street, which extends over the trees of an old churchyard.

Heading west on Gresham Street, turn right up Noble Street. Take another right on to Oat Lane and straight through the light-grabbing scoop of Norman Foster's 100 Wood Street (2000) to one of the City's most fascinating assemblages of architectural heavy-hitters. In the middle of the road is the surviving tower of Wren's St Alban's church – one of two bombed-out Wren churches in the City that are now private residences – and on the east side of Wood Street is McMorran & Whitby's police station (1966), a compelling pale-stone riff on a Renaissance palazzo (compare with Bracken House). Beside Foster's building is Richard Rogers' 88 Wood Street (2000), while across the road is the back of Eric Parry's coolly elegant 5 Aldermanbury Square (2007), with its silvery external steel frame and classical entasis tapering towards the roof. The street ends with the very 1980s, postmodern bombast of Terry Farrell's Alban Gate at 125 London Wall.

Cut through Parry's building to see its Aldermanbury Square frontage, then return by continuing along the side of 88 Wood Street, allowing you to see the full extent of Rogers' airy masterpiece, sheathed in glittering Saint-Gobain glass. Now you get a splendid view of yet another Foster building: curvy, deco-ish 1 London Wall (2003). Turn left down Noble Street again and along Foster Lane, ending at Michael Aukett's 150 Cheapside (2008) and Jean Nouvel's huge One New Change (2010).

540

...then see the Lloyd's building lit up at night

Time your day tour of the city's buildings carefully so that you're heading east along Cornhill to 1 Lime Street just as the lights are coming on. The Lloyd's of London building is still the City's best-known example of high-tech architecture, its commercial and industrial aesthetics combined by Richard Rogers to create what is arguably one of the most significant British buildings produced since World War II. Mocked on completion, the 'inside out' building still manages to outclass much of the more recent, much-vaunted competition. You can usually see the inside of the building during Open House weekend (*see p21*), but get there early and expect to queue.
Lloyd's of London *1 Lime Street, EC3M 7HA (7327 6586, www.lloyds.com).*

541

Play bike polo
The rules are simple: in teams
of three, put the ball
in your opponents'
net with a wooden
mallet while
mounted on a
bike. The first
to five goals
wins. See www.londonbikepololeague.com
for more information on what's played
where in London.

542
Experience peace and reconciliation at St Ethelburga's

A place for people of all faiths and none, St Ethelburga's Centre for Reconciliation and Peace is a tiny spiritual oasis in the heart of the City. Step through an unassuming medieval door on Bishopsgate and you'll find yourself in an interfaith prayer tent before you enter the building proper. A church dedicated to St Ethelburga stood here for nearly 800 years before it was destroyed by an IRA bomb in 1993. Rebuilt as a centre for reconciliation and peace – it is no longer a parish church – it hosts lectures and discussion evenings on conflict and faith, as well as concerts ranging from flamenco to Afro-Caribbean music, and nights of African storytelling. One recent session brought together dissidents and secret police from South Africa; another looked at violence and the sacred in film. And if it's old-fashioned spirituality you're after (or simply a break from urban life), there are several free weekly meditation sessions, including one every Thursday lunchtime.

St Ethelburga's Centre for Reconciliation and Peace *78 Bishopsgate, EC2N 4AG (7496 1610, www.stethelburgas.org).*

543 *Don't get Court!*

Marlborough Street Magistrates Court, opposite the northern end of Carnaby Street, was once infamous for cases involving unfortunate notables such as Oscar Wilde, Christine Keeler and the *International Times* obscenity defendants. It was drugs offences that saw the Rolling Stones, Johnny Rotten and Lionel Bart kept here under lock and key, while John Lennon was pulled up for exhibiting a little too much of Yoko Ono in his sketches on show at the London Art Gallery. Now, at the Courthouse Hotel, you can enjoy Indian fusion food in Number One Court, and a drink in the cells – complete with hard bunk, 'ice-bucket' lav and warden's peephole in the lead door.

Courthouse Doubletree Hotel *19-21 Great Marlborough Street, W1F 7HL (7297 5555, www.courthouse-hotel.com).*

544
Hear classics in the City's halls

The City of London Festival (7796 4949, www.colf.org) is a well-established favourite, both for music fans and those intrigued by the Square Mile's many historic buildings. A huge range of concerts takes place from late June to early July each year, in some of the finest churches and halls in the Square Mile. While concerts in the grander venues (among them St Paul's Cathedral) are likely to be ticketed, many of those held in the atmospheric City churches and livery halls are absolutely free. The programme is mostly traditional classical music, but there are also more unusual offerings from the worlds of jazz, dance, visual art, literature and theatre.

545
Visit the address Richard Rogers must wish he could have

One Hyde Park – the name of Rogers Stirk Harbour & Partners' superprime, exquisitely located block of duplex flats – is pretty impressive, but how much do you think the architect would have paid to get his hands on No.1 London instead? You and those Russian oligarch flat owners have equal rights to visit the latter: stump up £6.30 and step right in. Right on Hyde Park Corner, Apsley House was called No.1 London back when Kensington was still a village, since it was the first building you reached on the way into the city. For more than three decades it was the Duke of Wellington's residence (a Goya portrait of the Iron Duke is among the treasures on display) and parts of the building – strictly out of bounds to the public – are occupied by his descendants to this day.

Apsley House *149 Piccadilly, W1J 7NT (7499 5676, www.english-heritage.org.uk).*

546 *Get slammed, the literary way*

You think you know all about book readings? The silences, the shuffling feet and smothered coughs, the pitiful bribe of precisely two wineboxes – one lukewarm white and one ice-cold red. Well, you've clearly never been to Book Slam (www.bookslam.com). This is a monthly musical-literary club night for which you're best advised to book tickets well in advance. Still organised by co-founder Patrick Neate – now with Elliot Jack and Angela Robertson of funky Scottish publishers Canongate – it rotates between the Tabernacle (35 Powis Square, W11 2AY, 7221 9700) and Clapham Grand (21-25 St John's Hill, SW11 1TT, 7223 6523). Tickets are £6-£8 in advance (more on the door), for which meagre sum you might get lucky and see authors such as Zadie Smith, Will Self or Dave Eggers, supported by musicians like Adele or Plan B.

Book Slam

547 *Get near to the neolothic*

Ask most East Enders if it is possible to walk the ramparts of an Iron Age hill fort in their manor, and they'd most likely suggest you were having a proper larf. Head out to Epping Forest on the further reaches of the Central Line, though, and you'll find two of them – the huge wooded circles of Ambresbury Banks and Loughton Camp. A natural spring rises in the former, and both can be cut off by their broad moats in rainy weather. An awesome discovery, half an hour from Oxford Street. Visit www.eppingforestdc.gov.uk for details of how to get to them.

548 *Add a string to your bow at the Royal Academy of Music*

Here you can inspect hundreds of different musical instruments, including over 200 violins and a number of pianos dating back to the early 19th century, and see temporary exhibitions.
Royal Academy of Music *Marylebone Road, NW1 5HT (7873 7373, www.ram.ac.uk/museum). Free.*

A few of my favourite things

549-554

Lesley Lewis, owner of the French House

I asked my granddaughter what she would like to do in London if she could do anything and she said, 'Feed the ducks'. So I took her to St James's Park and it was wonderful. Then we watched the changing of the guard at Buckingham Palace and walked down the Mall. **Annie, one of the barmaids here, suggested walking along the river path from Hammersmith and having a beer outside the Dove (19 Upper Mall, W6 9TA, 8748 5405), then continuing on to Richmond Park.**

Danny, an ex-barmaid, recommends a comedy night called Old Rope at the Phoenix Bar on Cavendish Square (37 Cavendish Square, W1G 0PP, 7493 8003, www.phoenixcavendishsquare.co.uk). It's £8 to get in and you get to see top-notch comedians trying out their new material. If they have to resort to using tried and tested gags then they have to hold on to an old rope as punishment. **The Soho Festival (www.thesoho society.org.uk), held every July, is wonderfully old fashioned. It takes place in the gardens of St Anne's Square off Wardour Street and it's like a village fête for the Soho community; so you'll find everything from drag acts to Chinese food to live bands.**

There is also the Soho Food Feast (www.sohofoodfeast.co.uk, admission £6), started by Margot Henderson (owner of Rochelle Canteen and Soho resident) in 2011. Money raised from this celebration of food and drink goes to our local Soho Parish School. **Pop into the French House for a glass of prosecco (£4.20) – it's especially fun on Bastille Day (14 July), when we have music.**

555

Admire an original Crapper

You can see the founder Methodist John Wesley's nightcap, preaching gown and personal experimental electric-shock machine in his austere home, but if you head downstairs (to the right) you'll see some of the finest public toilets in London, built in 1899 by Sir Thomas Crapper. Some parts are now replicas, but the cisterns are original.
John Wesley's House & Museum of Methodism *Wesley's Chapel, 49 City Road, EC1Y 1AU (7253 2262, www.wesleyschapel.org.uk).*

556

Look up at Gresham's grasshopper

Spend less time staring at the pavement and look up! You'll be endlessly rewarded. We're particularly fond of the stone relief grasshopper at the top corner of the Royal Exchange, EC3. It's the family symbol of Thomas Gresham, pioneering Tudor financier, sometime arms smuggler and founder of the original version of this building. Another grasshopper makes the Exchange's weathervane, and a third hangs from a wall on nearby Lombard Street.

557

Drink vodka in a Polish bar

More often than not bars in the West End merely nod towards a theme, but Bar Polski (1 Little Turnstile Street, WC1V 7DX, 7831 9679) is the real deal. Polish sausages, bigos, pierogis and Polish sweetmeats are available all day, but by the evening all anyone's seriously interested in are the vodkas. Divided into 'dry and interesting', 'clean and clear', 'kosher' and 'nice and sweet' (try the Lancut rose petal) – they're here by the vatload. Most cost around £2.90 a shot.

558 Visit Dulwich Picture Gallery

Sir John Soane's neoclassical, purpose-built art gallery (the first of its kind) has been described as the most beautiful art gallery in the world, but its contents are worth a look too: you'll find work by Rubens, Van Dyck, Rembrandt, Gainsborough, Hogarth, Raphael, Canaletto and Reynolds, among others. It's also worth timing a visit around the series of musical evenings held in the galleries (check website for a list of events). It's a fiver's worth of admission very well spent.

Dulwich Picture Gallery *Gallery Road, SE21 7AD (8693 5254, www.dulwichpicturegallery.org.uk).*

559 Take time out at the Clockmakers' Museum

Overseen by the Worshipful Clockmakers' Company, this one-room museum houses the oldest collection of clocks, watches and sundials in existence. Among the hundreds of ticking and chiming horological pieces dating back to the 16th century is an early 19th-century gas-powered clock, and the watch Sir Edmund Hillary carried with him to the top of Everest in 1953, as well as some stunning timepieces by British modern craftsmen. Admission is free.

Clockmakers' Museum *Guildhall Library, EC2V 7HH (7332 1868, www.clockmakers.org).*

Dulwich Picture Gallery

Carry on cabaret

Time Out Cabaret Editor Ben Walters explores a scene where creativity matters more than cash.

London's cabaret scene has been going from strength to strength over the past decade as a thriving underground scene has broken decisively into the mainstream. What was once the preserve of vintage-fixated retro-queens and musical-theatre know-it-alls has exploded into a snowballing melange of dressed-up fun, groundbreaking performance and sexy sensation.

So what is cabaret? Well, definitions vary but generally speaking, it involves a mix of forms, with burlesque, variety and comedy acts that share borders with music, theatre and dance, satire, visual arts and circus skills. You should expect performers to deal with transgressive subject matter – some with more explicit politics than others – and address the audience directly and, yes, sometimes involve them in the act (though a good performer will know not to pick on anyone too reluctant). And nine times out of ten, alcohol will be available during the show in one way or another – after all, it's meant to be fun!

At a practical level, London's cabaret scene is really an ecosystem of sub-scenes, from burlesque and new variety to avant-garde performance, alternative drag and exciting new video-interactive forms. Different sub-genres have different venues specialising in their work but, over recent years, cabaret artists have also collaborated with major institutions from the Royal Opera House and National Portrait Gallery to the Old Vic Theatre and Royal Albert Hall. In 2011, the Edinburgh Fringe added a cabaret section to its programme – the first new section in decades – and in 2012 the inaugural London Cabaret Awards (for which I was on the judging panel) cemented a sense of arrival. And there are plenty of exciting new cabaret projects planned to coincide with the London Olympics, including a huge Spiegeltent venue, dubbed the London Wonderground (www.underbelly.co.uk/londonwonderground), between the London Eye and the South Bank Centre.

Volupté

There's no shortage of stuff to see, then, and given how fast-moving the scene is, your best bet is always to check out the latest listings in the pages of *Time Out London* or at www.timeout.com/cabaret. But there are plenty of safe bets for reasonably priced nights out.

Compared to most other forms of live performance, cabaret tickets are cheap: every week will see a number of shows you can get into for less than a tenner, or even for free. Admittedly, increased popularity has seen a rise in tickets priced over £15 – at the top end, some nights will set you back the best part of £100, though these will generally include a three-course meal and at least some drinks. If your wallet stretches, you should check out the supperclub shows at the Café de Paris (7734 7700, www.cafedeparis.com), Volupté (7831 1622, www.volupte-lounge.com) or Proud Cabaret (www.proudcabaret.com).

Most of the shows are free at CellarDoor (7240 8848, www.cellardoor.biz), an intimate subterranean venue at the foot of the Strand whose origins as a public toilet are but a lingering memory. Its regular weekly shows include Kitty La Roar and Nick of Time slinking their way through jazzed up swing standards on Thursdays and exquisitely moustachioed good-time guy Champagne Charlie's open mic musical theatre night on Tuesdays. Wednesdays are a good bet for high-calibre wild cards, with the likes of pansexual femmes fatales EastEnd Cabaret, unstoppable chanteuse Holly Penfield and devilishly droll ukulele-strummer Des O'Connor (not the TV host) on hand.

Much of the programme at the Royal Vauxhall Tavern (www.rvt.org.uk) comes in at less than £10. The venerable south London home of gay performance, the pub has been a staple of drag shows since before the war and remains one of the most dynamic venues in town. On Saturdays, it hosts Duckie (£6), a queer club night that began almost 20 years ago and has powered much of the most interesting progressive cabaret work since then, including Olivier Award-winning productions at the Barbican. On Mondays, bearded drag queen Timberlina hosts a free, freaky and friendly bingo night (£1 a card

Royal Vauxhall Tavern

to play) – despite its ramshackle vibe, its blend of bonkers patter, crappy prizes and delirious set-pieces is a delicate balancing act. The rest of the week sees a range of performers take to its stage: it's the London home of the scabrously sensational genius David Hoyle, from whom no sacred cow is safe. Others who regularly perform there include self-appointed 'head fatso' Scottee – a sort of modern-day cross between Leigh Bowery and Hattie Jacques – and whip-sharp young drag queen Myra Dubois.

Bethnal Green Working Men's Club (7739 7170, www.workersplaytime.net) hosts a number of dressed-up parties and speciality cabaret nights. As the cradle of the burlesque revival, it was home to nights by the Whoopee Club and Tournament of Tease, both of which have now bowed out, but legendary themed dance parties by Oh My God I Miss You continue and there are plenty of newer options. The monthly Double R Club (£10, www.the doublerclub.co.uk), for instance, bridges the burlesque and alternative performance scenes, presenting turns from some of the best

performers in town inspired by the nightmarish screen work of David Lynch (*Twin Peaks*, *Blue Velvet*, *Mulholland Drive* et al).

There are plenty of other monthly nights at a tenner or less, some with regular homes, others that rove around. Names to look out for include the hot mess that is alt-drag legend Jonny Woo's Gay Bingo at the Soho Theatre (7478 0100, www.sohotheatre.com), which regularly offers crazy new numbers alongside Jonny's trademark latter-day nonsense-patter delights; and the cheeky burlesque of the Folly Mixtures (www.thefollymixtures.co.uk), one of the stronger new tease outfits whose routines often combine wit and satirical verve with sauce. They often play at the Soho cabaret institution that is Madame Jojo's (7734 3040, www.madamejojos.com).

One of cabaret's defining features is its refusal to stay constant, so while these suggestions should point you in the right direction, there are bound to be new nights popping up. Check our weekly listings, ask around, get exploring. After all, what good is sitting alone in your room…?

567
Get digging

Annie Dare digs for victory with some of the capital's community gardening projects.

This meeting of the Transition Town's (TT, www.transitionnetwork.org) Belsize Park branch has something of the Women's Institute about it. Twenty-two of us sit in a circle in a dimly lit room in a local library; there's a marked preponderance of ladies in cardies and practical heels, and we're knitting a (somewhat symbolic) scarf together. And then there's the baking: side-tables groan with homemade fare. Yet the ambition here is somewhat loftier than the staging of a village fête.

TT's goal is to inspire local communities to prepare for the end of the 'Oil Age' and at its heart is 'local resilience' – in other words community cohesion and sustainable environmental practice, particularly with

regard to food and energy use (hence tonight's hand-fired hurricane lamps, to spare the National Grid a few gigawatts). It may sound like a radical fringe but there are now hundreds of Transition Towns worldwide and lots in London, including Brixton, Kingston and Belsize Park.

Although there is some hand wringing about the urgent need to change Londoners' shopping habits and convince us all to eat and waste less – at which point those who lived through rationing 'tsk' approvingly – by and large the group seems optimistic and avoids being overly earnest. There's home-grown hooch to wash down the homemade cakes and jams and a local gent waxes wonderfully lyrical about the history of fruit trees. Nor is it all knit-one, pearl-one in the Transition movement: the Brixton branch's festive shindig was at a bar.

Tonight's main aim is to establish a local food-growing strategy, so we're scoping out possible plots that we can take over within the borough: housing association plots, school yards, derelict gardens, and even cemeteries are the prime contenders – and World War II survivors suggest we arm-twist the Corporation of London into allowing us to turn Hampstead Heath back into vegetable plots, as happened during the 1940s' Dig for Victory campaign.

Over the past few years, growing your own reached a tipping point, and actually became cool. Cool – and cheap. It looks likely that the food-growing phenomenon will continue to expand at grassroots level too. Lucie Stephens, head of co-production at the left-wing thinktank the New Economics Foundation (NEF), sees the Transition Town movement and community food cultivation schemes across London as symptoms of a larger trend: that of local communities making positive, non-financial based interventions to prevent social breakdown. She cites Rushey Green in Catford, where a local doctor's surgery began prescribing voluntary work and community involvement to patients suffering from poor mental health largely caused by isolation.

Whatever their reasons for getting involved, it seems that Londoners are queuing up to get dirt under their fingernails. Dozens turn up for bimonthly conservation digs set up by the British Trust for Conservation Volunteers (www2.btcv.org.uk), Britain's largest practical conservation charity. BTCV also runs the Green Gyms in London (see p92), which rebranded gardening as a sport every bit as legitimate as pilates or ab crunching. There's no membership fee and you can't help feeling that brandishing shears in a park, dog walkers and joggers beaming at you as you work, certainly beats a session on the running machine.

568
Flash mob

Have you ever stumbled across a mass pillowfight outside Tate Modern or a rabble dancing like maniacs in the middle of a railway station? Welcome to the surreal world of the flash mob. First staged in 2003 in New York, when 100 people gathered, for no apparent reason, around an expensive rug at Macy's department store, flash mobs are bizarre spectacles that involve a crowd of strangers assembling briefly in a public space and performing some strange ritual (the second ever flash mob comprised 200 people suddenly bursting into applause for 15 seconds in the lobby of the Hyatt hotel). They may seem like a relic of the early noughties, but London's mobs continue, coming up with new and intriguing spins on the format. Public pillowfights became particularly popular for a while and then waterfights were all the rage. For the next weird happening, visit the website. *www.flashmob.co.uk.*

569
See a new piece of architecture every year at the Serpentine Pavilion

With its consistently acclaimed and thought-provoking exhibitions, the Serpentine Gallery has long been a great pit stop on a leisurely stroll around Hyde Park, but since 2000 there's been even more to entice you here each summer. The temporary summer pavilion, designed by a host of high-profile architects, is now one of the most anticipated annual events in the architectural calendar. Past designers have included Frank Gehry and Oscar Niemeyer.
Serpentine Gallery *Kensington Gardens, near Albert Memorial, W2 3XA (7402 6075, www.serpentinegallery.org).*

570-579

Investigate ten of London's lesser-known squares

Bonnington Square, SW8

Incorporating a 'Pleasure Garden' designed by local residents, this bohemian pocket of Vauxhall is a community hub, complete with a vegetarian restaurant operating a chef-rotation system and hosting weekly vegan nights. An inexplicable wooden rowing boat suspended above the entrance welcomes visitors into what is an overgrown jungle of a square.

Cabot Square, E14

Although Canada Square, with Ron Arad's impressive Big Blue sculpture as its centrepiece, has its advocates, we're more taken with neighbouring Cabot Square. Located to the west of Canary Wharf tower, it has a broad, calm fountain, as well as views over the docks on either side. Wander south to see the beautifully manicured Japanese-style garden by the Jubilee Line exit from Canary Wharf station.

Cleaver Square, SE11

Just off Kennington Park Road, this quiet residential square was beautifully restored using Lottery money. It's a peaceful place for a game of pétanque (see p29) or to sup a beer.

Cloudesley Square, N1

Holy Trinity Church, which sits in the middle of this square, was built by Charles Barry in 1828 and is said to be an imitation of King's College Chapel in Cambridge. The diminutive square (built in 1826) was the earliest of the Barnsbury squares, all of which boast late Georgian and early Victorian architecture.

Edwardes Square, W8

Built by Louis Changeur in the early 19th century, this superb garden square in Kensington features a Greek Revival-style gardener's lodge, a rose pergola and a croquet lawn. It's normally closed to the public, so visit on the annual Open Squares Weekend (see p134).

Fitzroy Square, W1

Designed by Robert Adam in 1793, Fitzroy Square was built in two stages: the first, from 1793 to 1798, saw the construction of the east side (a unified Portland stone palazzo of individual houses); the second produced the stucco-fronted north and west sides. Former residents include George Bernard Shaw, Virginia Woolf and Lord Salisbury.

Gordon Square, WC1

A verdant alternative to the neighbouring Russell and Bloomsbury Squares, this quiet space is frequented by students from the surrounding colleges intent on loafing and exerting themselves with some light Frisbee action. One of Virginia Woolf's residences (the blue plaque is to be found at Fitzroy Square nearby), Gordon Square was the epicentre of the Bloomsbury Group's literary activities.

Hanover Square, W1

Dominated by the art deco presence of Vogue House, this shady spot behind Oxford Street unites fashionistas, shoppers and workmen looking for an impromptu lunchtime picnic spot. St George's, an 18th-century church to the south of the square, was once the most fashionable place in town to exchange your vows: George Eliot and Teddy Roosevelt were both married here.

Hoxton Square, N1

The square that spawned a thousand haircuts. Since the 1990s, this nocturnal green has been well known for its fashionable bars, clubs and, at the White Cube and now Yvon Lambert galleries, contemporary art. But the area's rambuctiousness was already being felt several centuries earlier: in 1598 playwright Ben Jonson killed actor Gabriel Spencer in a duel here, narrowly escaping a public hanging.

Lincoln's Inn Fields, WC2

This 17th-century square, laid out by Inigo Jones, is now a favourite spot for lunching lawyers from the Inns of Court. As well as the lawns, there are trees and tennis courts, in an area that's almost big enough to be considered a park. Sir John Soane's Museum (see p26) and the Royal College of Surgeons (see p62) face off across the greenery.

Fitzroy Square

580-583
Revisit Clerkenwell's radical roots

Now a trendily gentrified enclave for London's creative industries, Clerkenwell has travelled far from its time as a hotbed of radicalism. But much survives from the area's revolutionary heyday and you can still trace the footsteps of its radicals, rebels and reformers.

From the 18th century, the skilled artisans who lived and worked in the area met to discuss politics and far-reaching ideas of social justice in the coffee houses and inns around Clerkenwell Green, giving rise to the term 'Clerkenwell Radical'. The green became the focal point for demonstrations and mass meetings – like that welcoming the Tolpuddle Martyrs (agricultural labourers transported to Australia for forming a trade union) on their return to Britain in 1836, after being pardoned.

Under the beady eye of the Old Court House on the green stands the Marx Memorial Library. It once housed a coffee house where radical organisations such as Karl Marx's International Working Men's Association met, and William Morris and Eleanor Marx addressed crowds from the building. In 1902-03 Lenin edited his revolutionary journal *Iskra* (The Spark) here in an office that is still preserved. One of Lenin's favourite watering-holes was the nearby Crown Tavern and an apocryphal story lingers that he met Stalin there for a quiet pint in 1903.

The struggles of Irish Nationalism came to London in 1867 at the House of Detention on Clerkenwell Close when a huge explosion – an attempt to free two jailed members of the Irish Republican Brotherhood (or Fenians) – killed six and injured 40, marking the diminution of working class support for the Irish cause.

By the 1930s, the area, with its Communist councillors and radical health programme, was known as the People's Republic of Finsbury. You can see a legacy of this in one of London's finest Modernist buildings, the Finsbury Health Centre on Pine Street, designed by Berthold Lubetkin.

584
Badger a beadle in the Burlington Arcade

The Regency-era Burlington Arcade (www.burlington-arcade.co.uk) off Piccadilly is England's longest covered shopping street, Britain's first ever shopping arcade – and the precursor of many similar oases of cashmere, jewellery and other classy craftsmanship throughout Europe. Upscale window shopping is the order of the day here – that, and sneaking a peek at the top-hatted beadles, aka Georgian security guards.

585
Applaud a real Choc Star

Run from a converted ice-cream van by owner Petra Barran, the Choc Star (www.chocstar.co.uk) mobile chocolate service has recently been travelling the length and breadth of our sweet-toothed nation selling cakes, cookies, ice-cream, milkshakes and other chocolate goodies. When it's next back in London (check the website for details), you can expect the likes of Malteser muffins, millionaires' shortbread, chocolate brownies, Mexican chocolate ice-cream, a 'triple-chocolate malted bliss' milkshake (topped with a Valrhona-dipped cherry and worthy of its name) and espresso-style Venezuelan choc shots, flavoured with vanilla, chilli and cinnamon.

586
Subscribe to Time Out magazine

Subscribing to *Time Out* magazine is a much cheaper way of getting your weekly copy than buying it at the newsstand. At the time of writing you can get ten issues for £5 (that's an impressively inexpensive 50p per magazine). Call 0844 815 5861 or subscribe online at www.timeout.com.

587 *Take a peek into Hell*

If you catch a double decker bus on St James's, you can take a peek into Hell, the first-floor gaming room of aristocratic club White's (37-38 St James's Street, SW1) – where gauntlets were once thrown down for dawn duels and vast fortunes have been won and lost.

588 *Check out the Mighty Wurlitzer*

This Brentford-based collection of melodic curios provides a fascinating history of pre-electronic musical gadgetry and houses one of the largest collections of automatic instruments in the world. Exhibits include ghostly self-playing pianolas, tiny Swiss musical boxes and the museum's grand centrepiece: the majestic 'Mighty Wurlitzer' that emerges from the orchestra pit of the 230-seat concert hall much as it once did in a 1930s picture house. Check the website for upcoming concerts.
Musical Museum *399 High Street, Brentford, TW8 0DU (8560 8108, www.musicalmuseum.co.uk).*

589 *Explore Lesnes Abbey*

The ruins of Lesnes Abbey are an unexpected find in suburban south-east London, overshadowed as it is by tower blocks and beside a busy main road. The Abbey was founded in 1178 by Richard de Luci, a supporter of Henry II, in penance for the murder of Archbishop Thomas à Becket in 1170. A small Augustian foundation, after passing through various private hands, it was bequeathed in the 17th century to Christ's Hospital, which sold it in 1930 to the London County Council. Nowadays the Abbey's scant ruins are surrounded by attractive gardens, featuring a 17th-century mulberry tree, as well as the surprisingly extensive Lesnes Abbey Wood. Particularly delightful in spring, when the daffs and bluebells are in bloom, it's worth a visit at any time of year for its even more ancient fossil bed – it's not unusual to unearth 50-million-year-old shark's teeth and rare seashells from the Eocene period.
Lesnes Abbey *Abbey Road, Belvedere, Kent (8303 7777, www.bexley.gov.uk).*

Lesnes Abbey

590 Revisit iconic scenes from London movies

Starting out with a classic establishing shot, Lewis Gilbert's *Alfie* takes some beating for an iconic opening scene. The Tower of London is, of course, still a tourist attraction, and the Thameside stretch overlooking the moat and ramparts is still a focus for buskers, artists, tat-floggers and thousands of happy snappers – if not quite Michael Caine's tourist photo scam. David Lynch's *The Elephant Man* also used real London buildings to brilliant effect: squint up into the overhead gantreys on a grey winter's day and it's almost possible to see Butler's Wharf on Shad Thames as the grim Dickensian world through which John Hurt shuffles. Likewise the façade of John Merrick's sanctuary, the Royal London Hospital on Whitechapel Road. Another 'slice of life' location well worth a visit is *Quadrophenia*'s pie and mash shop at the Goldhawk Road end of Shepherd's Bush Market, where mod Jimmy (Phil Daniels) meets greaser Kevin (Ray Winstone).

There's no more iconic or atmospheric a London film than Antonioni's *Blow Up*, and the unique Maryon Park in Charlton is virtually unchanged since 1966, when the Italian director happened across the strange landscape of Cox's Mount and immediately moved the focus of his swinging London film away from the West End.

Another south London location associated with surreal ultra-violence is the Thamesmead South estate, site of the slo-mo slicing 'tolchock' action between Alex and his three 'droogs' in Stanley Kubrick's *A Clockwork Orange*. Binsey Walk is the path in question, running at the side of the concrete Southmere Lake. Even 38 years on, the walkways and tower blocks of the planner's dream have a faintly futuristic – and grim – feel about them. Finally, no round-up of London film violence would be complete without a mention of *The Long Good Friday*. Sadly, there's no chance of visiting the Lion and Unicorn pub, because it was built temporarily on the Wapping riverfront just along from the Town of Ramsgate pub (*see p247*). But the interior of St Patrick's Church on nearby Greenbank was used when gangster Bob Hoskins took his old mum to church and the churchyard of St George in the East was where his Rolls-Royce got blown up. (Interestingly, the derelict location of the future Canary Wharf is visible when Hoskins takes to the Thames to view his proposed marina development.)

Grounds for a grand, all-encompassing conspiracy theory may be found in the fact that the Great Hall of Freemasons Hall, WC2 (*see p21*), was used as a ringer for the Kremlin in *From Russia With Love*. And there's yet more dastardly intrigue to be had at the Salisbury pub in the heart of Theatreland on St Martin's Lane. It wouldn't be giving too much away to say that in the landmark 1961 gay thriller *Victim*, Dirk Bogarde is blackmailed over his sexuality – or that the true, scene-stealing star of the film is the pub itself, all glancing mirrors and art nouveau table lamps.

And finally to music. American documentary-maker DA Pennebaker ushered in a whole new era with the groundbreaking sequence he filmed for the opening of *Don't Look Back*, in which Bob Dylan flicks though cue cards scrawled with the lyrics of *Subterranean Homesick Blues*. It was a '60s high, ultra-cool and oft-copied and these first shots of the coming video age were filmed, in 1965, in an alleyway called Savoy Steps, behind the hotel on the Strand.

It took Nic Roeg and Donald Cammell to signal the end of the '60s dream in *Performance*, in which Mick Jagger got to frolic with naked, drugged-up chicks, perform the cracking non-Stones tune *Memo To Turner* and swap personalities with psychotic hoodlum James Fox. It all happened (or was it just a bad trip?) behind the classical portico of 25 Powis Square, off the Portobello Road in Notting Hill.

591

See a magic show

Keep an eye out for the magic shows at Wilton's Music Hall (7702 2789, www.wiltons.org.uk) – they're only staged occasionally, but are a real treat. Most recently, the featured magician has been Katherine Rhodes; her past exploits have included making Wilton's artistic director float, and producing singer Marc Almond from an empty coffin. Tickets cost £10 (£5 children).

592 *Horse around with avant-gardists...*

Since 1993, a former Horse Hospital (Horse Hospital Colonnade, WC1N 1HX, 7833 3644, www.thehorsehospital.com) near Bloomsbury's Brunswick Square has been staging esoteric arts events that range from rare film screenings to gigs, from left-field theatre to séances and strange pagan celebrations. Lots of the events are free, and few – if any – cost more than a tenner. Check the website for details.

593 *...or hang out at the Design Museum while you still can*

For a former banana warehouse, the Design Museum has come a long way most of it upwards. Conran and Partners' conversion was described by one architecture critic in 1989 as 'cool and logical, a counterblast to the feverish and feeble sub-vernacular styling which is almost de rigueur in Docklands'. Well quite – our thoughts exactly. Even the toilets are classy, thanks to Australian design star Marc Newson. And it's hardly necessary to look round the exhibits to enjoy the place: have a coffee in the café and look out over the river and Tower Bridge. But be aware there's a time limit – in late 2014 the Design Museum moves to the amazing Commonwealth Institute building in west London.
Design Museum *28 Shad Thames, SE1 2YD (7403 6933, www.designmuseum.org).*

Design Museum

594 *Call in at Dover Street Market*

Comme des Garçons' designer Rei Kawakubo's retail space combines the edgy energy of London's indoor markets – concrete floors, tills housed in corrugated-iron shacks, Portaloo dressing rooms – with a beautifully curated array of rarefied labels. True, it isn't the first place we'd direct the cash-strapped shopper to – you'll not walk out with any change from a tenner if you're hunting for clothes. But that doesn't mean you can't look. And what a space it is to look at: the theatrically designed displays give some of the capital's art galleries a run for their money and make for great browsing. If you really must buy something, nip into the Labour and Wait concession on the fourth floor for one of their cheaper items (some soap, say) or visit the Rose Bakery for a sit-down and one of its renowned carrot cakes (£4.50).

Dover Street Market *17-18 Dover Street, W1S 4LT (7518 0680, www.doverstreetmarket.com).*

595

Boost your brain power at a free public lecture

British Academy
Organising public lectures for over a century, the British Academy persuades serious intellectuals (of the likes of Jonathan Bate and Stuart Hall) to impart their wisdom. The series of endowed talks includes the annual Shakespeare Lecture on or around the Bard's birthday on 23 April. If titles such as 'Moral Panics: Then and Now' or 'From Shells and Gold to Plastic and Silicon: a Theory of the Evolution of Money' tickle your fancy, these mostly ticketless talks usually start at 5.30pm.
10 Carlton House Terrace, SW1Y 5AH (7969 5200, www.britac.ac.uk).

Dana Centre
This state-of-the-art centre – affiliated to the Science Museum – encourages adults to take part in innovative evening debates about contemporary science, technology and culture. Topics might include 'Future Skies – Airplanes of the Future' and 'Alternative Therapies – Busting the Myths', covered in always entertaining and often interactive ways. Events are free – and popular; always pre-book.
165 Queen's Gate, SW7 5HD (7942 4040, www.danacentre.org.uk).

Gresham College
Gresham College was set up 400 years ago precisely to provide free lectures. There are eight permanent lecturers in disciplines ranging from geometry and commerce to (brilliantly) physic and rhetoric, who talk about anything from 'The Search for Other Worlds' to 'Are Normal People Sane?'. Up to half a dozen lectures are held a week during termtime, mostly in the 90-seat Barnard's Inn Hall in Holborn; more popular lectures are sometimes forced to move elsewhere and may be ticketed.
Barnard's Inn Hall, EC1N 2HH (7831 0575, www.gresham.ac.uk).

National Gallery
The National Gallery runs several series of well-respected and informative free talks. These include lunchtime lectures (1pm Mon-Sat) on subjects such as 'Distant Lands, Uncharted Waters' (how can you paint an imaginary landscape?), as well as ten-minute talks (4pm Mon, Tue, Fri-Sun), lectures on the selected 'Painting of the Month' (perhaps Bronzino's *An Allegory with Venus and Cupid* or Degas's *Ballet Dancers*).
Trafalgar Square, WC2N 5DN (7747 2885, www.nationalgallery.org.uk).

Royal Institution of Great Britain
The hugely popular, flagship Christmas Lectures series is for paying punters only, but the superbly refurbished Royal Institution, established in 1799 to spread scientific knowledge among the masses, also runs a lively programme of free events. Regular monthly features include a book club, 'Fiction Lab', for which Dr Jennifer Rohn (founder of Lablit.com) leads discussions of great fiction with a scientific bent. The evening lectures generally cost £10 (£6-£8 reductions).
21 Albemarle Street, W1S 4BS (7409 2992, www.rigb.org).

Royal Society of Arts
In the business of promoting public thought for two centuries, the RSA runs free lectures on a wide variety of subjects. Their 'Themes' strand has hosted speakers of the stature of Kofi Annan, Al Gore and Richard Rogers, while Thursdays offer a lunch hour top-up of arts or politics, perhaps 'Living with a Black Dog' (on depression) or 'The Element' (on how to fulfil your creative potential). See website for details.
8 John Adam Street, WC2N 6EZ (7930 5115, www.rsa.org.uk).

University College London (UCL)
Ingest your sandwich and get some intellectual nutrition at the same time by attending one of UCL's 40-minute lunchtime lectures, intended to offer an insight into research carried out at the university. Lectures start at 1.15pm (days vary) and subjects range from the intriguing 'The Man who Invented the Concept of Pi' to the abstruse 'The Reception of Homer in Byzantium' via the plain scary 'Physiology on Top of the World: Xtreme Everest'.
Darwin Lecture Theatre, Gower Street, WC1E 6BT (7679 9719, www.ucl.ac.uk).

596

Enjoy the view
Could this be the best
view in London? Next to
the Royal Observatory,
the panorama from the
summit of Greenwich
Park is as splendid as
anything you might see in
the night sky. The genteel
foreground, like something out of a period drama, makes a great
contrast with the razzle dazzle of the Canary Wharf skyline.

597-604

Poke your nose into the City's livery halls

The City of London's 108 livery companies are the remnants of once-powerful guilds, or unions, for trades that mostly no longer exist. Many date back to medieval times, but most were formally established in the 16th century. Today, most of us would be hard pushed to describe exactly what a chandler does, never mind a fletcher or cordwainer; the relevance of a longbow maker and barber-surgeon is now, at best, symbolic, while the attraction of a decent currier is sadly illusory.

However, several of the worshipful companies still have a regulatory role and do a lot of fundraising for charity, pulling on their ruffles and big-buckled shoes for the Lord Mayor's Show. They also own a lot of property in the City. Most importantly, from our perspective, 33 of them have their own historic headquarters, or livery hall, secreted in some City backwater. It's fun to track them down – to spot and photograph their telltale ancient signs and coats of arms.

In terms of gazing at a secretive company's HQ façade, there are no greater thrills to be had than at the Cutlers' Hall (Warwick Lane, EC4M 7BR, 7248 1866, www.cutlerslondon. co.uk), which boasts a magnificent 3D terracotta frieze of cutlers going about their work. It's groovier than it sounds. Ditto gazing through the outrageous ornamental gates of the Tallow Chandlers' Hall (4 Dowgate Hill, EC4R 2SH, 7248 4726, www.tallowchandlers.org) into the haunted courtyard, with its large Indian Bean tree.

Most livery halls are closed shops, though a surprising number are available to hire for functions, and some are occasionally open to visitors (call to check details of opening times). Top of the curiosities is at the Thames-side 18th-century Fishmongers' Hall (London Bridge, EC4R 9EL, 7626 3531, www.fishhall. org.uk, tours for parties £10 each), where, amid a jumble of precious loot, you'll find the preserved 12-inch dagger used by fishmonger-Mayor William Walworth to stab Wat Tyler in the back and end the Peasants' Revolt of 1381. There's even a lifesize wooden statue of the murderous Walworth, dagger in hand.

Meanwhile, the treasures at Butchers' Hall (87 Bartholomew Close EC1, 7600 4106, www. butchershall.com) include a key cupboard from Newgate Prison; Vintners' Hall (Upper Thames Street, EC4V 3BG, 7651 0748, www.vintners hall.co.uk) boasts the Swan Banner (they own the swans on the Thames – it's a long story), archaeological finds and a collection of bottles; and Mercers' Hall (Ironmonger Lane, EC2V 8HE, 7726 4991, www.mercers.co.uk) a wonderful and expansive art collection, effectively lost to the world. Conversely, the Clockmakers' Company Museum is handily housed in the Guildhall Library (Aldermanbury, off Gresham Street, EC2V 7HH, 7332 1868, www.clockmakers.org) – free admission, and true superstar timepieces. The Renaissance-style Goldsmiths' Hall (Foster Lane, EC2V 6BN, 7332 1456, www. thegoldsmiths.co.uk) is probably the most open to outsiders' prying eyes, and stages regular free art exhibitions to promote both the history and modern-day work of jewellers, gold and silversmiths.

Open House weekend (www.openhouse. org.uk) in September always features several livery companies. In addition, every June/July, the City of London Festival (www.colf.org) uses some halls for events, while at this time others open up their doors for architectural tours (and general nosying). In previous years the secret courtyards, ballrooms, roof gardens and treasures of the Butchers', Drapers', Leathersellers', Painter-Stainers', and Watermen & Lightermens' Halls (to name but a few) have all been opened up to the public.

605-606

Bag a vintage bargain

Brick Lane's vintage finds are hardly a secret, but that doesn't mean there are no bargains to be had. After window shopping your way along the Bethnal Green Road end of the street and gazing at 1920s dresses priced at well over £200, try the Shop (3 Cheshire Street, E2 6ED, 7739 5631) or the Vintage Emporium (14 Bacon Street, E1 6LF, 7739 0799, www.vintage emporiumcafe.com).

607-609

Wander, float or cycle along Regent's Canal

Opened in 1820 to provide a transport link between east and west London, Regent's Canal developed as a scenic public foot- and cycle path in 1968. The route's industrial trappings have been transformed into a delightful green corridor over the four decades since. Any stretch of the canal is worth a stroll or a cycle (bear in mind that you can't follow it between Angel and King's Cross), but the most popular patch is from Camden Lock west to Little Venice, passing Regent's Park and London Zoo. Narrowboat cruises also travel along the water in summer and on winter weekends. They depart from Camden Lock and cost around £6.50 for a single fare, £8.50 return (Jason's Canal Boat Trip, 7286 3428; Jenny Wren, 7485 4433, www.walkers quay.com; London Waterbus Company, 7482 2660, www.londonwaterbus.com).

610 *Watch glassblowers at work*

In the fiery workshop at Peter Layton's London Glassblowing studio you can watch, mesmerised, as master craftsmen patiently and painstakingly create beauty out of molten silica molecules. Every object produced is unique and free blown and all are signed by their creators (there's currently a team of five working at the studio). This means, of course, that they don't come cheap (around £100 for a small perfume bottle and up to several thousand pounds for larger pieces) but the demonstrations themselves are completely free to watch – just drop in during working hours (but not between 1pm and 2pm). A word of warning: although there's no pressure to buy, the showroom next door is likely to prove a dangerous temptation. **London Glassblowing** *62-66 Bermondsey Street, SE1 3UD (7403 2800, www.londonglass blowing.co.uk).*

Brought to books

You'll only have a penny left to spend out of your ten pounds if you bought this book. So, by way of recompense, Charlie Godfrey-Faussett suggests some places where you can borrow it, along with many others, for free.

Who could disagree with Stephen Fry when he put public libraries firmly in his 'Room Lovely' on TV show *Room 101*? All that knowledge, all that power, the shelf stacks packed with promising titles, each one quite possibly a key to wisdom, information or inspiration. All effectively ordered, categorised and indexed, quietly awaiting enquiry. And all for free. Though most libraries now offer internet access (usually also free) and various other local services, their essence remains that thrill of discovery and the firing of imagination going on gratis under one communal roof. (And when it comes to roofing, libraries often do it much better than many other municipal buildings.)

Few cities contain such a fabulous array of libraries as London: there's the mother of them all, the British Library at St Pancras; the more than 300 local authority lending and reference libraries spread across the capital; and then there are the delights of the city's individual,

specialist, independent and academic libraries – the Marx Memorial, the Women's, the Lindley, the Weiner and many others. All in all, if you haven't found what you're looking for in a London library, you probably haven't been looking for long enough.

The British Library (96 Euston Road, NW1 2DB, 0843 208 1144, www.bl.uk) is one of the most extensive research resources anywhere on the planet. One of four copyright libraries in the country (the others being the National Libraries of Scotland and Wales, the Bodleian in Oxford, and Cambridge University Library) established by the Copyright Act of 1911, it receives a copy of everything published in the UK, as well as much more besides. Currently it requires about eight miles of extra shelf space each year for its growing collection of some 14 million books. It's free to join, but you need to have a professional reason to gain access to the reference-only reading rooms. All other visitors are more

Swiss Cottage Library

than welcome at the great red-brick building at St Pancras, however. Much derided when it opened after years of expensive delays in 1997, it is in fact a superb light-filled space inside and special exhibitions (which usually cost less than ten pounds admission) draw on the library's remarkable holdings: in 2009, for example, it celebrated the 500th anniversary of Henry VIII's accession to the throne by displaying a collection of books, letters and manuscripts actually read or annotated by the king himself. Another gallery contains a permanent free exhibition of some of the library's most precious treasures and displays, the likes of the Magna Carta, Shakespeare's First Folio, a Gutenberg Bible and Leonardo's notebooks – some extraordinary stuff, in other words.

Then there's the fantastic procession of public libraries in London. Many are the legacy of the Victorian drive to encourage self-help in the illiterate masses, but they've come a very long way since then. The City of London maintains several, but three are particularly noteworthy. Their flagship is the Guildhall Library (Aldermanbury, EC2V 7HH, 7332 1868, www.cityoflondon.gov.uk/guildhalllibrary), founded in the early 15th century by Dick Whittington and given its modern form in

1824 as a reference library on 'all matters relating to the City, the Borough of Southwark and the County of Middlesex'. As such, its collections on the history and topography of the capital are exceptional, including maps dating back to the 16th century and some 26,000 images of the City, viewable in its Print Room. This is also the place to see Lloyd's of London's historic marine collection of manuscripts relating to shipping; the wine and food libraries collected by André Simon, Elizabeth David and the Institute of the Masters of Wine, among others; and special collections devoted to Samuel Pepys, John Wilkes and Charles Lamb. The City Business Library (1 Brewers' Hall Garden, off Aldermanbury Square, EC2V 5BX, 7332 1812, www.cityoflondon.gov.uk/citybusinesslibrary) provides one of the most accessible and comprehensive practical sources of current business information in the UK. And the Barbican Music Library (Barbican Centre, EC2Y 8DS, 7638 0672, www.cityoflondon.gov.uk/barbicanlibrary) holds a huge number of recordings of all types of music (eight listening booths are provided), including the unique Music Preserved collection of recent live performances of classical music as well as musical scores and books about music and musicians for both lending and reference.

The City of Westminster's libraries are also pretty special. Bang in the middle of the West End, the Charing Cross Library (4-6 Charing Cross Road, WC2H 0HF, 7641 1300, www.westminster.gov.uk/libraries) is a public lending library that also serves Chinatown. It holds one of the largest collections of books in Chinese for loan in the country, has four Chinese-speaking staff, and stages a variety of China-related events. Nearby, just off Leicester Square, the Westminster Reference Library (35 St Martin's Street, WC2H 7HP, 7641 1300, www.westminster.gov.uk/libraries) is particularly strong in art and design and the performing arts. At the Westminster Archives Centre (10 St Ann's Street, SW1P 2DE, 7641 5180, www.westminster.gov.uk/libraries/archives), you can access www.ancestry.co.uk for free (for censuses from 1851 to 1901), as well as see illustrations dating back to the 16th century and search parish registers of baptisms, marriages and deaths.

Want to find out more about any given house, street, footpath or park in the mighty borough of Camden? Holborn Library (32-38 Theobalds Road, WC1X 8PA, 7974 4001, www.camden.gov.uk/holbornlibrary), with its wonderfully helpful local studies centre, is the place to come.

Staff will happily produce maps and resources relevant to your enquiry and point you in the direction of a variety of exhaustive card indexes.

Also in Camden, Swiss Cottage Library (88 Avenue Road, NW3 3HA, 7974 4001, www.camden.gov.uk) is worth a visit for its architecture alone. Designed by Sir Basil Spence, it's a superb modernist structure, looks a little like an enormous Rolodex, and was opened in 1964. It has a particularly strong psychology and philosophy collection.

Other public libraries around London have also pushed architectural boundaries: Peckham Library (122 Peckham Hill Street, SE15 5JR, 7525 0200, www.southwark.gov.uk) led the way with its colourful reading pods and glass walls. Opened in 2000, and designed by Will Alsop to undermine stuffy assumptions about libraries, it has become the busiest in Southwark. Tower Hamlets (www.towerhamlets.gov.uk) have gone a step further, ditching the word library altogether, with their Idea Stores: Whitechapel Idea Store (321 Whitechapel Road, E1 1BU, 7364 4332 , www.ideastore.co.uk), opened in 2005. Designed by conceptual architect David Adjaye, it has glass walls and rubber studded floors, and as well as books it boasts 'learning spaces' (and classrooms), a crèche, dance studio, complementary therapy room, café, baby changing room and wheelchair accessible

Swiss Cottage Library

toilets. Further east, 2008 saw the opening of the Barking Learning Centre (2 Town Square, Barking, IG11 7NB, 8724 8710, www.barking-dagenham.gov.uk/blc), another award-winning new build.

If other local authority libraries have struggled to become less, how shall we say, pedestrian, no such problem faces London's extraordinary collection of specialist and independent libraries. We highlight a handful here,, while noting that, sadly, the most venerable of them all, the London Library (14 St James's Square, SW1Y 4LG, 7930 7705, www.londonlibrary.co.uk) costs close to £450 per annum to join, though it is possible to book an introductory tour of the splendid old reading rooms.

If the muse takes you, then the Poetry Library (Level 5, Royal Festival Hall, SE1 8XX, 7921 0943, www.poetrylibrary.org.uk) could help harness your inspiration. Funded by the Arts Council, it's the major library of modern and contemporary poetry in the UK, and now holds some 100,000 books for loan and reference. Its sister in the visual arts is the National Art Library (Victoria & Albert Museum, Cromwell Road, SW7 2RL, 7942 2000, www.vam.ac.uk/nal). A reference library only, though with very well-appointed reading rooms, it's also the museum's curatorial department for the art, craft and design of the book. It holds fantastic documentary material on the fine and decorative arts of many different countries and periods. Simply register as a reader on your first visit if you want to explore the collections.

Anyone interested in the art and design of books will benefit from a visit to the St Bride Printing Library (St Bride's Passage, Salisbury Square, EC4Y 8EE, 7353 4660, www.stbride.org), which has 'something for everyone in the world of graphics'. Exhibits include everything from typefaces to artefacts illustrating the history of printing, along with thousands of books and magazines.

If you're more concerned with cultivating your garden, then the Lindley Library (80 Vincent Square, SW1P 2PE, 7821 3050, www.rhs.org.uk), the main library of the Royal Horticultural Society, is the place for you. It contains 22,000 botanical drawings, and some 50,000 books on gardening. Take along two forms of identification to register.

Meanwhile, all matters medical are comprehensively covered at the Wellcome Library (183 Euston Road, NW1 2BE, 7611 8722, http://library.wellcome.ac.uk), the UK's most important resource on the history of medicine, in all its grisly detail. Recently acquired are the pioneering notes of the great forensic pathologist Bernard Spilsbury.

For the more politically inclined, the Wiener Library (4 Devonshire Street, W1W 5BH, 7636 7247, www.wienerlibrary.co.uk) is part of the Institute of Contemporary History and bills itself as 'the world's oldest holocaust memorial institution'. It was founded in 1933 by Alfred Wiener in order to record the persecution of Jews in Nazi Germany; since 1956 the collections have been housed in Devonshire Street, where all are welcome to search the shelves for modern European history and current affairs. Also founded in 1933, partly in response to Nazi book-burning, was the Marx Memorial Library (37a Clerkenwell Green, EC1R 0DU, 7253 1485, www.marx-memorial-library.org, open for guided tours 1-2pm Mon-Thur only, or by appointment) dedicated to the history of socialism and the science of Marxism. It was in this building that Lenin's *Iskra* magazine was printed before World War I.

Another hotbed of radicalism and free thinking is the Bishopsgate Library (230 Bishopsgate, EC2M 4QH, 7392 9270, www.bishopsgate.org.uk) which holds famous collections on London, labour, free thought and co-operation and was founded in 1895 as part of the Bishopsgate Institute for the education of the working man. It's a reference library, restored in the 1990s to its original appearance, with research materials for local and family historians, as well as more general reference books and current national and local newspapers.

Not far away is the Women's Library (London Metropolitan University, 25 Old Castle Street, E1 7NT, 7320 2222, www.londonmet.ac.uk/thewomenslibrary) which contains the most extensive collection of works specifically relating to women's history in the UK. As well as the reading room, there is a lively exhibition and events programme. Access here is free and open to everyone – just what libraries should be all about.

633

Celebrate the Thames

Without its river, London quite literally wouldn't exist, so it seems only right that there should be a proper celebration of the mighty Thames. The annual festival, nominally run by the Mayor's office, takes place over the middle weekend of September and populates the area between Westminster Bridge and Tower Bridge with an assortment of movies, food stalls, sculptures, the odd bar and an eclectic musical line-up. Sail on the water, dance in the streets and take a moment to reflect on the river that brought London to the world, and the world to London. The firework display is always a splendid finale.

Mayor's Thames Festival *99 Upper Ground, South Bank, SE1 9PP (7928 8998, www. thamesfestival.org). Free.*

634

Stick it to the whelks at Tubby Isaacs's seafood stall

What price a genuine taste of Cockney London? A couple of quid when it's Tubby Isaacs' whelks we're talking about. Standing outside the Aldgate Exchange pub on the corner of Goulston Street and Middlesex Street, E1, a few yards from the hustle and bustle of Petticoat Lane Market, Tubby Isaacs seafood stall has been trading since 1910. Currently owned by Paul – friendly faced grandson of Tubby himself – the seafood is top quality (eels, whelks, cockles, crabs… he's got the lot). The whelks are served in a polystyrene cup: flavour them with a slosh of vinegar, chilli vinegar if you're feeling adventurous, and some salt and pepper, then dive in with your toothpick. How do they taste? Like the sea, of course. A cheap, charming sliver of London's seafood heritage, the stall is usually open on all market trading days (that means normally every day except Saturday).

635 Take in a Midnight Matinée at Tristan Bates Theatre

For your next up-all-Saturday-night escapade, ditch the club scene and dive into the world of cutting-edge drama at one of Tristan Bates Theatre's Midnight Matinées. The sellout performances were established as an incubator for experiments in theatre, and the venue gives actors, writers and directors a space to test challenging ideas and new theatre companies an opportunity to strut their stuff. Ticket prices are kept low and the bar buzzes post-show as performers mix with the audience of locals and luvvies. TBT's also perfectly positioned for checking out that other forum of experimental theatre – the night bus home.

Tristan Bates Theatre *1A Tower Street, WC2H 9NP (7240 6283, www.tristanbatestheatre.co.uk).*

636

Kick off with the girls…

Women's football has really taken off over the past decade and there are now dozens of local teams looking for players. If you are interested, either contact the London County Football Association (11 Hurlingham Business Stadium, Sulivan Road, SW6 3DU, 7610 8360, www.londonfa.com) or visit the Football Association website (www.thefa.com/womens) to find a club that's convenient for you.

637

…or watch the professionals play

At a fiver a ticket to watch games in the FA Women's Premier League, it's cheaper than even non-league men's football (*see p36*), and yet professional women footballers are now playing at a seriously high (dare we say better?) standard. Most of London's pro clubs also have a women's team: Arsenal are far and away the best, but Chelsea and Fulham also have Premier League sides.

638 *Help reach a Critical Mass*

Part political movement, part breezy bike ride, Critical Mass (www.critical masslondon.org.uk) is a global cycling organisation that aims to reclaim the roads for pedal pushers. The website has links to cycling activism around the world as well as details of events in London – suffice to say the vibe is fairly anti motorised vehicle. The ride through the centre of town meets at 6pm on the last Friday of every month under Waterloo Bridge on the South Bank – if you want to take part just turn up with a bike.

639-648 *Hear great bands live for less*

Live music for less than a tenner? Bella Todd tours the town in search of the capital's best pub back rooms.

Amersham Arms

A roomy yet homely pub, the Amersham is something of a beacon for music fans navigating the unfriendly straits of New Cross Road. Its 300-capacity room plays host (usually Thursday to Saturday) to everything from big name DJs to folk festivals and ukulele jams, but it's probably best loved (especially by the students from the nearby Goldsmiths College) for pulling in well-known electro pop acts such as Ladyhawke and Hot Chip.
388 New Cross Road, SE14 6TY (07739 158380, www.theamershamarms.com). Free-£10.

Bedford

Gigs at this tardis-like Balham pub take place in the sizeable 'globe theatre', a round space ringed by a balcony and also in the 'ballroom' upstairs. The music policy is fairly middle of the road but there's an emphasis on breaking new talent – James Morrison and KT Tunstall both played here on the way up – what's more, there's no charge. Live music happens four nights a week (though comedy in the form of the Banana Cabaret takes precedence on Fridays and Saturdays). Names such as the Finn Brothers and Pete Townshend have played impromptu gigs here, too.
77 Bedford Hill, SW12 9HD (8682 8940, www.thebedford.co.uk). Free.

Betsey Trotwood

Set over three floors with a gig venue in the cellar and an acoustic room upstairs, this cosy Victorian pub hosts superior monthly alt-country and bluegrass nights (the latter in the form of an unplugged hoedown) and is a favourite with antifolk heroes over from the States. It's also home to modern folk club the Lantern Society (on the first and third Thursday of the month), which commandeers the upstairs room for its candlelit harmonies.
56 Farringdon Road, EC1R 3BL (7253 4285, www.thebetsey.com). Free-£6.

Dublin Castle

Indie heaven in the stickiest, sweatiest sense, this Irish pub (or, more importantly, its back room) is slap bang in the heart of Camden Town and has seen more bands pass through its doors than its clientele have skipped hot dinners. Once Madness's second home, it's now the best place to go if your aim is to catch as many up and coming acts as possible (there are at least four bands a night) regardless of whether they're playing metal, psych-pop or techno-reggae. The day the Dublin Castle turns itself into a gastropub is the day the Rolling Stones take to their rocking chairs.
94 Parkway, NW1 7AN (7485 1773, www.thedublincastle.com). £4.50-£7.

Gladstone Arms

More like someone's candlelit front room than a venue, 'the Glad' in Southwark is often packed but always relaxed, with the chance to enjoy rootsy acoustic music (perhaps over a Pieminister pie and a game of chess) nearly every Thursday, Saturday and Sunday. There's also a trad night on the last Monday of each month, and every Friday there are DJs playing soul, ska and rock'n'roll from 7.30pm. Ellie Goulding and Noah and the Whale have played here, as have the Shortwave Set and Findlay Brown. A proper little charmer.
64 Lant Street, SE1 1QN (7407 3962, www.thegladpub.com). Free.

Haggerston

Formerly known as Uncle Sam's – and with a retro neon sign outside to prove it – this post-pub, pre-club venue, with its late licence,

Hackney postcode, low-level lighting and leather sofas, somehow manages to straddle the divide between pretentious edginess and genuine good fun. Journey into Dalston for DJs and alt-ish bands on Saturdays and Sundays, but the jewel in its crown is Uncle Sam's Jazz and Blues, a weekly late night Sunday session, led by Alan Weekes's modern jazz quartet, where even the bar staff may take to the mic for the odd Billie Holiday classic.

438 Kingsland Road, E8 4AA (7923 3206). Free.

Half Moon Putney

Well, where do we start? KD Lang made her UK debut here; Kate Bush played her first ever show here; Elvis Costello had a residency, Nick Cave played a surprise gig, and the well-kept Wall of Fame pays testimony to shows by everyone from the Rolling Stones and U2 to, er, Gay Dad. The Half Moon has been putting on bands since the 1920s, and seems to have a special pull on performers. There are concerts every night of the week, and the Monday night acoustic sessions have been going since the '60s. It's now owned by Geronimo Inns; good pub grub is served seven days a week.

93 Lower Richmond Road, SW15 1EU (8780 9383, www.halfmoon.co.uk). £2.50-£12.

Macbeth

An intimate hipster Hoxton boozer where all kinds of rock and indie acts play amid

Amersham Arms

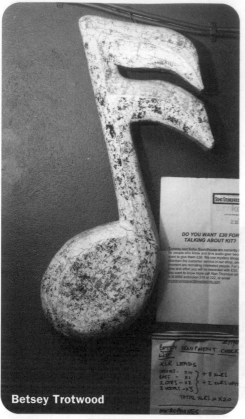

Betsey Trotwood

Renaissance-style paintings and some very attractive tiling. Past performers have included Florence and the Machine, Gang of Four and Roots Manuva. On Sundays there's a new, more gentle night – Beatnick – a folk-based session with barbecue, cake, face painting, poetry and short films, as well as acts – all for free. There's no entrance fee charged for the Monday jam sessions either.
70 Hoxton Street, N1 6LP (7749 0600, www.themacbeth.co.uk). Free-£10.

Old Blue Last

At times unbearably trendy (even more so since *NME* voted it 'the coolest pub in the world'), but this shabby-looking Hoxton watering hole is highly adept at generating a buzz. The Old Blue Last is famed for secret performances by the likes of the late Amy Winehouse and the Arctic Monkeys, but it also runs a pretty hip live music ship the rest of the time too. There

are no frills here, and often barely room to shake your hips, but when you're enjoying early gigs by the likes of Kate Nash, Dan Le Sac vs Scroobius Pip and Santogold, who cares?
38 Great Eastern Street, EC2A 3ES (7739 7033, www.theoldbluelast.com). Free-£10.

Slaughtered Lamb

Upstairs, it's a trendy drinking post for local office workers; down in the basement – a cavern-like space packed with mismatched sofas – it's a top spot for leftfield acoustica and folky electronica, thanks to promoters Pull Up The Roots, who programme many of the gigs. Lau played here shortly after winning Best Group at the BBC Radio 2 Folk Awards 2008, for example. Accompany the music with real ale, plus dishes such as fish finger sandwiches or sausage and mash.
34-35 Great Sutton Street, EC1V 0DX (7253 1516, www.theslaughteredlambpub.com). £5-£10.

649

Laugh, guffaw, chuckle...
...but don't snigger

Believe it or not, there are two groups in the capital dedicated entirely to the process of learning how to laugh. It's all about laughing for no reason (jokes are forbidden) – and tapping into your natural joy and inner playful child. Laughing also reduces stress hormones, boosts natural endorphins, strengthens the immune system and tones the stomach muscles, apparently. The Laughter Workout (07789 954972, www.laughingmatters.co.uk) is held twice a month from May to August in Lincoln's Inn Fields and costs £8 for an hour (the winter sessions are at indoor

venues and therefore cost more than £10). At the London Laughter Community, also held at Lincoln's Inn Fields (07904 334222, www.shinetime.co.uk, £5-£15 depending on income), chucklers lie on the floor and do laughter meditation. 'It's all about feeling happy because you laugh, and not laughing because you feel happy,' says Leela Bunce, who leads the sessions and tries to foster a sense of community through chortling. 'In these tough times, it's more important than ever to laugh. It doesn't take our problems away, but it makes them lighter.'

A few of my favourite things

650-655

Victoria Thornton, Founder, Open House

Leighton House (12 Holland Park Road, W14 8LZ, 7602 3316, www.rbkc.gov.uk) just off Kensington High Street, is beautiful. It was the 19th-century home of Frederic, Lord Leighton, who was the president of the Royal Academy, and it's designed like an Italianate villa. The interiors are very richly coloured and there are Arab-style tiled fountains in the hallways that people always fall into. **Another amazing building is the house of the late architect Sir John Soane (13 Lincoln's Inn Fields, WC2A 3BP, 7405 2107, www.soane.org). It's preserved exactly as it was in the 1800s, with all his paintings and sculptures. It's usually free to get in, and on the first Tuesday of each month they do an atmospheric candlelit evening tour.** St Martin-in-the-Fields church in Trafalgar Square (WC2N 4JJ, 7766 1100, www.st martin-in-the-fields.org) has been renovated. It's got a lovely café in the crypt and a little exhibition space that has given the building a new lease of life. The church itself is also fantastic. It hosts a lot of really good concerts and the lunchtime ones are free. **What's nice about London is that you don't have to get very high up to get an amazing view. Since the Royal Festival Hall has been renovated, it's a great place to go for a drink and from the café on the second floor (Riverside Terrace Café, Royal Festival Hall, Southbank Centre, Belvedere Road, SE1 8XX, www.southbankcentre. co.uk) you can enjoy a view of the north side of the river, with all its grand buildings.** I love going to Kenwood House for tea (Brew House, Kenwood, Hampstead Lane, NW3 7JR, 8341 5384, www.companyof cooks.com). The café is in the gardens of the grand old house and you can sit and have a pot of tea and fantastic cakes before a wander up Parliament Hill for an incredible view over London. On a good day you can actually see the skyline on the other side of the city right down to the South Downs. **Open House (www.open-city.org.uk) is a fantastic way to get to know the city – not just from the outside but from the inside. On the third weekend of September we open up 700 buildings to the public, from beautiful private houses to venues like the National Theatre and institutions that the public can't normally access. One of the most incredible is the Foreign Office in Whitehall. It has a wonderfully ornate interior and there's a lovely courtyard area in the middle with a glass ceiling. The great thing about it is that you can wander round at your own leisure, rather than being forced through on a tour.**

656 Respect your elders at the Age Exchange

The Age Exchange centre in Blackheath (11 Blackheath Village, SE3 9LA, 8318 9105, www.age-exchange.org.uk; closed until late 2012) offers the senior citizens of south-east London a chance to meet, greet and wax nostalgic about the old days. There's also a museum here decked out like a 1930s shop that showcases products of yesteryear: a wind-up gramophone, vintage records, retro clobber and wartime paraphernalia (from gas masks to ration books). It features regular exhibitions (an end of war tea party, a recreation of London's docks) and invites schoolchildren to learn about the past. A nostalgia kick goes well with a nice cup of tea, served in the café. Admission is free (though there's a charge for groups).

657

Wrap up warm and watch the Peter Pan Cup

Every Christmas morning in the frosty waters of Hyde Park's pond you can see members of the Serpentine Swimming Club (www.serpentineswimmingclub.com) thrashing it out for the Peter Pan Cup Christmas Morning Handicap Swim. The club requires participants to endure several months of winter training to help their bodies acclimatise, as water temperatures rarely exceed 4°C. Every swimmer must be a club member and have competed in a series of competitions... and, last but not least, they must be sporting a Santa hat. Kicking off at 9am on 25 December on the south bank of the lake, it's great fun to watch from dry land in nice snug clothes.

658
Attend the olde Strawberrie Fayre in Ely Place

This hidden little place – or Place – is the site of St Etheldreda's Church (14 Ely Place, EC1N 6RY, 7405 1061, www.stetheldreda.com), commended in Shakespeare's *Richard III* for its garden's fine fruit ('My Lord of Ely, when I was last in Holborn, I saw good strawberries in your garden there: I do beseech you send for some of them.'). In recognition of this, an annual Strawberrie Fayre is staged in late June (check the website for the exact date). There's plenty of traditional fun, games and strawberries, with all proceeds going to charity.

659
Sit on a ferryman's perch

Bankside was once London's Pleasure Quarter, where gaming, drinking and womanising could take place out of sight and mind on the far side of the river. On the corner of Bear Gardens (named for its bear pit), there's an ancient waterman's seat let into the modern wall, where boatmen once drummed up trade with their nudge-and-wink cry of 'Oars! Oars!'.

660

Swap stuff

Call them what you like: swapping, swishing, or ditching 'n' switching events, where you exchange your clobber for someone else's – no cash required – are an excellent way to save money, the environment (it's recycling, see) and prevent wardrobe ennui. Of course, it's also a great way to meet total strangers. See www.swishing.org for a list of upcoming events

The cheapest way to go about it is to hold your own clothes swapping party. Like the 21st century's answer to the Tupperware bash, you invite all your friends round, asking them to bring a bottle and the clothes they no longer want – then hope that someone else's cast-off is your own sartorial holy grail. And the rules are simple enough too: everyone brings a few items they're willing to relinquish and they can take home as much as they like. Reserving the best stuff before kick-off is frowned upon and, of course, remember your manners – all-out brawling is not in the spirit of swishing.

More shy and retiring sorts can get swapping online; try websites such as www.iswap.co.uk and www.swapshop.co.uk.

661 *Buy your lunch from an award-winning author*

A deliciously bucolic remnant of Old Spitalfields Market, upscale corner deli Verde & Co forms the ground floor of author Jeanette Winterson's restored Georgian home. Artfully presented – think linen-lined baskets of organic seasonal vegetables out front – and with an emphasis on Italian produce (to avoid competing with next door Brit specialist A Gold), the fruit and veg on sale here is carefully selected by ex-St John chef Harvey Cabaniss. He clearly takes pride in his artisanal lunchtime sandwich menu: try the chorizo, gorgonzola and sweet chilli, the suckling pig and balsamic onion, or check the daily specials board.

Verde & Co *40 Brushfield Street, E1 6AG (7247 1924, www.verde-and-company-ltd.co.uk).*

662

Have an epiphany in Neasden
A miraculous vision in marble,
the Shri Swaminarayan Mandir
(8965 2651, www.mandir.org)
is the biggest Hindu temple
outside India. Fascinating
architecturally and culturally,
the Mandir is open to people
of all faiths and none.

663

Visit the home of baseball

Baseball (unlike basketball) is a game of evolution rather than invention, and it may come as a surprise to learn that much of that evolving took place in Surrey rather than across the pond. Local records show that the game was played near Guildford in the 1750s, and there's even a reference in Jane Austen's *Northanger Abbey*. More than 250 years later, that tradition continues. The Croydon Pirates are one of the leading clubs in Britain's thriving baseball scene, competing in the National Premier League from their home at Roundshaw Playing Fields. The Pirates also host the London Tournament every July, with 16 top teams enjoying a weekend of pitching, pinch hits and put-outs. All games are free to watch and the season runs from April to September.
Croydon Pirates *www.croydonpirates.co.uk.*

664 Get your hands dirty in a 17th-century knot garden

Next door to Lambeth Palace, the old parish church of St Mary-at-Lambeth and its churchyard is home to the Garden Museum (formerly the Museum of Garden History), which exhibits the works of various green-fingered luminaries in its beautifully refurbished galleries. Outside, a lovely churchyard garden laid out in a formal 17th-century knot garden design was the last resting place of the John Tradescants (father and son), gardeners to Charles I. If you are itching to share some of your horticultural knowledge or would like to learn more about the historic plant species growing here, why not volunteer your services to help tend the garden (it is run entirely by volunteers). Visit the website for more information and application details.
Garden Museum *Lambeth Palace Road, SE1 7LB (7401 8865, www.gardenmuseum.org.uk). £6.*

665-666
Wake yourself up at a market

Stir your stumps at the crack of dawn, or even earlier, and head for 'the largest fresh produce market in the UK'. New Covent Garden Market is open 3am-11am Monday-Friday, 4am-10am Saturday (most of the wholesale action is over by 8am), and claims to supply almost half of all the food that London likes to eat while it's out. Covering 53 acres, the market opened here in Vauxhall after moving from Covent Garden in 1974, and is about to be given a thorough makeover. Even if you're not buying (and there's plenty of opportunity to – whether you are thinking wholesale or not), your £5 entry fee (free if arriving on foot) guarantees a feel for the market's buzz and there are plenty of market caffs where you can breakfast alongside the traders. In a separate building, the flower market offers the most spectacular profusion of plants for sale under one roof in the country. As well as supplying florists and flower-stall holders, it does brisk business with funeral directors, wedding planners and brides-to-be.

Sunbury Antiques market takes place on the second and fourth Tuesday of every month at Kempton Racecourse and features more than 700 stalls (350 indoor, 350 outdoor). It opens at 6.30am, and if you're serious about your rummaging, you'll need a car – one, the trains don't start running until later, and you'll need to transport your treasures home. On the plus side, there's no entrance fee, and parking is free. The big appeal of the place is the vast variety of the stuff on offer, from old French maps and tables of stuffed owls to gargantuan Belgian farmhouse tables. Plus you can often buy in bulk – 20 science lab light-fittings, or 100 school chairs, for example. There's also the great atmosphere that comes from a jumble of different accents, a shared enthusiasm for unusual objects, and the solidarity of enduring an excruciatingly early start.
New Covent Garden Market *Nine Elms Lane, SW8 5NX (7720 2211, www.newcoventgarden market.com).*
Sunbury Antiques Market *Kempton Racecourse, Sunbury TW16 5AQ (01932 230946, www.sunbury antiques.com).*

667 *Attend a poker festival*

Poker in the park (www.pokerinthepark.com) is a free, outdoor poker festival, held once a year over two days at the end of the summer. Expect games, talks, music and card magic. To play, just register on the door.

668
Eat Bánh Mì

Bánh mì, a delicious Franco-Viet baguette, is a big part of Vietnam's street food culture. Now, they're becoming ever more ubiquitous in London – popping up not only in market stalls, but in Vietnamese cafés and restaurants, too. A great place to try one is Bánhmi11 (www.banhmi11.com), which has a stall at Berwick Street Market, W1 (10am-3pm Mon-Fri) and at Broadway Market, E2 (10am-5pm Sat). The own-made pâté, in particular, stands out, and bread is made fresh in the morning by the Spence, a local baker. Variations on filling include 'Imperial BBQ' pork (based on a marinade from Hue, Vietnam's old imperial city) and sirloin steak (the 'Op La Di).'

669
Explore Kings Place

In line with the recent regeneration of the King's Cross area, this major arts centre opened in 2008 to great fanfare and much critical acclaim. Incredibly, the airy modern building is home to the first new public concert hall to be built in central London since the Barbican Concert Hall opened in 1982. The building consists of a public open-plan ground-floor area with comfortable seating, a café and a restaurant, while the two lower levels house a gallery and two concert halls, whose acoustics can be adjusted for music or speech. There are classical, choral and jazz concerts, with whole cycles dedicated to individual composers, as well as spoken word evenings and events for children. All art exhibitions are free, while lectures and music events can be attended for just £9.50 if booked in advance online. Elegant inside and out, this is a great addition not only to King's Cross, but to London as a whole.
Kings Place *90 York Way, N1 9AG (7520 1490, www.kingsplace.co.uk).*

Kings Place

670-672
Get to know William Morris

Born in Walthamstow in 1856, Morris made it his mission to beautify the ends and means of mass production, most famously with his wallpaper designs inspired by natural forms, but more generally through a deep respect for craftsmanship and the dignity of labour.

In 1877, he rented a house on the lovely riverside path that runs from Hammersmith to Chiswick. He called it Kelmscott House (26 Upper Mall, 8741 3735, www.williammorris society.org, free) after his manor in Oxfordshire, and died here in 1896. Now home to the William Morris Society, founded in 1955, the basement and coach house, containing a library and a variety of Morris memorabilia, can be visited from 2pm to 5pm on Thursdays and Saturdays.

Other key places in London associated with the pioneering socialist include the Red House (Red House Lane, Bexleyheath DA6 8JF, 8304 9878, www.nationaltrust.org.uk, £7.20), which Morris designed with architect Philip Webb and where he lived from 1860 for five years (before being forced to sell) and the wonderful William Morris Gallery (Lloyd Park, Forest Road, E17 4PP, 8527 3782, free), where he lived as a teenager and which now exhibits his famous designs in fabrics, glass, tiles, wallpaper and furniture as well as other works by other Arts and Crafts designers such as Arthur Heygate Mackmurdo and William de Morgan.

673
Ogle classic cars in South Kensington

In the mews off the Old Brompton Road lie three of the world's top classic car dealers: Peter Bradfield, 8 Reece Mews (www.bradfield cars.com); Fiskens, 14 Queens Gate Place Mews (www.fiskens.com); Hexagon Classics, 6 Kendrick Place (www.hexagonclassics.com). Even if motors aren't really your thing, you'll be hard pressed not to drool over the Ferraris, Jaguars and Alfa Romeos, though your tenner won't be much use here.

674
Catch a film at the Exhibit Cinema

London has been at the forefront of a British cinema revolution and now boasts several exclusive and luxurious movie dens. One of the most favoured chocolates in the box is Balham's doo wop-style boutique picture house. The Exhibit offers the chance to see a mix of new-ish releases and arthouse works on comfortable, chocolate-brown leather sofas for £7 (or £5 if you have dinner in the adjoining restaurant). It's the perfect setting for a wallet-friendly date.

The Exhibit *12 Balham Station Road, SW12 9SG (8772 6556, www.theexhibit.co.uk).*

675
Get your jewellery valued at Hatton Garden

When the chips are *really* down, take the family loot to be valued at one of the sparkling stores of Hatton Garden, London's gem trading centre since the Middle Ages.

676 *Go Dutch*

Dutch bars aren't unusual these days, but what they don't have is the century-old history of De Hems. This ornate-fronted hostelry was first a refuge for homesick Dutch sailors, then an overseas base for the wartime Dutch Resistance. Now a convivial two-floor pub with dark wood interior, the sturdy counters are lined with Grolsch Weizen, and Kriek taps (£3.75/pint), with more unusual bottled beers such as Kwak, Vedett and Orval stored behind the bar. Traditional Dutch bar snacks such as *bitterballen* (deep-fried meat balls) cost from £3.75 a dish, or, if they don't appeal, it's conveniently located on the edge of Chinatown.

De Hems *11 Macclesfield Street, W1D 5BW (7437 2494, www.nicholsonspubs.co.uk).*

677-679 *Get your skates on*

Outdoor skating has become an expensive business, so it's good to know that the ice rink at Broadgate Circle (www.broadgateice. co.uk) remains under a tenner (£5-£8). Also affordable are the Lee Valley Ice Centre (Lea Bridge Road, E10 7QL, 8533 3154, www.leevalleypark.org.uk), where it's £7.30 to skate and £1.70 to hire skates, and the Sobell Leisure Centre (Hornsey Road, N7 7NY, 7609 2166, www.aquaterra.org/sobell-leisure-centre), where a session costs £5.10, with skate hire at £1.10.

680

Pay homage to the Tyburn martyrs

A neat and tranquil afternoon antidote to the toxic bustle of nearby Oxford Street, this peaceful convent is home to 25 cloistered nuns, who watch over the relics of more than a hundred Roman Catholic martyrs who were executed here under the Reformation laws between 1535 and 1681.

In the chapel on the ground floor you'll find at least one sister mantaining contemplation before the cross while others are available at 10.30am, 3.30pm and 5.50pm daily for tours of the crypt below. The shrine, which contains some extraordinary wall-mounted displays of various body parts of unfortunate Catholics dispatched here, is located near what was once the site of the infamous King's Gallows. Over 50,000 executions took place from 1196 to 1783 and most of the Catholics remembered here were hung from a triangular gallows that became known as the Tyburn Tree. The gallows became so infamous that 'to be taken to Tyburn' became a euphemism for execution. A replica of the Tyburn Tree can be seen in the convent's eerie crypt.

Tyburn Convent *8 Hyde Park Place, W2 2LJ (www.tyburnconvent.org.uk).*

681

Discover Eadweard Muybridge at Kingston Museum

Kingston Museum is worth anyone's time – containing as it does a remarkably well-preserved Anglo-Saxon logboat – but for movie buffs it's an absolute must. The remarkable Eadweard Muybridge (1830-1903) was born in Kingston as plain Edward James Muggeridge, but changed his name to Muygridge then to Eadweard Muybridge (taking the spelling of his Christian name from the name of Eadweard the Elder on Kingston's coronation stone).

He headed for America hoping to find a market for his topical photographs and soon made a name for himself with his landscapes of Yosemite, cityscapes of San Francisco and work with moving images (in 1872 he was asked to photograph the racehorse Occident, belonging to a former governor of California, to prove that all four of the horse's feet left the ground at once when galloping – his experiments proved that they did).

Back at the museum in Kingston, there's a collection of his equipment and some of the prints that Muybridge bequeathed to the place on his death. You can see two of the revolving slotted drums or zoetropes that he experimented with – they show an ostrich running and a man jumping up and down, as well as a phenakistiscope, one of the world's earliest moving picture devices. Muybridge's second Zoopraxiscope, also on display here, was designed to project the movement and actions of various animals. The museum also holds one of only nine surviving copies of his 'Panorama of San Francisco', which is over 17 feet in length, and taken with a series of 13 cameras in 1878.

Kingston Museum *Wheatfield Way, Kingston upon Thames, KT1 2PS (8547 6440, www. kingston.gov.uk/museum). Free.*

682

Be a mystery shopper

Mystery Shopping is probably the closest you are likely to get to being a secret agent (well, a sort of consumer sleuth anyway). Posing as a real customer, your mission, should you choose to accept it, is usually to check out customer service (sometimes in person, sometimes on the phone) and buy all manner of goodies incognito – some of which you may get to keep. With many big name clients out there determined to maintain their high levels of service, you can find yourself in some exciting places (free flights are not unheard of) – and any expenses spent while on a case are reimbursed (you may also earn a small fee for completing an evaluation form). Register online.
www.mystery-shoppers.co.uk.

Fringe benefits

Grant Gillespie uncovers the best theatre deals in town and discovers that we're spoilt for choice.

Battersea Arts Centre

One of the most common laments you'll hear from the would-be theatre going community relates to the expense of the tickets – if we had a pound for every time we'd heard a complaint along these lines we could afford the theatre every night of the week and dinner at the Ivy afterwards. But with more and more venues introducing 'pay-what-you-can nights' along with various other tempting deals to entice both the jaded and the cash-strapped back into theatres, things are looking up. What's equally encouraging is that the venues employing this non-elitist practice are generally also those that produce some of the most interesting and thought-provoking work in London. You won't come away humming a Lloyd Webber tune but you'll certainly have food for thought and enough money for food to boot (though not at the Ivy). OK, so you might not be seeing Kevin Spacey or Nicole Kidman gracing the stage but chances are you will be watching the next Kevin Spacey and hotly tipped Nicole Kidman replacement.

Pay what you can

Pay-what-you-can means just that: you pay what you can afford and it's entirely at your discretion – some punters pay a pound, some pay full price, but a fiver or so is a good average. All of the theatres below offer this deal on certain nights – although you may need to be quick off the mark to take advantage. Keep your ear to the ground or, more usefully, your finger on the mouse.

The well-established and respected Gate Theatre (7229 0706, www.gatetheatre.co.uk) in Notting Hill is the only London theatre venue exclusively dedicated to international writing. The great and the good either started off here or still work here, attracted by the diversity and quality of the company's output. It's an intimate but flexible space above the Prince Albert pub and seats about 70 people. At Saturday matinées, tickets cost £10.

Tuesday night is pay-what-you-can night at the Battersea Arts Centre (7223 2223, www.bac.org.uk). Housed in a beautiful Grade II building that was originally Battersea Town Hall, BAC's ambitious mission is to 'invent the future of theatre' and that means showing everything from huge site-specific pieces that make use of the whole space (including the café, two theatres and the gallery) to intimate

performances for just one audience member. 'Whether you want to pay £10 or just 50p we believe pay-what-you-can nights are a great way of introducing audiences to the best in theatre at BAC. It's a central strand of our commitment to knocking down barriers to attendance and has, over the last decade, introduced thousands of people to our work,' say David Jubb and David Micklem, the joint artistic directors. Generally speaking, on pay-what-you-can nights at the BAC, all tickets are pay-what-you-can tickets, and they are available from the moment the run goes on sale (there are occasional exceptions to this rule – check the website for details).

> *'Venues offering pay-what-you-can nights are often also those that produce some of the most interesting work in London.'*

Arcola Theatre (7503 1646, www.arcola theatre.com) in Hackney, has been growing steadily in repute since it opened in 2000. The programming is varied, running from comedy through to the classics, and is staged by new and established practitioners alike. The Arcola offers pay-what-you-can tickets on Tuesdays (40 tickets for Studio 1, 15 for Studio 2), which can be purchased from 6.30pm on the evening of the performance.

At the Riverside Studios (8237 1111, www.riversidestudios.co.uk) in Hammersmith the large warehouse space holds – among other things – two theatres, a large café and a cinema. The theatre remit is all-encompassing, presenting a plethora of cutting-edge productions, not only in theatre but also dance, comedy, and music; you can see some new names, some established, some home-grown and some flown in. 'Great entertainment is at its best when it surprises. But that means people need to be up for the risk of seeing a show that has no guarantees attached to it – no big names, no stars etc. That's the reason we offer cheaper tickets as often as we can – to instil a sense of discovery and adventure,' says artistic director, William Burdett-Coutts. Riverside has various pay-what-you-can nights and early bird tickets (*see below*), but you need to be fairly assiduous about checking the website for details of what the deal is and when because they change for each show.

Early-bird tickets

Another way to get your cultural kicks on a limited budget is to look out for the early-bird seats you'll find at the theatres below. Again, you need to be prepared to book promptly, but being quick off the mark will give you all the more time to look forward to the upcoming thrill. And bear in mind that seats are often easier to come by in the first week of the production before the reviews come out.

The Tricycle Theatre (7328 1000, www.tricycle.co.uk), says artistic director Nicolas Kent, remains 'committed to making theatre accessible to all of London's culturally diverse population regardless of income. Theatre is a two-way transaction, and the composition of the audience, whether rich, poor, old, or young is a vital part of that experience.' The theatre, based in Kilburn, shows works by Irish, Afro-Caribbean, Jewish and Asian writers that invariably tackle political or topical issues, but don't expect overly worthy, mirth-free theatre – there are plenty of laughs along the way. The building is spacious, with a gallery, cinema and café/bar, and the theatre space seats 225. Early-bird tickets are available for £10 on certain dates for the first 80 tickets – keep a close eye on the website.

The Southwark Playhouse (7407 0234, www.southwarkplayhouse.co.uk), in the arches below London Bridge train station, is an atmospheric Victorian vault of a place and houses a versatile 150-seat auditorium and a truly cavernous bar. The theatre, in the words of its education director, Ellen Hughes, puts on 'inventive theatre for courageous audiences', and offers seats for keen bookers at £9.

Lunchtime shows

There are a few London fringe theatres that run regular lunchtime shows. The Bridewell (7353 3331, www.stbridefoundation.org), a 136-seater theatre in a converted Victorian swimming pool on Fleet Street, holds 'lunch-box' theatre, which costs just £6 in advance and £7 on the door, and you can bring your own picnic. It showcases emerging talent and classic short plays, often comedies, by the likes of Oscar Wilde or Neil Simon, that last about 45 minutes. Tickets can be bought at the theatre office or on the day at the box office. Visiting companies set the ticket prices for the evening shows, and it is worth having a look on the website as some start from as little as £7.50.

At Islington's King's Head Theatre (7478 0160, www.kingsheadtheatre.org), a tiny space tucked away at the back of a Victorian boozer on Upper Street, all tickets are £10 in preview week (the first week of all performances). The theatre had a major change of direction in 2011, when Adam Spreadbury-Maher became artistic director and turned it into a fringe opera venue. OperaUpClose is its resident company and opera, musical theatre, dance and occasionally plays alternate in its current rep.

Other deals

The Royal Court (7565 5000, www.royalcourt theatre.com) on Sloane Square is Britain's leading national company dedicated to putting on new writing of the very highest quality. It was here in 1956 that John Osborne's *Look*

Tricycle Theatre

Battersea Arts Centre

Back in Anger was first performed, marking the beginning of a new wave of British theatre. The space is great, with a big restaurant and bar in the basement. It doesn't do pay-what-you-can, but it does have £10 Mondays in the downstairs space. Tickets are available from 9am online and 10am in person, plus, if you are prepared to stand, there are sometimes a few tickets available for a paltry 10p – it's always worth checking. (Other theatres sell standing tickets 'in the slips' as well, but a lot of them don't advertise the fact, so it's a good idea to ask at the box office.)

At the National Theatre (7452 3000, www. nationaltheatre.org.uk), you can buy standing tickets on the day for £5. At Shakespeare's Globe (21 New Globe Walk, 7401 9919, www. shakespeares-globe.org), you can feel like an Elizabethan peasant by parting with five British pounds to stand in the pit and be a groundling. The Donmar (41 Earlham Street, 0844 871 7624, www.donmarwarehouse.com) in Covent Garden offers 20 standing tickets a night at the back of the circle for £7.50, while prices for the Almeida (7359 4404, www. almeida.co.uk) in Islington start at £8, though they are mainly restricted view. In terms of the West End, you can try for Standby seats,

go to the cut-price ticket boxes or, if you have good eyesight and don't mind heights, sit in the gods.

> ### *'Cheap seat deals are often easier to come by in the first week – before the reviews come out.'*

And finally, at the Bush Theatre (8743 5050, www.bushtheatre.co.uk) tickets start at £10, and there are various offers and multi-buys that push the price down even further. This award-winning theatre, above the Bush pub in Shepherd's Bush, has long been committed to showcasing promising new writing and boasts an impressive list of alumni including Stephen Poliakoff, Mike Leigh and Jim Broadbent.

And note – it's always worth looking at the theatre section of *Time Out* magazine, not only for the latest reviews and listings, but also for two-for-one ticket offers and other regular deals.

698 *Drink in the gardens at the Chumleigh café*

In the otherwise slightly barren Burgess Park, the quaint Chumleigh almshouses (now used as conference facilities) and magnificent gardens come as a pleasant surprise. Capturing the spirit of five distinct gardening styles – Islamic, English, African/Caribbean, Mediterranean and Oriental – you'll find some unusual plant species here as well as two ponds, one for wildlife, the other a more formal, mosaiced Islamic-style affair. Another garden area north of the café is being landscaped by Groundwork London with a playground and walks. You can feast on some hearty snack fare (and roasts on Sunday) and Fairtrade drinks in the cheerful café (between the Mediterranean and Islamic Gardens), with its bright colours, samba music and peaceful outdoor seating.
Chumleigh Gardens *Burgess Park, SE5 0RJ (7525 2000).*

699 *Birdwatch*

Despite warnings of declining populations and lack of habitat, there's still a surprising amount of birdlife to appreciate in London – around 300 species of bird have been identified in the last few years, including large birds such as herons, cormorants, falcons and sparrowhawks. Even without a pair of binoculars (you'll have to pay more than a tenner for those) there's still a lot you can do to maximise your chances of getting some interesting sightings.

With the help of the RSPB's free guide to birds or a well-illustrated field guide you may soon be ticking off species (like tits, thrushes and finches) from your twitcher list before you've even left your back garden, but the best sites are obviously the places where there's a lot of vegetation. In the centre of town that means parks, where you can see some interesting species such as woodpeckers, redwings and fieldfares (in hard winters), goldcrests, wrens at different times of year as well as water birds like great crested grebes.

Further out, try wilder areas like Rainham Marshes, Brent's Welsh Harp Reservoir, Sydenham Hill Wood, the Lee River Valley, and – just 25 minutes from central London – the London Wetland Centre (www.wwt.org.uk), an international award-winning visitor attraction, considered the finest urban site in Europe for wildlife spotting. The Centre is home to some rare and beautiful birds including bitterns, redstarts, kingfishers, sky larks, red shanks and golden plovers.

If you want to learn more, you could always join a group – try the East London Birders Forum (www.elbf.co.uk), the London Natural History Society (www.lnhs.org.uk) or your local RSPB group (www.rspb.org.uk).

700-702 *Play bar billiards*

Providing an ideal, and not arduous, workout to accompany a pint, bar billiards involves sinking balls in holes of varying difficulty, without knocking down the skittles that protect the most high-scoring holes. A time limit is set on each game (eventually a bar drops inside the table preventing any more balls returning to be replayed), so unlike billiards and snooker, even clueless novices know they won't be stuck at a game for hours. There are bar billards at Pembury Tavern (90 Amhurst Road, E8 1JH, 8986 8597,www.individualpubs.co.uk), Dog & Bell (116 Prince Street, SE8 3JD, 8692 5664) and King Charles I (55-57 Northdown Street, N1 9BL, 7837 7758). Games cost £1.

703 *Learn to free run*

You know those montages you see of spring-heeled urban gymnasts running up lampposts, bounding over bollards and ping-ponging from wall to wall like hoodie-clad superheroes? They're free runners. And you know what? You can do it too. Founded in France and sharing much with the similarly acrobatic and equally dangerous practice of parkour (also sometimes known a *l'art de déplacement* or 'the act of displacement'), it has an official network, Urban Freeflow, which offers outdoor classes for small groups and individuals. The website has plenty of information on the UK free running scene.
www.urbanfreeflow.com.

704
Visit the new Photographers' Gallery

The new home of the Photographers' Gallery opened in May 2012 in central London, and is the city's largest public gallery dedicated to photography. Annual events include the Deutsche Börse Photography Prize exhibition. There are three floors of galleries devoted to British and International photography, plus the Studio Floor – a space for talks, events, workshops and courses, a camera obscura, the Study Room, and Touchstone – a changing display of a single photographic work. The building also holds a bookshop, a print sales room and a street level café.

Photographers' Gallery *16-18 Ramillies Street, W1F 7LW (www.photonet.org.uk).*

705
Listen to the experts at Stanfords

Stanfords Travel Bookshop in Covent Garden first opened for business in 1901, and even today its three floors of maps, guides and travelogues can conjure up an almost overpowering wanderlust. Its selection of maps and guidebooks make for pleasant browsing but the store also makes a fitting setting for the lectures, presentations and book readings that it hosts, which feature some of the most established figures in the travel writing world. Michael Palin, Colin Thubron and William Dalrymple among other well-travelled luminaries have all spoken here. Ticketed events, which usually include a glass of wine and few nibbles, take place most weeks, either here or at the Royal Geographical Society. There's generally a Q&A session afterwards.

Stanfords *12-14 Long Acre, WC2E 9LP (7836 1321, www.stanfords.co.uk). From £5.*

706
Try karate...

Karate is an exciting blend of kicks, punches, knee and elbow strikes and is popular as ever. Guided by Sensei Linda Marchant, a 6th Dan black belt and former world champion, the structured programme of tuition here includes short sequences to allow you to practise defence and attack techniques with your partner but without the risks that are involved in free fighting. The classes at Tooting Karate Club start at £7.

Tooting Karate Club *Smallwood School, Smallwood Road, SW17 0TW (07771 932963, www.southwestlondonkarate.co.uk).*

707
...or kick-boxing

The Martial Arts Place teaches a form called *mo-gei-do* (meaning 'the way of no boundaries'). It's a combination of European and Eastern techniques, including karate and boxing. Kick boxing is an excellent all-round fitness workout and is as popular with women as it is with men. A trial class costs £10.

Martial Arts Place *88 Avenue Road, NW3 3HA (7586 1222, www.themartialartsplace.com).*

708
Take a day-trip to Portugal

The Portuguese population hits around 50,000 in Lambeth – that's nearly one in every five residents of the borough – and on 10 June (or the nearest weekend if it falls on a weekday) there's a celebration of all things Portuguese in the 'Little Portugal' area that surrounds Kennington Park. With live *fado* (and other music) and numerous seafood stalls selling *bacalhau* (salted cod), it's lusophone laughs all round.

709-718
Follow a London blog

A Little Bird
www.a-littlebird.com
A carefully curated run-down on the hottest shops, exhibitions, pop-up projects and more.

Dave Hill's London Blog
www.guardian.co.uk/uk/davehillblog
Scrutinising London politics.

Dos Hermanos
www.doshermanos.co.uk
Opinionated, entertaining reviews of London's restaurants, written by the food-obsessed Majumdar brothers.

Going Underground
www.london-underground.blogspot.com
News, trivia and irreverent comment on the tube.

The Great Wen
http://greatwenlondon.wordpress.com
From London's worst statues to weird museum exhibits, Peter Watts has an eye for the unusual.

London-in-Sight
http://londoninsight.wordpress.com
London's quirkier corners and characters, seen through the lens of photographer Stephanie Wolff.

London Review of Breakfasts
londonreviewofbreakfasts.blogspot.com
Breakfast places of all sorts dissected by very readable reviewers.

Spitalfields Life
www.spitalfieldslife.com
Offbeat, well-written articles on the East End past and present.

Time Out London – Now. Here. This.
www.now-here-this.timeout.com
The ultimate guide to eating and drinking, clubbing, fashion, the arts and more in London.

Tired of London, Tired of Life
www.tiredoflondontiredoflife.com
Not sure what to do in the city? TOLTOL's daily posts provide varied suggestions.

719
Beautify yourself on a budget...

'It's better to be beautiful than to be good', claimed Oscar Wilde. But he wasn't living through a credit crunch. However, mindful of the sentiment, we recommend a trip to the Esthetique salon – part of the London School of Beauty, where students (under supervision of beauty therapists) will soothe away worry lines brought on by these troubled times. Eyebrow and eyelash treatments start at £7, and, though not eligible for this book, there's also a great value 45-minute facial (£17). Booking is recommended as slots fill up fast.

London School of Beauty and Make-Up
Esthetique Student Salon, 18-19 Long Lane, EC1A 9PL (7580 0355, www.lond-est.com).

720-721
...then get a cheap, chic haircut

There are also places in London where you can have your tresses tended to for next to nothing. And if you like staring at yourself in the mirror for hours on end, then so much the better. Salon training schools such as Vidal Sassoon and Toni and Guy need a constant supply of models for their students to practise on and trained stylists are always on hand to advise and deal with any mishaps. At Vidal Sassoon, the standard haircut price is actually £12 (£5 if you're a student), but there are often special £5 offers available to entice more models when there's a high volume of students – check by phoning ahead or sign up for their newsletter. Every fourth haircut is also free.

Toni & Guy *71-75 New Oxford Street, WC1A 1DG (7836 0606, www.toniandguy.com). From £5.*
Vidal Sassoon *56, 48 Brook Street, W1K 5NE (7491 0030, www.sassoon.com). From £5.*

722 Save yourself for 'Thirsty Thursday'

The American health food superstore Wholefoods Market on Kensington High Street offers wine and organic canapé sampling evenings every Thursday in an attempt to pull punters in to buy healthy goodies from the colourfully stocked shelves. But for just £5 you can try a selection of five seasonal wine and food combinations at different counters around the shop. In the past, the gourmet treats have included smoked eel with beetroot and horseradish crème frâiche paired with a sample of Codorníu cava clasico, and parmesan crisps with a snort of Taittinger Brut champagne. Five of these little babies should set you up nicely for the evening. Tasting from 5-8pm every Thursday.

Wholefoods Market *The Barkers Building, 63-97 Kensington High Street, W8 5SE (7368 4500, www.wholefoodsmarket.com).*

723 Turn your garden into a nature reserve

There are more that three million gardens in London – that's a whole lot of habitat for the capital's wildlife to take refuge in. As well as managing over 50 London-wide reserves, the London Wildlife Trust is on a mission to get gardeners to turn their backyards into more inviting environments for plants and animals. It suggests planting mixed hedgerow and broad-leafed trees to create more shade, buying drought-resistant plants that are less water hungry, digging ponds to provide further habitat diversity and a place for animals to drink and bathe, and sticking compost on the roof of your shed to create a living roof and to allow further space for plants to grow. Visit the website to download the free 'how to' guides.

London Wildlife Trust *Skyline House, 200 Union Street, SE1 0LX (7261 0447, www.wildlondon.org.uk).*

724 Dust off your crest at the College of Arms

The Court of the Earl Marshal in the College of Arms is the 17th-century, wood-panelled HQ of the royal heralds, guardians of the right to bear arms (of the heraldic variety). If you ask to speak to the officer-in-waiting, one of the qualified genealogist heralds, pursuivants or officers-in-arms, he may be happy to explain his function for free, especially if there's a chance of his later being able to undertake research into your ancestors and whether or not they carry a coat of arms (for a fee). The College can also arrange for the examination of pedigrees and prepare heraldic artwork. Recent grants of arms include those to Loyd Grossman, who chose a polar bear for his crest, and the motto 'If not now when', and to Sir Christopher Frayling, Rector of the Royal College of Art, who, perhaps equally inexplicably, chose a dodo for his crest, three owls on his arms, and a cactus for his badge.

College of Arms *Queen Victoria Street, EC4V 4BT (7248 2762, www.college-of-arms.gov.uk).*

725 Visit Bermondsey's Fashion & Textile Museum

British designer Zandra Rhodes is known for her outlandish use of colour and so it comes as little surprise when you catch sight of the gaudy pink and orange façade of her brainchild (now run and co-owned by Newham College). As well as housing permanent exhibits by Rhodes, the Fashion and Textile Museum also has a changing programme of exhibitions (these usually showcase British designers), runs courses for both fashion students and businesses, and holds a series of fashion-related events and talks (many of which cost less than a tenner – see website for details).

Fashion and Textile Museum *83 Bermondsey Street, SE1 3XF (7407 8664, www.ftmlondon.org). Admission £7.*

726 Listen to the SOAS World Music series

Want to expand your musical horizons? Then head to SOAS's series of gigs. Try north Indian dhrupad, a classical vocal genre dating back to the 15th century. And that's just the tip of the musical iceberg. How about hearing a master of the Middle Eastern oud, or watching a dab hand at the Afro-Cuban batà drums? There's exorcistic salpuri dance from Korea; Pontic lyre sessions; Argentinian chacarera, candombe, zamba and chamame dances; the maqam music of the Uyghurs; Judeo-Spanish Ladino song; or scprcwa sounds from the Ashanti region of Ghana. The concerts are organised by the SOAS World Music Series and are free. You can't book, so you'll need to turn up in good time and even then there can sometimes be something of a crush at the door.

SOAS *Brunei Gallery Lecture Theatre, Thornhaugh Street, Russell Square WC1H 0XG (7898 4500, www.soas.ac.uk/concerts). All performances start at 7pm usually on a Tuesday, Wednesday and/or Friday*

727 Visit the new Serpentine Sackler Gallery

Zaha Hadid is the architect remodelling what was a 19th-century gunpowder depot into the new Serpentine Sackler Gallery. The handsome, Grade-II listed building is in a plum position on West Carriage Drive in Kensington Gardens. The plan for the art is to show 'the best in emerging international talent across all art forms, complementing the existing programme at the Serpentine Gallery'. The Gallery will also house a café/restaurant, and the whole thing should be open by the end of 2012. See www.serpentinegallery.org for more details.

728-735

Fabien Riggall

I have a soft spot for Gordon's Wine Bar (47 Villiers Street, WC2N 6NE, 7930 1408, www.gordonswinebar.com). There are few better places to hole up with friends and a bottle of wine on a dreary Sunday afternoon. **Or if it's a sunny Sunday afternoon, take your bottle of wine to the Serpentine and get your friends to row you around.** Nag's Head Market (opposite Odeon Cinema, Holloway Road, N7 6LJ, 01992 717198, Saturday and Sunday) is a fab place to offload junk from home and pick up the odd gem of new junk to replace the last lot with. **Victoria Park is my favourite London park. It's hard to beat a jog here on a crisp weekday morning. I also love cycling along Regent's Canal.** I'm always on the lookout for interesting London venues for Secret Cinema and Future Cinema film nights but for some reason it took a Rock'n'Roll cinema event (no longer running) at the Hackney Empire (291 Mare Street, E8 1EJ, 8985 2424, www.hackneyempire.co.uk) for me to realise what a beautiful old place this is. **Another beautiful place, which we have just used for a Secret Cinema event is the Royal Horticultural Halls (80 Vincent Square London, SW1P 2PE, 0845 370 4606, www.horticultural-halls.co.uk). The Lawrence Hall is a stunning, high glass-ceilinged art deco space – we blacked it out and put on a Ghostbusters night.** I'm a keen swimmer and lucky to have London Fields Lido (London Fields Westside, E8 3EU, 7254 9038) – the only heated outdoor pool in town – as my local.

Fabien Riggall is the founder of Future Cinema as well as the Secret Cinema and Future Cinema film events.

736

Keep TV (and radio) live

See TV and radio shows for free by offering your services as an audience member (and canned laughter substitute). A quick Google search will reveal many companies offering free tickets but we recommend the following sites for the best shows: www.sroaudiences.com may be giving away tickets for the *Alan Titchmarsh Show* and *Countdown* but it also has places for new comedy and panel shows such as the *A Short History of Everything Else* with Griff Rhys Jones; and www.bbc.co.uk/tickets, which offers a huge variety of entertainment from *Strictly Come Dancing* to the surreal world of Radio 4 comedy. (Note that in order to be part of the *Question Time* audience, you have to fill in an application form.) Book early for the most popular slots (which includes almost all Radio 4 comedy shows).

737

Take a tour round the pet cemetery in Hyde Park

A century before Stephen King's creepy cat, Church, scared us silly by clawing his way back from the dead in *Pet Sematary*, the Victorians, obsessed with death and mourning, were laying their dear-departed mutts and moggies to rest in this macabre little corner of Hyde Park. It started with Cherry, a Maltese terrier, in the 1880s and the last interment was in 1967. George Orwell described it as 'perhaps the most horrible spectacle in Britain' and while we wouldn't go that far, it's certainly a spooky spot, hidden behind the railings at Victoria Gate on the Bayswater Road. If you fancy a fright, visit at twilight and you might agree with Mr King's assertion that 'sometimes dead is better'.

738

Look a million dollars for less than a tenner

It can be tough to pull off a look on an evening when the purse strings are tighter than a David Hasselhoff perm, so we asked London's fiercest trendonistas how to concoct DIY club couture on the cheap.

Jodie Harsh, socialite and DJ, suggested that the best shop for obscure items is So High Soho on Berwick Street – the fancy dress shop to end all fancy dress shops: 'I've bought rainbow-coloured false lashes, light-up sunglasses and random bits of jewellery there. You can put a whole look together for a tenner.'

The fashion designer Nova Dando goes to the stall outside Sainsbury's in the Kingsland Shopping Centre in Dalston, which sells assorted earrings and hair bobbles for cheap.

Club kid Joshyou Are says: 'John Lewis's fabric section is great for upholstery fringing, or hit up B&Q for chains for necklaces or handbag straps, while the alt performance artist Scottee can often be found roaming around bargain basement bins in Shepherd's Bush's fabric and haberdashery stores. 'They're cheaper than Soho's and you're more likely to find something a bit, weird.' He also suggests the 'bits and bobs' lady at Goldhawk Road Market. Everything's rounded down to the nearest pound.

739

Attend a foyer performance at RADA

The Royal Academy of Dramatic Art (7908 4800, www.rada.ac.uk) often holds performances in the bar/foyer (entrance on Malet Street), where you can see the stars of the future for a fraction of the price of a West End theatre ticket, and sometimes for free. Events include 'rehearsed readings', poetry slams, musical performances ranging from classical to folk, and comedy. Previous play readings, that have included *World Music* by Steve Waters, *The Schuman Plan* by Tim Luscombe and *Eyes Catch Fire* by Jason Hall, have gone on to be performed at the Hampstead Theatre, Donmar Warehouse and the Finborough Theatre.

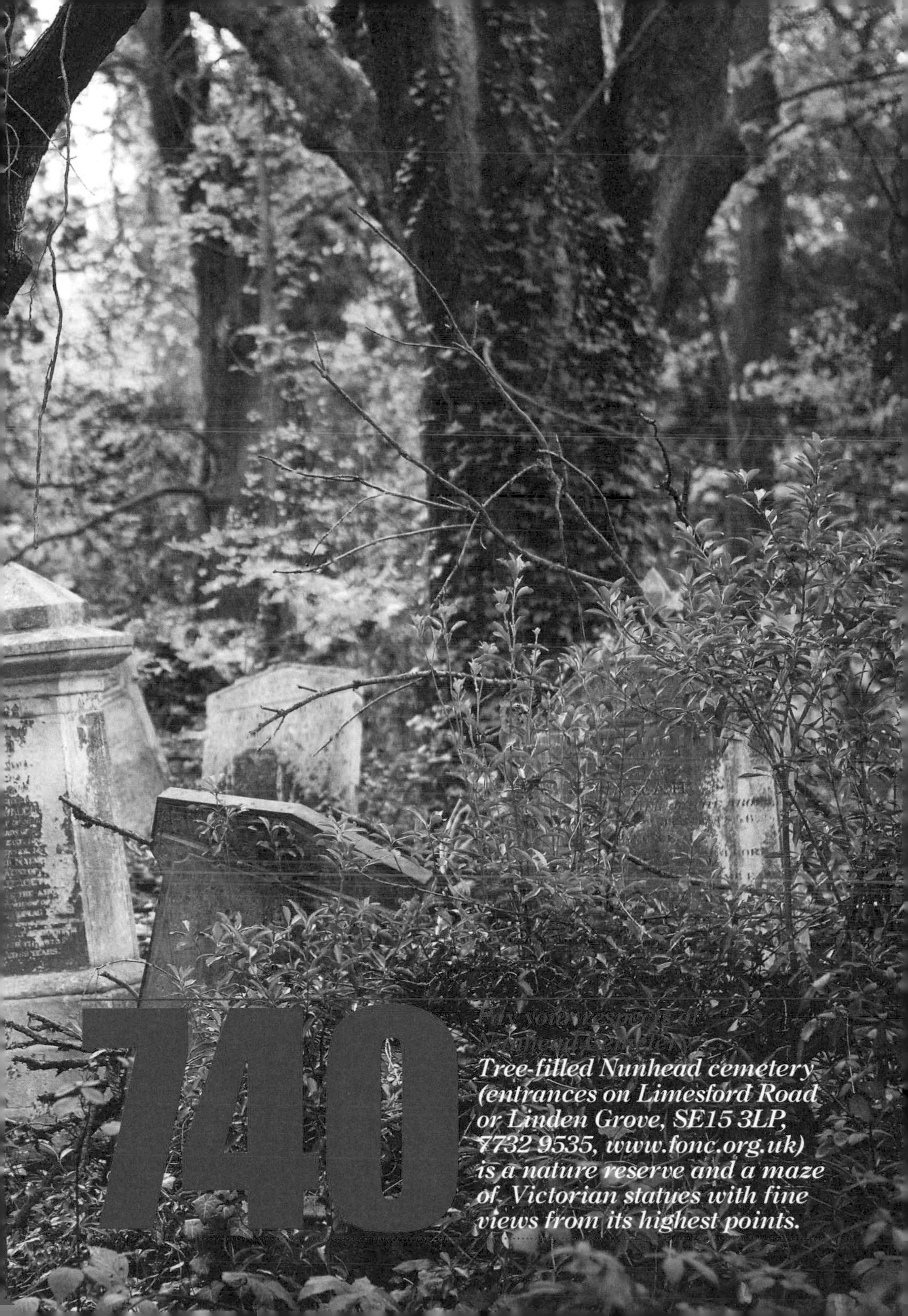

740

Pay your respects at Nunhead Cemetery

Tree-filled Nunhead cemetery (entrances on Limesford Road or Linden Grove, SE15 3LP, 7732 9535, www.fonc.org.uk) is a nature reserve and a maze of Victorian statues with fine views from its highest points.

741-747 ...then pay some more at London's other great graveyards

Abney Park

If ivy-clad sculpture is your thing, head to this cemetery in Stoke Newington. A series of atmospheric, rambling walks takes you past the last resting place of William Booth, founder of the Salvation Army, whose massive headstone assures us that he has not died but been 'promoted to glory'. Further on, you'll see monuments to slavery abolitionists and missionaries as well as music hall stars.
Stoke Newington High Street, N16 0LN (7275 7557, www.abney-park.org.uk).

Bunhill Fields Burial Ground

Tucked away off City Road (near Old Street tube) is another atmospheric oasis of eternal peace. Used as a nonconformist – and therefore unconsecrated – cemetery from the late 17th century to the middle of the 19th, it features the graves of such notables as poet and mystic William Blake, John 'Pilgrim's Progress' Bunyan, some assorted lesser Cromwells, Thomas Hardy, Daniel Defoe and Susannah Wesley – mother of John Wesley, the founder of Methodism.
City Gardens Office, 65 London Wall, EC2M 5TU (7374 4127, www.cityoflondon.gov.uk). Guided walks June, July 12.30pm Wed. £4.

Brompton Cemetery

Full of magnificent Victorian monuments, Brompton Cemetery has seen many of the great and the good laid to rest within its boundaries, not least among them suffragette Emmeline Pankhurst. And it's said that many of the names you'll see here inspired Beatrix Potter, who lived nearby – look out for Jeremiah Fisher, Peter Rabbett, Mr McGregor and Mr Nutkins.
Fulham Road, SW10 9UG (7352 1201, www.royalparks.org.uk).

Highgate Cemetery

The fame of many of Highgate Cemetery's 'residents' makes this a popular visitor attraction and explains the entry fees (East cemetery £3; West cemetery, by guided tour only, £7). But with its angels, shrouded urns, broken columns and dramatic tombs, this is a delightfully atmospheric place to wander. The checklist of celebrated graves includes Christina Rossetti, Michael Faraday, Karl Marx and George Eliot. Both sites are closed during funerals, so call ahead to check before you visit.
Swain's Lane, N6 6JP (8340 1834, www.highgate-cemetery.org).

Kensal Green Cemetery

Kensal Green Cemetery hides its fair share of notable figures behind its neoclassical gateway. It's particularly strong on 19th-century intellectuals – towering examples of which include Isambard Kingdom Brunel, William Thackeray, Anthony Trollope and Wilkie Collins – but don't forget to visit the grave of Charles 'the Great' Blondin whose high jinks on a tightrope above Niagara Falls way back in 1859 put David Blaine to shame.
Harrow Road, W10 4RA (8969 0152, www.kensalgreen.co.uk).

Tower Hamlets Cemetery

Though the gravestones here may be a little light on famous names, Tower Hamlets Cemetery has a serene charm all of its own – an expanse of calm just off the busy Bow Road. You'll find 33 acres of beautiful woodland and meadow here, making it a much-needed green heart in the middle of the East End.
Southern Grove, E3 4PX (07904 186 981 office hours only, www.towerhamletscemetery.org).

West Norwood Cemetery

West Norwood cemetery in Lambeth, with its impressive Gothic revival architecture, holds memorials to Mrs Beeton, Sir Henry Doulton, Dr William Marsden, Baron Julius de Reuter, Charles Spurgeon and Sir Henry Tate.
Norwood Road SE27 9JU (8670 5456, www.fownc.org).

748 *Visit Trinity Buoy Wharf*

Once a ship and buoy maintenance depot, Trinity Buoy Wharf has had many different incarnations over the years and now it's a thriving centre for the arts and creative industries. With spectacular views over the Thames and with Canary Wharf twinkling in the background, the site is home to exhibitions and performance venues, and houses what is probably London's smallest museum – a former docker's hut dedicated to 19th-century scientist Michael Faraday. Artists' studios are in old shipping containers that have been revamped and painted bright colours, forming an area known as container city.

The Wharf is also home to London's only lighthouse (there are great views from the top) and the Longplayer Tibetan bell sound installation: Jem Finer's 1,000-year-long musical composition has been playing since 31 December 1999 and should continue, without repetition, until the year 3000. It's open to the public at weekends.

Trinity Buoy Wharf *64 Orchard Place, E14 0JW (7515 7153, www.trinitybuoywharf.com). Free.*

749

Create a Spark

Tired of listening to celebrity self-publicity? Well, Spark is your chance to star – along with other 'ordinary people' – in your own tragi-comic story. Creator Joanna Yates explains that Spark is the place to hear and tell true stories. On the first Monday of every month at the Canal Café Theatre in Maida Vale, performers – including teachers, car dealers, mothers and barristers – stand up in front of an audience and spill their beans. Each show is loosely structured around a theme (such as 'mistaken identity' or 'under the influence') and individual stories are (perhaps advisedly) limited to seven minutes. After the show, audience and performers float downstairs to the bar for a drink and a chat. Tickets are £8 (plus a once-yearly £1.50 membership fee to the Canal Café Theatre).
Canal Café Theatre *Delamere Terrace, W2 6ND (7289 6056, www.canalcafetheatre.com).*

750

Visit the 18th century at Dennis Severs' House

Journey through time at one of London's most magical houses in the heart of the old Huguenot district in Spitalfields. The 'still-life drama' that takes place here is the creation of American Dennis Severs, who lovingly restored the decaying 18th-century building, with each room reflecting a different era of the house's past. The rooms are inhabited by the invisible (and invented) members of the Jervis family, silk-weavers and residents of the house between 1725 and 1919, who leave half-eaten pieces of bread and murmur just out of sight as you drift from room to room on your dream-like tour. Silence and concentration are encouraged on a trip that's not really aimed at children.
Dennis Severs' House *18 Folgate Street, E1 6BX (7247 4013, www.dennissevershouse.co.uk). £7-£10.*

751 *Watch short films*

Short film screenings are thriving in London. The capital offers a variety of venues and festivals where audiences can enjoy anything from quirky music videos and short stories to animations and documentaries – and not necessarily in a traditional cinema setting.

The good folk behind Future Shorts (www.futureshorts.com) have taken it upon themselves to create a culture around the medium of short films. They're not afraid to take film out of the cinema and have previously let their reels loose in galleries, bars and clubs (such as Fabric, where they showed *Metropolis*, with a band re-scoring the film), and a cave in Cornwall while on tour with the Guillemots. 'We want to change the way people watch short films and to create an immersive experience,' says founder and director of Future Shorts Fabien Riggall.

Films are grouped by theme, so around Valentine's Day, for example, you'll see 90 minutes' worth of shorts from all over the world, each showing different interpretations of love. The team is also behind Secret Cinema (www.secretcinema.org, although this costs more than £10), a monthly event that invites people to a secret and often bizarre venue to watch a film (are you up for spending an evening in a five-star hotel car park?).

Short and Sweet (www.shortandsweet.tv) hosts weekly short film evenings. It's run by Julia Stephenson, a passionate enthusiast who single-handedly brings together filmmakers and film lovers. As she puts it, 'the idea is to inspire all who attend, expose the best talent and ultimately celebrate film.' Interaction is also encouraged and it can be a great place to meet and network with people who are fanatical about film. Sign up to the mailing list for more information.

And finally, there's the London Short Film Festival (www.shortfilms.org.uk), set up in 2004, which runs over ten days each January in some of the city's best cinemas, and brings together excellent contemporary talent.

752 *Moonwalk*

A charity marathon walk held each year in aid of breast cancer research, Moonwalk is for the hard core. Yes, a 26.2 mile walk through London is doable – but try doing it sleep deprived in the dead of night, wearing a lavishly embellished bra. The shenanigans start at midnight and places get sold out fast, so book early. Register on www.walkthewalk.org.

753 *Have a Friday Night Skate*

It's been seven years since this weekend warm-up skate around town began, and it's still one of London's best free nights out. Open to rollerskaters (in-line and quad varieties both welcome) of all ages and levels, the evening kicks off every Friday at 8pm. Hundreds of individuals (many of them clad in Lycra) bunch together, racing, socialising and rolling along to tunes pumped out by a boombox taped to an accompanying bike. The route (which changes every week) is between ten and 15 miles long with things getting more intense in the second half as the pace picks up for the serious skaters. Afterwards everyone usually piles into the nearest pub for a well-deserved pint. The skate starts at the Wellington Arch, Hyde Park Corner; see www.thefns.com for details.

754-776 *Treat the children*

Family fortunes

Riding the DLR, splashing in fountains, picnicking with llamas – there's a wealth of budget family fun to be had in the capital, says Ronnie Haydon.

London has an embarrassment of riches for the thrifty family. You only need the price of a travelcard, a packed lunch and a following wind to spend the whole day freely entertaining your children. Museums, galleries, parks, gardens, farms, dancing fountains and prancing minstrels await their pleasure.

Your travelcard is your ticket to all the free fun that London can offer. Just experiencing big red buses (old-fashioned Routemasters still operate on routes 9 and 15), trains and trams is a treat for the very young, especially those deprived darlings who don't ordinarily travel on public transport. The range of vehicles you can hop on and off using your travelcard is wider than in any other city. Choose your carriage: bus, tube, Docklands Light Railway (DLR), overground train, tram and riverboat (where you'll get a discount).

A pleasant overview of that excellent source of free entertainment, the South Bank, is afforded by the commuter/tourist bus number RV1. The clue's in the name. It takes you along past some great riverside sights – the London Eye, National Theatre, Royal Festival Hall, Tate Modern – on its route from Covent Garden to Tower Gateway. You could use it on a fun-filled self-guided tour starting at Covent Garden piazza, where crowds gather for the street entertainers on a daily basis, then on to Watch This Space, outside the National Theatre (7452 3400, www.national theatre.org.uk), which has a free summertime arts programme (July to mid September) showcasing the best street theatre, circus, music, art and dance from all over the world. After which you can stroll all the way along the South Bank to see what else is going on. If it's hot, the dancing fountains outside the Royal Festival Hall are a source of pure pleasure for children. Take a change of clothes and tempt them out of the water for a South Bank picnic in Bernie Spain Gardens nearby. Take a moment to look in on the Clore Ballroom in the Royal Festival Hall (0844 875 0073, www. southbankcentre.org.uk, free) while you're

Discover the Story Centre

Angel Theatre

promenading: this is often the site for free school holiday events, such as treasure trails, storytelling and quite bizarre performances.

The RV1's terminus at Tower Gateway will lead you to your next fun transport option – the DLR. Happy is the child who baggsies a front seat on these driverless trains. They love to pretend to be the driver and enjoy the swoops down the humpy track that takes you on to Docklands. Stop off at Canary Wharf for an ogle at the shiny tower blocks at One Canada Square and the various neat little gardens, pontoons and public art, then hop on to the DLR again and continue your journey.

If you take the southerly branch toward Lewisham, you can get down on the farm in the heart of the city at Mudchute City Farm (7515 5901, www.mudchute.org, free), one of the most rewarding of London's bumper crop of agricultural idylls. This is the only place in the city where you can picnic with llamas. Other animals grazing and rootling with the City's skyscrapers as their backdrop include ponies, poultry, sheep, goats, pigs and cattle. The

Mudchute Kitchen is plump with homemade cakes and delicious savouries, if your budget will allow. For a list of some of London's other city farms, *see p106*.

The next DLR stop from here is Island Gardens, by the river. If you fancy a trip south, take the Greenwich Foot Tunnel (a spooky experience if ever there was one) under the river and emerge at Greenwich, to see how the *Cutty Sark* restoration is coming along, and visit one of the best free museums in the city, the National Maritime Museum (8858 4422, www.nmm.ac.uk), which has art activities and storytelling for children. If the weather's good, don't miss the chance to enjoy the airy heights of Greenwich Park and the Royal Observatory courtyard (8858 4422, www.rog.nmm.ac.uk, free), where costumed storytellers often hold forth during the school holidays. The Meridian Line here is the classic photo opportunity.

If you choose to travel north on the DLR from Docklands, you can stop off at Stratford to look in on preparations for London's Olympic jamboree in 2012. Better fun, perhaps, is

Discover the Story Centre (8536 5555, www. discover.org.uk, £4.50), which, although it has an admission charge for the indoor story-building centre, has a lovely – little garden with a space ship, slides and willow tunnel that kid adore. It's a splendid place for a picnic too.

Back in town, the DLR links up with the Jubilee Line of the tube system, the most modern and attractive line. It'll take you to London Bridge, where several overground trains an hour can whisk you to Forest Hill and the most original and one of the best free museums in town – the Horniman (8699 1872, www.horniman.ac.uk) – where there's always something going on in the school holidays: summer sees wildlife art activites in the extensive, beautifully managed grounds and woods, and open-air shows in the bandstand. If the weather's iffy, take time to enjoy the music rooms and yet more arts-based fun inside this quirky museum. The Aquarium (£2.50) here is fantastic fun, with mesmeric jellyfish, graceful seahorses and loads of variations on the Nemo theme.

If the children are keen to sample every form of public transport in the city, be prepared to fit in a tram ride – down in deep south London. Take a train from Forest Hill to East Croydon (provided you have a Zone 1-6 travelcard), from where you can pick up a tram to Wimbledon, an oft-neglected London outpost but an essential stop-off point for families because of the excellent children's theatre, the Polka (8543 4888, www.polkatheatre.com). You don't have to buy tickets for a show to enjoy spending time in the indoor and outdoor play areas, the super little café and at the teddy bear collection.

From the Polka, Morden South tube station will whisk you a lot more quickly into town again. Get out at London Bridge and walk westward from Bankside to Tate Modern (7887 8888, www.tate.org.uk, free).

Smart arty programmes for children can be found here and at older sister Tate Britain (7887 8888); check online for details of children's multimedia guides, activity packs and under-fives play zone. Once you've done the Modern you can float off to the Britain – on Damien Hirst's dotty Tate to Tate boat (with your travelcards it costs just £3.70 for adults and £1.80 for children). Tate Britain provides kids with the Art Trolley at the weekends, which is laden with a wide variety of make-and-do-ideas.

If you want to take in a show in the evening, a just-a-tenner artistic treat not to be missed (if your party consists of just one adult and one child) is Friday Fives at the Little Angel Theatre in Islington (7226 1787, www.little angeltheatre.com), where all tickets for the 5pm Friday performances cost just a fiver. This diminutive but legendary arts venue, (the only permanent puppet theatre in London), is an atmospheric place to take in a show, particularly around Christmas time.

Bear in mind that packing a picnic is essential if you're going to spend the day in London with the children without spending more than a tenner. With so many museums and galleries to explore the kids are going to fade fast without one. And we haven't even mentioned the big three: Science (7942 4000, www.sciencemuseum.org.uk, free), Natural History (7942 5000, www.nhm.ac.uk, free) and Victoria & Albert (7942 2000, www.vam. ac.uk, free) museums, all of which have a busy school-holiday programme of events for younger visitors. Also, in good weather there's nothing better than relaxing in the park with your lunch. Hyde Park and Kensington Gardens (0300 061 2000, www.royalparks.gov.uk) is your best bet, mainly for the excellent Diana, Princess of Wales Memorial Playground and for paddling in the Memorial Fountain, by the Serpentine. Most big museums have a picnic room too, so food brought from home can still be eaten in comfort even if the weather's foul.

Still, if you've forgotten to bring food or fancied treating everybody, and there's just one adult and one or two children to feed, you can just about do lunch for under a tenner. The Deep Blue Café in the Science Museum offers a good children's set meal; some places in Chinatown offer budget lunch deals, as do, of course, the Pizza Huts and McDonald's of this world. Belgo Centraal and Belgo Noord, in Covent Garden and Camden respectively (www.belgo-restaurants.co.uk), go one better, however, and offer their mini menu for children (chicken, sausages, mussels or cod with frites, followed by ice-cream) free of charge if the accompanying adult orders a main course. However, in order to keep within the budget it means everyone has to settle for tap water. Sometimes it's hard to be a parent.

777-783 Take advantage of the capital's free music festivals

Who said festivals had to happen in leafy green fields in the middle of nowheresville? London's streets might not be paved with gold, but in the summer they are a hive of free musical and cultural activity.

The Big Dance

This week-long dance party encourages all ages to get fit in toe-tapping fashion. You can get your jig on at hundreds of events. In the past these have included tango demos on the tube, performances in Oxford Street shop windows and alfresco shows in Regent's Park.
Various venues (www.bigdance2012.com). Jul.

London Jazz Festival

The London Jazz Festival continues to stretch its elastic definition of jazz, so an excitingly eclectic and top-notch line-up is guaranteed. Not only that, but LJF has now expanded out of its original central London bases like the South Bank and Ronnie Scott's to embrace far-flung venues across the capital, from Finchley's Artsdepot to Blackheath Halls. Many tickets are under a tenner and there's an amazing range of free events – a great opportunity to discover different jazz genres.
Various venues (www.londonjazzfestival.org.uk). Nov.

London Mela

Dubbed the Asian Glastonbury, tens of thousands flock to Ealing for this exuberant celebration of Asian culture – contemporary and traditional. Garage beats play happily alongside traditional Qawwali and you'll also get an opportunity to check out innovative commissioned projects (such as a collaboration with Circus Space that brought Indian dancers together with aerial performers). As well as the music and dance, there are also bustling bazaars and tasty food stalls.
Gunnersbury Park, W3 (www.londonmela.org). Mid Aug.

More Music

What could be better than music in the open air on a summer's day? Stroll down to City Hall in July and you'll find a diverse range of alfresco concerts livening up the outdoor Scoop amphitheatre. From big band swing to R&B, Latin beats and classic rock, you'll catch a few famous faces here alongside established performers and stars of the future, playing for free on the banks of the river.
City Hall, SE1 (www.yourlondon.gov.uk). Aug.

London Mela

Barclays bike

Music Village

Dedicated to showcasing the best in global beats, Music Village is an annual event that offers the chance to absorb musical traditions from all over the world. There's a carnival atmosphere, live shows and dance and spoken word events. Check the website for locations.
Various venues (www.culturalco-operation.org). Mid June.

Shoreditch Festival

London's hippest neighbourhood is transformed into one massive venue for this annual shindig. Aimed as much at families as trendies, it's packed with musical happenings and events. Past highlights have included Proms in Shoreditch Park, performances by English National Ballet, tea dances, fireworks and the famed Shoreditch Bark Dog Show.
Shoreditch Park, N1 (7033 8520, www.shoreditch festival.org.uk). Mid July.

Watch This Space

The National Theatre takes the action outdoors in summer with this packed programme of cultural riverside events on the South Bank. The entertainment is a playful mix of gigs, club nights, dance, cabaret and street theatre.
Theatre Square, South Bank, SE1 (www.national theatre.org.uk/wts). End June to end Sept.

784 Ride the new Routemaster...

The new Thomas Heatherwick-designed bus runs on the no.38 route from Victoria to Hackney. But you may have be patient: there are only eight prototypes planned to be in service in 2012.

785 ...or a Barclays bike

Casual users can hire a bike by going to a docking station, touching the 'hire a cycle' icon and inserting a credit or debit card. The machine will print out a five-digit code that you tap into the docking point of a bike, which releases the machine. £1 buys 24-hour access, and the first 30 minutes are free. See www.tfl.gov.uk for more details.

786 Serve yourself a pint

At the Thirsty Bear (62 Stamford Street, SE1 9LX, 7928 5354, www.thethirstybear.com) drinkers can pour their own pints from iPad-controlled pumps at each table.

787

Celebrate the great British butty

The bacon butty is more than just a sandwich. It is a British institution. The St John Bread & Wine's version has become the stuff of sandwich lovers' legend – thick Gloucester Old Spot bacon sandwiched between chargrilled slices of home-baked white loaf, served with a months-in-the-making in-house ketchup. So if you can't afford St John at lunch or dinner (and let's face it, a meal here doesn't come in at under a tenner), you can have the experience at breakfast, over a pot of tea and a meticulously created example of one of Britain's crowning culinary glories.

St John Bread & Wine *94-96 Commercial Street, E1 6LZ (3301 8069, www.stjohnbread andwine.com).*

788

Keep the party going

With the East London party scene having now firmly made its way up the Kingsland Road into the Turkish heartland of Dalston, it was inevitable that at some point the two cultures would come together. There are a number of small Turkish pool and snooker halls dotted along Stoke Newington Road, but Efes Snooker Club is the largest and most well known. Its late opening hours mean that on Thursday to Saturday nights it's jam-packed full of party goers looking for somewhere to carry on after the surrounding pubs have shut. Don't expect more than a few pool and snooker tables, some arcade machines and a lot of voguing. Pool costs £1 a game and snooker is £5 per hour with a £5 deposit.

Efes Snooker Club *17B Stoke Newington Road, N16 8BH (7249 6040).*

789

Visit an artist's studio

Whether you want to buy work, commission a piece or just gawp at the art (and the art crowd), open days – where artists, sculptors and artisans throw open the doors of their workspaces for a weekend – are great fun. Most studios open twice a year to the general public, often in December and also May. Arts Unwrapped (7274 7774, www.artsunwrapped. com) is Europe's biggest open studio event, involving 2,000 artists over three weekends in May and June. Shuttle buses ferry people from one studio to the next.

790

Take a closer look at the Albert Memorial

The overblown Gothic wonder that is the Albert Memorial, opposite the Royal Albert Hall in Kensington Gardens, was opened to public view 11 years after the premature death, from typhoid, of Queen Victoria's beloved Prince Consort in 1861. At 176 feet tall, it's a shrine to the certainties of the Victorian age – and definitely worthy of closer inspection.

Surrounded by a microcosmic Empire and all its achievements – four continents, frozen life-size models representing the industries and the respected professions of the day – a 14-foot figure of Albert sits amid a fantastic sparkling shed of jewels, polished stones and glass, surmounted by four brightly coloured mosaics of the arts, an angel-strewn spire and a golden cross. It's as kitsch as anything you're ever likely to lay eyes on.

Stand and stare, and you'll soon find hidden wonders: a marble camel and bison, models of Native Americans, voluptuous Miss Asia and her elephant, as well as a 'hive' of industry. If you want to know more, tours are held every first Sunday of the month from March to December; they cost £6, and pre-booking is not required.

791 *Sample Sampled*

Are you a fan of dance but not of dance ticket prices? Or perhaps you're not inclined to blow money on an art form you know nothing about? Fear not, for internationally renowned dance venue Sadler's Wells is now planning to hold 'Sampled' weekends once a year, following the success of the first event held in 2007. The idea is to give people an opportunity to check out a variety of different dance styles – in manageable bite-size chunks, and all in the space of one evening. Pretty much everything is covered, from hip hop to flamenco, tango to classical ballet. Tickets cost £6 standing (£12 seated).

Sadler's Wells *Rosebery Avenue, EC1R 4TN (0844 412 4300, www.sadlerswells.com).*

792-795

Drink champagne

Bars selling champagne aren't rare, but a classy joint offering fizz for under a tenner is a less common occurrence. Here are a few of our favourites.

Sit amid the wood-panelled surrounds of the bar at the City branch of steak specialist Hawksmoor (10 Basinghall Street, EC2V 5BQ, 7397 8120, www.thehawksmoor.com) and sip champagne for £8.50 a glass. At the elegant Kettners (29 Romily Street, W1D 5HP, 7734 6112, www.kettners.com), class comes in a flute-shaped glass (from £9.50) and is accompanied by a pianist every evening. Small but perfectly-formed 69 Colebrooke Row (69 Colebrooke Row, N1 8AA, 07540 528593, www.69colebrooke row.com) also has fizz at £9.50 a glass, together with jazz musicians on Sundays. And while the surroundings may not be as glam, it's hurrah for the Amuse Bouche (51 Parsons Green Lane, SW6 4JA, 7371 8517, www. abcb.co.uk), the Fulham champagne bar where the house fizzy starts at £6 a glass, and there are more than ten champagnes offered by the glass.

796 *Do the Docks*

It's a shame so few tourists make their way any further east than the pub-, restaurant- and shopping-happy St Katharine's Dock, close by Tower Bridge. A mere ten-minute walk away on Wapping Wharf there are whole streets of waterfront wharves prospering as flats, but still full of atmosphere with their stock-brick pavement arcades, deep-water inlets, old gantries, river stairs and lookouts.

For example, from next to the Town of Ramsgate pub (62 Wapping High Street, E1W 2PN, 7481 8000), take the historic Wapping Old Stairs down to the Thames foreshore – make sure the tide's out, and don't wander too far – to explore the site of the old Execution Dock, marked with an 'E' on the pierhead façade. This is where the East End river pirates – known variously as Heavy Horsemen, Mudlarks and Scuffle Hunters – were chained and washed by tides in punishment for robbing an impressive 50 per cent of the Docks' spices, tea, butter, tobacco, tropical woods and coal. That was until the West India Dock Company began defending their new, stoutly fortified premises with cannon.

797 *Watch a Bollywood film at the Boleyn Cinema*

A beacon of charm amid fast-food shops on Barking Road in Newham, this ornate picturehouse screens a strict diet of Indian Bollywood blockbusters (£5, £4 Tuesdays). **Boleyn Cinema** *7-11 Barking Road, E6 1PN (8471 4884, www.boleyncinema.com).*

798-803 *Visit the city's best beer shops*

Twickenham's Real Ale Shop (371 Richmond Road, TW1 2EF, 8892 3710, www.realale.com) sells around 100 beers, ales, ciders and perrys, including bottle-conditioned varieties that are as close as the home-drinker can get to cask ale flavour without installing handpumps in their kitchen. Even better, you get 500ml sizes of most bottles for around £3. Beer Boutique in Putney (134 Upper Richmond Road, SW15 2SP, 8780 3168, www.thebeerboutique.co.uk) has a carefully selected range of Trappist, Belgian, fruit and pilsner beers; London ales are well represented too. Drink of Fulham (349 Fulham Palace Road, SW6 6TB, 7610 6795, www.drinkoffulham.com) has an exceptional range of brews (more than 500) from around the world. At Kris Wines (394 York Way, N7 9LW, 7607 4871, www.kriswines.com), ales are arranged by country of origin and range from Odell's 90 Shilling Ale (from the States) to bottles from Manchester's Marble Brewery. Handily placed for all those BYO Vietnamese restaurants is the City Beverage Company (303 Old Street, EC1V 9IA, 7729 2111, www.citybeverage.co.uk), a Hoxton off-licence that keeps all its beer in the fridge, including ales from the Kernal and Redchurch breweries From Thursday to Saturday, the Utobeer (Unit 24, Middle Road, SE1 1TL, 7378 6617) stall in Borough Market sells hundreds of different beers from all over the world.

Drink of Fulham

A few of my favourite things

804-808

Emmy the Great, musician

You can go to London Zoo for free if you just walk around it on the outside. I take all my friends when they come over from America. The bigger animals live on the outskirts, and if you go in the afternoon they all come out of their stables. You can see the llamas and the giraffes, and of course all the birds that have long necks, like emus. I've got a route: start at the Parkway end of Regent's Park in Camden Town and begin with the birds and work clockwise. Go after lunch – the best time is around 2pm, around feeding time and before nap time.
The Roundhouse (Chalk Farm Road, NW1 8EH, 0844 482 8008, www.roundhouse.org.uk) has a great youth programme for under-25s. If you sign up you can use one of its rehearsal rooms for £1 an hour. Most people use it to practise DJing or for band rehearsals, but I go in there and pretend I have an office. I write all my songs there. The Roundhouse café has free Wi-Fi too.
Next door to the Roundhouse there's a nice branch of Japanese restaurant Feng Sushi (Adelaide Road, NW3 3QE, 7483 2929, www.fengsushi.co.uk). Sushi is not cheap usually but they do something called 'the power lunch' for £8.75. It's a lot of food, everything you could possibly need to get you through the day – raw fish, soya beans, seaweed, brown rice, avocado and pomegranate. You're like: 'every bite of this lunch is adding a year to my life.'
The V&A Museum of Childhood (Cambridge Heath Road, E2 9PA, 8983 5200, www.vam.ac.uk/moc) is kind of weird. There are all these really creepy Victorian toys, and then lots of screaming children. It would be even better if only the adults were allowed in.
In the mornings I help my friend walk his dog, a mongrel called Maggie, on Hampstead Heath. It's really fun because you meet all the dog owners – and all the retired people on benches who are out waiting for the dog owners to go past. Walking is way, way more fun with a dog. You don't even have to think of proper things to say to each other, you can just go, 'Oh look, she's done a poo.' 'She did a poo yesterday too.' 'No way!'

809

Yodel!

Since 1967, Joseph, with the help of his lederhosened lads and dirndled lasses, has been providing an impressively high-camp version of Austrian hospitality in this cellar venue. The likes of David Walliams, Elle McPherson and Kate Moss have descended the stairs to this basement restaurant – along with countless stag nights and work parties: and we're pretty sure they didn't come for the bratwurst. It's the floorshow of yodelling, cowbells and accordian-accompanied singalongs that keeps the place packed out. A meal would cost around £25-£30 per head (reservations are recommended), but you can squeeze in at the tiny bar and wet your whistle on a few Dortmunder Unions for a tenner. You might even be persuaded to belt out to a few tunes from *The Sound of Music*.
Tiroler Hut *27 Westbourne Grove, W2 4UA (7727 3981, www.tirolerhut.co.uk).*

810 *Learn to box*

Attention, Rocky Balboa wannabes. Boxing London serves up sweaty, seedy glamour, from the rickety weight machines to the well-thumped bags. And the training is Rocky intense: the coach is Enzo Giordano, a one-time super-middleweight contender. The vibe is friendly and good-humoured, though, and the punters are of both sexes and all ages – from child prodigies to comeback kings, out-of-shape actors to East End wide boys. Classes cost £8 each **Boxing London** *20 Hazelville Road, N19 3LP (07956 293768, www.boxinglondon.co.uk).*

812 *Walk the Jubilee Walkway...*

Pity taxi drivers. London is a colossal patchwork rug of a city, and even long-term residents find it tricky to gain an understanding of how its various districts stitch together. The Tube map might be a design classic, but those linear patterns and handy spacings bear little relation to things at ground level – the average street layout in an A to Z is cartographic spaghetti.

The Jubilee Walkway, then, offers a dual function: meaningful exploration for newcomers to the city and a refresher course for those who call it home. Just as important, though, is the fact that it's a great walk. Initially created to celebrate the Queen's Silver Jubilee in 1977, the route has since been honed and enlarged to provide a pavement-pounding 15-mile loop through some of the centre's more absorbing pockets. You'll get your fair share of postcard sights – Big Ben, the Tower et al – but you'll also get a genuinely enlightening look at London in its various guises: old and new, hushed and chaotic, grand and grotty.

The 'official' starting point is Leicester Square, although in our view it makes more sense to begin with the stretch between Lambeth and Tower bridges – it's the only section south of the river and a view-packed hors d'oeuvre for what's to follow. From there it's over the water into St Katharine Docks, across into the Square Mile and on to the Barbican before winding back down to St Paul's. Then, head along Fleet Street, up into Holborn and hard north to St Pancras, at which point the route plunges back through Bloomsbury and Covent Garden, touching St James's and heading on into Westminster and Lambeth. Easy.

There are metal 'Jubilee Walkway' sign-plates embedded in the pavement at regular intervals, although if you'd rather not stare down at your feet all day you'd do well to pick up a dedicated map beforehand (see www.walklondon.org.uk). The loop can be done in a full day but it's a fair trek, so many choose to split it over two or three days. It can be whatever you make of it – a history tour, a photographic walk or even the mother of all pub crawls. And the beauty lies not in the classic set pieces but in the finer details: the architectural quirks, the sense of ages gone by, the stately calm of backstreet Bloomsbury, the suit-and-tie mêlée of St Paul's, the sheep of Coram's Fields and the pelicans of St James's Park.

Potential pit-stops are countless, and a big part of the fun – the route passes some of the best cafés, museums, shops, pubs and galleries that London has to offer – but we'd cherry-pick the following: the madcap interior design at Sir John Soane's Museum (13 Lincoln's Inn Fields, 7405 2107, www.soane.org); an arthouse flick at the Renoir Cinema (the Brunswick, 0330 500 1331, www.curzoncinemas.com); a pint in Victorian opulence at the Princess Louise (208-209 High Holborn, 7405 8816); then head over to Monmouth Street, where you'll find boutiques aplenty along with Covent Garden caffeine stalwart Monmouth Coffee House (27 Monmouth Street, 7379 3516, www. monmouthcoffee.co.uk). Finally, walk to Cecil Court (www.cecilcourt.co.uk) and have a browse through its antiquarian bookshops.

813

...and the Jubilee Greenway

This walking and cycling route marks the Queen's Diamond Jubilee. It's exactly 60 kilometres (37 miles) long – one kilometre for each year of Her Majesty's reign – and is waymarked with distinctive glass pavement slabs. The start (at Buckingham Palace) links in with the Jubilee Walkway, and section one runs through the heart of London up to Little Venice, but some of the later sections are arguably more interesting, as they offer a route into less visited parts of town. One section of the route goes past the Olympic Park (and is planned to go through it once the park is open to the public), another past the Thames Barrier. At the time of writing there were a frustrating number of diversions in place in some of the sections (notably section six, River Thames to Greenwich), so have a good look at the website (www.walklondon.org.uk) before setting off.

814

Browse the Petrie Museum with a torch

While the British Museum's Egyptology collection is strong on the big stuff, we love the Petrie for its focus on the minutiae of ancient life. Set up in 1892 by eccentric traveller and diarist Amelia Edwards, it's named after Flinders Petrie, one of the indefatigable excavators of ancient Egyptian treasure. Borrow a torch from staff and explore the gloomy Second Gallery (dimly lit for conservation purposes). Shine your light into old-fashioned glass cases housing all manner of everyday items, including the world's oldest tunic (a 5,000-year-old linen dress), tools, cosmetics (kohl pots, combs) and – hurrah! just what you need to complete the Indiana Jones fantasy – human remains in a pot (a 4,000-year-old female skeleton).

Petrie Museum of Egyptian Archaeology *University College London, Malet Place, EC1E 6BT (7679 2884, www.petrie.ucl.ac.uk). Free.*

815

Tower over the city atop Westminster Cathedral

Often overlooked in favour of the more famous Westminster Abbey, Westminster Cathedral is spectacular in its own bizarre way. Looking like a wedding cake with a stick of rock stuck on the side, this neo-Byzantine confection – finished in 1903 – has incredible views from the four-sided viewing gallery in its 273-foot bell tower. The bell's inscription reads, 'While the sound of this bell travels through the clouds, may the bands of angels pray for those assembled in thy church.' Don't worry about aural assaults though, the public aren't allowed in while the bell is being rung. Access (by lift) costs £5, £2.50 reductions.

Westminster Cathedral *Victoria Street, SW1P 1QW (7798 9055, www.westminstercathedral.org.uk).*

816

Watch Scene and Heard

Scene and Heard is an unusual and inspiring theatre trip. Based on New York's similar 52nd Street Project, it's a scheme that was set up ten years ago to encourage and challenge – emotionally and creatively – disadvantaged children from the Somers Town area south of Camden Town. The kids, all aged between nine and 15, write a short play and are then united with a dramaturg, a director and two actors – all of whom are professionals. The result is an often hilarious, heart-warming and hugely impressive piece of theatre, proving that children have a lot to teach us about imagination and clarity of vision. Performances are held at Theatro Technis, and are endorsed and attended by many well-known faces; donations are appreciated.

Theatro Technis *26 Crowndale Road, NW1 1TT (0845 009 0775, www.sceneandheard.org).*

817
Check out the Thames Barrier from all angles

The Thames Barrier has saved the city from watery catastrophe some 70 times since its construction in the early '80s. It's also a fantastic sculptural presence on the river that's worth travelling to see. Ideally a visit should be timed to see it in action – you can find out when that is from the Information Centre.

One approach is via Charlton station (from Charing Cross or Cannon Street) followed by a ten-minute hike up Anchor & Hope Lane, then right along Nagasaki Walk and Hiroshima Promenade. Alternatively, take the DLR to Pontoon Dock, which is set in the freshly landscaped Thames Barrier Park on the north side. Designed by Allain Provost, of the Parisian landscape architecture practice Groupe Signes, the park opened in 2000 and offers superb views of the Barrier. You can also check out the east side of the barrier from the Woolwich Free Ferry (8921 5965) – just hop back on the DLR for a couple of stops to King George V, from where it's a short walk south to get to the ferry.

Alternatively, and for perhaps the most amazing views, visit Greenwich Yacht Club (084 4736 5846, www.greenwichyacht club.co.uk) after 8pm on a Tuesday. Their clubhouse is on the river a few hundred yards upstream from the barrier. Of course, come the flood, they'll be okay on their boats.

Thames Barrier Information & Learning Centre *1 Unity Way, SE18 5NJ (8305 4188, www.environment-agency.gov.uk/thamesbarrier).*

818-827 *Listen to free lunchtime recitals*

Robin Saikia spends his lunch hours in some of the capital's most lovely churches, listening to sublime music – for next to nothing.

Listening to live classical music in London can often be an expensive pastime, but there are several churches around town where astonishingly good recitals can be heard and you'll come away with change from a fiver. At most of the venues mentioned here, recitals and concerts are free but if this is the case, a donation will be appreciated.

The Church of St James's, Piccadilly (197 Piccadilly, W1J 9LL, 7734 4511, www.st-james-piccadilly.org) offers a holy grail of free recital programming with its free 50-minute concerts every Monday, Wednesday and Friday at 1.10pm. The suggested £3.50 donation is well worth paying for concerts that routinely include – and this is taken from the running order for one month alone – works from the likes of Bach, Chopin, Rachmaninoff, Beethoven, Glinka, Janaceck, Faure and Ravel.

St Martin-in-the-Fields (Trafalgar Square, WC2N 4JJ, 7766 1100, www.stmartin-in-the-fields.org) hosts a popular programme of music (from Franck and Parry, Mozart and Gershwin for example) at its free lunchtime recitals at 1pm every Monday, Tuesday and Friday. For a concert in such a magnificent church, the suggested donation of £3.50 is a snip – and the money goes towards the church's continuing renewal programme.

There are free lunchtime recitals too in St Paul's, Covent Garden (Bedford Street, Covent Garden, WC2E 9ED, 7836 5221, www.actorschurch.org) known to Londoners as the Actors' Church on account of the many thespians interred or commemorated here. The recitals are usually held on Thursdays and Fridays but check the website before you turn up.

The tiny St Olave's Church in the City (Hart Street, EC3R 7NB, 7488 4318, www.sanctuaryinthecity.net), is the burial place of Samuel Pepys and his wife Elizabeth and is also one of very few medieval churches still standing in London (it dates from around 1450). Lunchtime recitals are held here at 1.05pm on Wednesdays and Thursdays.

At St Lawrence Jewry (Guildhall Yard, EC2V 5AA, 7600 9478, www.stlawrencejewry.org.uk) there are piano recitals on Mondays and organ concerts on Tuesdays – both at 1pm. The church is the official church of the Lord Mayor of London and of the City of London Corporation. Not far away, lovely Wren church St Martin-within-Ludgate (40 Ludgate Hill, EC4M 7DE, 7DE, 7248 6054, www.stmartin-within-ludgate.org.uk) has classical recitals most Wednesdays at 1.15pm.

At St Giles-in-the-Fields Church (60 St Giles High Street, WC2H 8LG, 7240 2532, www.stgilesonline.org) the organ dates from 1678 (there's an appeal fund currently working to raise money for its restoration) and there are free concerts every Friday afternoon from 1.10pm to 1.50pm. The church also has strong American connections and is the burial place of the second Lord Baltimore, proprietor of Maryland.

St Anne's Lutheran Church (Gresham Street, EC2V 7BX, 7606 4986, www.stanneslutheranchurch.org) is another City church that holds free lunchtime recitals – every Monday and Friday at 1.10pm. Watch out for Bach, Telemann and Buxtehude in particular.

In addition to a busy calendar of lectures, seminars and exhibitions, Southwark Cathedral (London Bridge, SE1 9DA, 7367 6700, www.southwark.anglican.org) has an impressive musical programme. As well as the free organ recitals on Mondays there are also other classical recitals on alternate Tuesdays. Again, check the website for details.

Finally, don't forget that there are free organ recitals at Westminster Abbey (7222 5152, www.westminster-abbey.org) every Sunday evening from 5.45pm to 6.15pm. If you are lucky you may hear the Abbey organist, James O'Donnell, one of the finest musicians in Britain.

Cheap chills

In freezing December weather, Annie Dare plunges headlong into London's outdoor swimming pools.

Iceland's financial collapse, in the summer of 2008, was a surreal demonstration of the start of the global recession. In its wake, shocked Icelanders, noted the BBC, distracted themselves by attempting a little submersion of their own: in November Reykjavik harbour (at 3.5° centigrade) was bobbing with unprecedented numbers of swimmers, up by more than 300 per cent since the start of the banking crisis that had caused monthly job losses of 5,000. Observers saw a direct correlation between the crash and the soaring attendance levels, as people took drastic measures to forget their economic woes. As Britain's economy starts to tank, would more Londoners take the plunge too?

It is a cold white morning. People are stomping their feet at Gospel Oak's bus stops, exhaling breath plumes. Up on Hampstead Heath, a series of terriers wear tartan gilets and some hockey lads lazily jog round goalposts in an attempt to keep warm. On the brick ledge encircling Parliament Hill Lido (Parliament Hill

Fields, Gordon House Road, NW5 2LT, 7485 5757, www.cityoflondon.gov.uk), a troop of pigeons have puffed out their feathers so hard that you can't even see their necks. Their bird eyes follow the figures of bobble-hatted humans bounding beneath them. At the water's edge, a small group dressed in fleeces traces the slow arc of a martial arts sequence. Behind, as a pep-talk draws to an end, a crowd in swimming caps and Speedos suddenly breaks apart, towels are flung off shoulders and feet move fast, like children's, towards the pool's edge. With 'Two widths minimum!' as our only requirement, on the count of three, we're told, we are to jump into the December water. This is the Outdoor Swimming Society's December Dip at Parliament Hill Lido and the goose-bumped bodies have been gathered here by its high priestess, Kate Rew, as part of a crusade to reconnect Britons – and today Londoners in particular – with nature by way of water.

Standing on the brink, strangers giddily swap stories and the line of people sways

with excitement; thighs jog in trepidation, toes are dipped into the freezing meniscus, ice drops are dribbled on to the backs of necks. Then, on three, 100 or so ragtag swimmers jump into four degrees of pool, more or less instantaneously.

I see the tall man next to me power away in a front crawl. Then I realise that I'd be close to having an out of body experience, were it not for the acute lightening rod sensations running through the cavity of my belly and around my chest. I didn't realise shock had a physical expression, but it does, and it is this that is now stabbing up and down my legs and arms, scything at my pelvis and ribs. It is masochistically fun. Around me, people laugh and yell, frantically front- and back-crawling, and quite forget who, and where, they are – apart from the near-cardiac arrest sensations.

After 90 seconds, for me at least, it's over. A few stalwarts swim on, gently gliding to and fro. But most are quickly wrapped up in towels, whooping, comparing notes on pain and invigoration, eyes bright as they surge towards the queue for hot chocolate and mince pies.

The popularity of outdoor swimming in Britain predates the current testing economic times. The empassioned writing of the late environmentalist Roger Deakin was a key catalyst. His 1999 book *Waterlog: A Swimmer's Journey Through Britain* galvanised people to use swimming outdoors as an expression of anarchic delight in the natural world. Rew is one of a handful of new evangelists to follow in his slipstream.

While the OSS's new recruits shudder and chat at the pool's margins, a handful of men and women are nonchalently stripping off and plopping into the water to do unhurried laps. Members of Parliament Hill's local swimming fraternity, they greet each other with a familiar, if a little staccato, bonhomie, and there's some friendly bragging about the natural beauty of various British swimming sites, recent swims and friends' attendance levels. Among them is Frank Chalmers, a daily swimmer at the lido, but whose spiritual home is Ye Amphibious Ancient Bathing Association on Scotland's River Tay. Chalmers, who is writing a book about cross-Channel swimmers, has notched up a few remarkable dips since taking up outside swimming in the run-up to his 40th birthday: for example the four-hour swim he made across eight treacherous miles in high seas (temperature 12°) off the coast of Scotland, and the 'unnavigable' whirlpool he braved between two Hebridean islands (famously taken on by George Orwell's brother-in-law, drenched in sheep fat, in the 1940s). 'This is where it starts,' he nods knowingly towards the glacial lido. 'Next thing you know, you'll be down at Dover Sands and training for the Channel.'

' Under your toes fish are teeming, while grebes, herons and swans float above. '

The next day in Gospel Oak, it's another ghostly pre-dawn. Past brambles and under the canopies of ancient trees are two beautiful, and altogether more solitary, swimming wildernesses. Mallards skud low across the limpid swell of Highgate Men's Pond (7485

4491) – a spartan mirror of water to swim in – and crows, seagulls and magpies caw and hop unperturbed under the trees. At the end of a lane past a further tangle of bush and briar, bullrushes sway around Kenwood Ladies' Pond (7485 4491), a popular summer Shangri La for many Londoners; however, at this time of year you can count on swimming with maybe two or three ladies, and seldom more than ten.

Margaret Hepburn has been swimming on the Heath since 1946, and has just had her morning dip. Her father-in-law, a free-spirited Scot, once led midnight swimming expeditions to the Heath's ponds during the summer, but she herself joined the cold-water swimming minority when her husband's health began to falter 20 years ago. 'I began getting up early and swimming regularly, creeping away silently with the dog. The people at the pond were so supportive, and kept saying "see you tomorrow". That's when it became a habit. Having done one winter I just kept it up. You come out physically feeling better, it makes your joints looser, and you've let go of things mentally. I'm of sanguine temperament, but for some people it is something akin to therapy.'

Jane Shallice, chair of the Kenwood Ladies' Pond Association, has been swimming here since she came to London after university in 1964. She only started to swim during the winter when she retired in 2000 and explains that being ringside to a particular part of the heath is an inextricable part of the appeal of year-long outdoor swimming. 'By going throughout the seasons, you get to know a small area in a very intimate way: which trees lose which buds, when the catkins come. You become very, very conscious of the surroundings.' Here, then, wild swimming is about holding a deep reverence for nature. Under your toes fish are teeming, while grebes, herons and swans float above.

Today she lasted seven minutes in the 4° centigrade pond, and emerged feeling invigorated – and incredibly privileged.

It's a privilege Shallice doesn't take for granted. The issue of funding never goes away (the Corporation of London has maintained the facilities since the demise of the GLC) and the Association has to be vigilant against threats from developers.

Conversely, these straitened times could represent a real opportunity for the advocates of outdoor swimmers. The London County Council engineered the last great lido building programme between 1920s and 1939, during the Great Depression, to provide working-class leisure facilities. Many closed during and after the 1980s (58 to date) and London now has just 12 outdoor swimming venues left.

Janet Smith, who swims at London's oldest built pool the Tooting Bec Lido (Tooting Bec Road, SW16 1RU, 8871 7198, www.slsc.org.uk), is also the author of *Liquid Assets*, a paean to Britain's outdoor swimming pools and an elegy for those that have already closed. She argues that if the government is to meet its pledges for swimming pool provisions, resurrecting lidos would be a cost-effective way of doing so. 'They are cheaper to build: you build less. The great lido boom of the 1930s which followed the great crash, came under the government policy of work projects as a scheme to give the unemployed a job and to build facilities for the benefit of families afterwards. Possibly the coming crisis and high unemployment could provide an opportunity for similar buildings.' She points to the successes of campaigns to reinstate London Fields and Brockwell Park Lidos, both of which were the subject of vigorous campaigning on the part of their local communities and are now finding favour with a new generation of swimmers.

It's a sentiment echoed by the Rivers and Lakes Swimming Association (www.river-swimming.co.uk), which says cash-strapped local authorities should stop subsidising swims at pools and instead reverse restrictions that overzealous interpretations of health and safety directives have imposed on outdoor swimming in lakes. 'There'd be no heating bill to pay.'

Other outdoor swimming fans argue it's not just cost-effective: beyond the act of swimming itself, the hardship and adrenaline associated with cold-water swimming keeps morale up. As Smith sums up: 'There's a very high feelgood factor for swimming in the open air. It appeals to people's current desire for simplicity. It makes a great contrast to our stressful, complicated working lives to wind down with a swim outdoors. It gives a sense of freedom and liberation you simply don't get in an enclosed building. And the common devotion to a lido is quite a bond.'

Enthusiasts are also proudly egalitarian. Smith talks of the 'incredible spectrum' of people who swim together as part of the

South London Swimming Club in Tooting Bec. Meanwhile, on the south shore of Hyde Park's Serpentine lake (Serpentine Lido, Hyde Park, www.serpentineswimmingclub.com), Sir Anthony Cleaver, the chairman of the Nuclear Decommissioning Authority, is bounding towards the changing rooms just as a fellow member lowers himself off the jetty, fresh from his shift as a night porter. A 24-year-old visiting American student, who is training to swim the Channel, remarks that the comradeship is what binds her to the pond. 'I was also taken aback,' she says. 'You hear so much talk about the English class system. Here, you get a total cross section of society, and a really strong sense of community.' '£20 a year,' beams the secretary, her pen poised over a spiral-bound notebook as she tries to sign me up for membership and record the latest heats in the Club's handicapped winter series. A flock of swans flies low over the horizon. 'The cheapest annual sports membership fee of anywhere in London, and we'll throw in a cup of tea too.'

London's lidos

Brockwell Lido Brockwell Park, Dulwich Road, SE24 0PA (7274 3088, www.brockwell-lido.co.uk). £5.20.
Charlton Lido Shooters Hill Road, SE18 4LX (8856 7180, www.gll.org). Check website for prices.
Hampstead Heath Ponds Hampstead Heath, NW5 1QR (7485 4491, www.cityoflondon.gov.uk). £2.
Hampton Heated Open Air Pool High Street, Hampton, Middx TW12 2ST (8255 1116, www.hamptonpool.co.uk). £5.60.
London Fields Lido London Fields Westside, E8 3EU (7254 9038, www.hackney.gov.uk). £4.30.
Park Road Lido Park Road, N8 8JN (8341 3567, www.haringey.gov.uk). £5.50.
Parliament Hill Lido Hampstead Heath, Gordon House Road, NW5 1QR (7485 5757, www.cityoflondon.gov.uk). £5 (£2 winter/early morning).
Serpentine Lido Hyde Park, W2 2UH (7706 3422, www.royalparks.org.uk). £4.
Tooting Bec Lido Tooting Bec Road, SW16 1RU (8871 7198, www.wandsworth. gov.uk). £5.50.

837 *Play fives*

Similar to squash but played on smaller, oddly shaped courts and with the use of a gloved hand rather than a raquet, fives is a sport indelibly linked with the public schools that it originated in (Winchester, Eton and Rugby). However, that doesn't mean it's elitist. You can play the Eton version (sloping walls, split-level floor, no back wall and a buttress known as a 'pepperpot') on four purpose-built courts at Westway Sports Centre. Small group or private tuition is available, after which you can pay a £5 registration fee then book a court for £6-£8 per hour or test your skills in tournaments and leagues.

Westway Sports Centre *1 Crowthorne Road, W10 5XL (8969 0992, www.westwaysportscentre.org.uk/fives).*

838

Inspect (but don't lie on) Freud's couch

Sigmund's family home is preserved as it was when he died – and as his previous house was when he fled Vienna in 1938 (he had written down the position of everything in his study, so it could be recreated in London). The centrepiece of the museum is Freud's library and study; check out his collection of Greek, Roman and oriental antiquities, along with the Couch – such a surprisingly inviting and comfortable looking piece of furniture, piled with cushions and a lush Persian rug, it's a shame you're not allowed to lie on it.

Freud Museum *20 Maresfield Gardens, NW3 5SX (7435 2002, www.freud.org.uk).*

839 *Get up early to see the deer in Richmond Park*

The park opens at 7am (7.30am in winter). See www.royalparks.gov.uk for more on the deer.

840

Volunteer in a charity shop

Although you won't be paid (unless you become a manager – and even then we're hardly talking big bucks), time spent working in charity shops is nevertheless rewarding. Firstly, there's the warm glow you'll get from doing something worthwhile and helpful. And secondly, chances are you'll get first dibs on everything that gets donated, which can be anything from Moschino dresses to rare vinyl. For your nearest shop see www.charityshops.org.uk.

841

Watch Tower Bridge opening

Long before it was a tourist landmark, Tower Bridge was a dazzling feat of engineering. Unveiled in 1894, it still thrills when its bascules swing into action. Watching it work its magic, one can understand why London was once the most technologically advanced city in the world. The Tower Bridge Exhibition, meanwhile, spells out the history, but the highlight (in every sense of the word) is the walk along the top tier of the bridge – just revel in those river views. Check the website to see when the bridge opens (which it does around 1,000 times a year).

Tower Bridge *SE1 2UP (7940 3985, www.towerbridge.org.uk). £8.*

842

Join the Fight Club

For blood, sweat and tears, and plenty of raw, unadulterated testosterone, watch East End bruisers punch each other's lights out in the unreconstructed surroundings of York Hall in Bethnal Green (Old Ford Road, E2 9PJ, 8980 2243, www.gll.org). The professional fights command prices of up to £100 a ticket, but on amateur night (usually held once a month), tickets are only a tenner.

843 Celebrate London's canals

Decked out in bunting and flowers, more than 100 colourful narrowboats assemble in the pool of Little Venice to celebrate Canalway Cavalcade, a three-day boat bash, which takes place every May. There are food and craft stalls; kids' activities, bands, a real ale bar and boat trips. The beautiful illuminated boat procession on Sunday evening is a must-see.

Little Venice, between Blomfield Road, Warwick Avenue and Warwick Crescent, W9 2PB (www.waterways.org.uk). Admission free.

844 Hang out at the bar of the Theatre Royal Stratford East

Never mind the performances on stage, check out the free ones seven days a week in the bar. As well as a diverse roster of musical performances, the bar also hosts comedy nights (every Monday) and poetry nights (every second Sunday of the month). And of course (inexpensive) food and drinks are available, too.

Theatre Royal Stratford East *Gerry Raffles Square, E15 1BN (8534 0310, www.stratford east.com).*

Theatre Royal Stratford East

Bar Italia

Amid the West End's sea of crappuccino merchants there are some very special coffee shop gems. Here we pick out the best places to fuel up on quality caffeine.

Bar Italia

When in Soho ... do as the Romans (and other Italians) do and head to Bar Italia if you're in need of a short, sharp caffeine hit. The macchiato is all toffee richness, the dab of creamy foam smoothing the bitterness of the Italian-style blend produced by former neighbours Angelucci Coffee.

22 Frith Street, W1D 4RF (7437 4520, www.baritaliasoho.co.uk).

Espresso Room

A tiny coffee bar opposite Great Ormond Street Hospital that punches above its weight, with Square Mile beans and quality soup, sandwiches and cake. Pleasant, intelligent staff offer a glass of water with the brews and are happy to grind bags of beans for customers to take home.

31-35 Great Ormond Street, WC1N 3HZ (07760 714883, www.theespressoroom.com).

Fernandez & Wells

The baristas at Fernandez and Wells work their magic by way of textbook-perfect crema served at the just the right temperature and cappuccinos on which the foam stands proudly several millimetres above the cup rim – the mark of an expert indeed. With its hard metal stools and long slabs of wood on the walls serving as 'tables', this may not be a place to linger for hours but sit yourself at a window seat and, in true Italian coffee drinking tradition, people-watch in style.

73 Beak Street, W1F 9SR (7287 8124, www.fernandezandwells.com).

Lantana

This airy space is ideal for a quiet morning spent reading the paper. The Australian proprietress, Shelagh Ryan, has chosen what she calls the 'coffee super-couple' to create her brews: Monmouth beans and a La Marzocco espresso machine – as she points out, it's 'sexier than Brad and Angelina, better pedigree than Peaches and Pixie'.

13 Charlotte Place, W1T 1SN (7637 3347, www.lantanacafe.co.uk).

London Review Cake Shop

Books, newspapers and magazines are strewn about this sun-filled room. Monmouth beans are used and cakes are sourced from small, independent producers. The room, with its communal table, is perfect for literary chin-wagging and it's very handy for the British Museum too.

14-16 Bury Place, WC1A 2JL (7269 9030, www.lrbshop.co.uk/cakeshop).

Milk Bar

The Milk Bar gets everything right. The espresso (made from Square Mile Coffee Roaster beans) melds seamlessly into the thick, cashmere-soft layer of foamed milk creamed with microscopic bubbles. Everything – from the charming, mellow baristas to the ever-changing art on the walls – exudes a certain cool.

3 Bateman Street, W1D 4AG (7287 4796).

Nordic Bakery

The cappuccino served amid Scandinavian warehouse design is strong and sturdy, much like the Ikea-esque cup it comes in – and the cocoa dusted on top is smooth and bitter, not Nestlé-sweet. A word of caution: you won't find sugar on the table, nor will sachets be presented on your serving tray – welcome to coffee purism.

14 Golden Square, W1F 9JF (3230 1077, www.nordicbakery.com).

Sacred

Creative beatniks are the regulars at this 'Southern Hemisphere' café, staking out the sofas and downing ethical espressos (made from Fairtrade beans, blended in-house) under the mindful eye of a stone Buddha and other religious motifs. Rather fitting, considering their almost-evangelical attitude to promoting good coffee.

13 Ganton Street, W1F 9BL (7734 1415, www.sacredcafe.co.uk).

853

Remember the Winchester Geese at Crossbones Graveyard

At 7pm on the 23rd day of every month, a group, loosely collected under the banner 'Friends of Crossbones' and led by local Southwark playwright and historian John Constable, gathers outside the iron gates of an unprepossesing Transport for London storage lot on Redcross Way, SE1. They are here to honour the memory of the 'Winchester Geese' – prostitutes who were given a licence to work in the area by the Bishop of Winchester (this part of London being under his – let's call it liberal – jurisdiction). Eventually closed in 1853, once it was 'completely overcharged with dead', Crossbones Graveyard was an unconsecrated burial ground dating back to the medieval period and used for disposing of people not considered fit for Christan burial.

Each month candles are lit, flowers, ribbons, notes and other memorial tokens are tied to the gates, poems are recited – and gin is poured on the ground in tribute to the fallen ladies' favourite tipple. As well as this monthly get-together, each Hallowe'en sees performances from the *Southwark Mysteries*, an epic cycle of poems and mystery plays written by Constable and inspired, he says, by the spirit of a Winchester Goose who first visited him on 23 November 1996 on Redcross Way. Check the website for Hallowe'en performance venues. *www.crossbones.org.uk.*

of Virginia' in 1921. The great American philanthropist and pioneer of affordable housing, George Peabody, holds court at the Royal Exchange, EC3, in the heart of the City. His statue is by WW Story and was erected in 1869, the year of his death.

More famously, in Grosvenor Square, W1, the statue of Franklin D Roosevelt by Sir William Reid Dick was unveiled by his wife in 1948, three years after his death. It was paid for with 200,000 donations of five shillings each, apparently raised in a single day, from grateful Brits. Also in the square, Dwight D Eisenhower, Allied Commander during World War II and 34th President of the United States, was sculpted by Robert Dean in 1989. In 2011, a statue of US President Ronald Reagan was unveiled to mark the centenary of his birth

A fine bust of John F Kennedy overlooks Marylebone Road, NW1, near Regent's Park tube. It was made by Jacques Lipchitz, unveiled in 1965 by Bobby and Edward Kennedy, and paid for by £1 donations from 50,000 readers of the *Daily Telegraph*. And finally, nearby at 84 Hallam Street, off Great Portland Street, a blue plaque acknowledges that flat No.5 was the home (from 1938-46) of the legendary World War II CBS broadcaster Ed Murrow.

854-862
See Americans in London

Every patriotic American, and quite a few others besides, might want to track down some of the monuments to their illustrious countrymen scattered around London. And it won't cost them a dime. Abraham Lincoln has just risen to his feet in Parliament Square, SW1, to hold forth in fine democratic style.

You'll find an even older father of the nation, Captain John Smith, first governor of Virginia, next to the St Mary-le-Bow Church on Cheapside, EC2, in the City. He was created by Charles Rennick in 1960. George Washington's likeness stands proudly in front of the National Gallery; it was presented by the 'Commonwealth

863 *Deliver a speech at Speakers' Corner*

See www.speakerscorner.net for a list of illustrious past orators.

864
Dodge bullets in Pickering Place

Down the side of Berry Brothers wine merchants (3 St James's Street, SW1A 1EG) is a rare surviving timbered passageway, dating back to 1730. Ducking through, the warped and crooked wainscoting draws you into the quiet of gas-lit Pickering Place, site of the last duel ever to be fought in London. Fittingly, a plaque at the alley entrance proclaims the 19th-century site of the Texan Embassy.

865-867

Eat old-school sweets

The realisation not only of the owner's but also many other people's long-held dreams, Hope and Greenwood is a proper, old-fashioned sweet shop that opened its doors to a grateful local clientele in East Dulwich in 2004 and now has a branch in Covent Garden. Those yearning for cola cubes, sherbert pips and rosy apples won't be disappointed. Over in Soho, Mrs Kibble's Olde Sweet Shoppe is a handy source of clove rock, liquorice twists and swirly lollipops, and there's now a branch just off Oxford Street too. For a different confectionery vibe, try CyberCandy, which stocks a range of sweets from all over the world – perfect if you're a US national craving a Hershey Bar or you just need some Hello Kitty Candy in a hurry.

Cybercandy *3 Garrick Street, WC2E 9BF (0845 838 0958, www.cybercandy.co.uk).*
Hope and Greenwood *20 North Cross Road, SE22 9EU (8613 1777) and 1 Russell Street, WC2B 5JD (7240 3314); www.hopeand greenwood.co.uk.*
Mrs Kibble's Olde Sweet Shoppe *57A Brewer Street, W1F 9UL and 4 St Christopher's Place, W1U 1LZ (7734 6633, www.mrskibbles.co.uk).*

Hope and Greenwood

868-876
Drink in some history

What's the strangest, most historical watering-hole in all London? To locals and visitors of a certain disposition, it's a hotly debated question (in a casual, leaning-on-the-bar, giving it the large opinion after four pints kind of way). So, for argument's sake, here's our must-sample 'rub-a-dubs' to set you on the right road to an unforgettable knees-up – especially if you manage to crawl round them all in one go.

When it comes to layer upon layer of atmospheric history, the waterfront Town of Ramsgate (62 Wapping High Street, E1W 2PN, 7481 8000) takes some beating. This was once Captain Bligh and Fletcher Christian's local, pre-Mutiny. The cellars were at one time fitted with shackles for drunks in the process of being press-ganged. From the tiny Thameside patio, you look out directly on to Execution Dock and Wapping Old Stairs, where Captain Blood was nabbed making off with the Crown Jewels. In the panelled bar, 'Hanging' Judge Jeffreys was spotted dressed as a woman as he tried to escape England in 1685. The Bloody Assizes' hardliner's local was actually the 16th-century Prospect of Whitby (57 Wapping Wall, E1W 3SH, 7481 1095), five minutes downriver, where a dangling noose marks his memory. There's also a 400-year-old flagstone floor, London's last pewter bar and a smashing hoard of antique seafaring knick-knacks.

Directly over the river in Rotherhithe is the Mayflower (117 Rotherhithe Street, SE16 4NF, 7237 4088, www.themayflowerrotherhithe.com), whence local skipper Christopher Jones carried the Pilgrim Fathers to America in 1620. The rickety wooden terrace over the river is highly recommended.

Off Borough High Street, near London Bridge, lies the National Trust-owned George Inn (George Inn Yard, 77 Borough High Street, SE1 1NH, 7407 2056, www.nationaltrust.org.uk), London's sole remaining galleried coaching inn, handily positioned just down the road from what was then London's only bridge. Just a third of the rebuilt 1676 structure survives, but there's still a wonderfully creaky atmosphere

Mayflower

Prospect of Whitby

that evokes the pilgrims, travellers and theatre players who've crowded the cobbled courtyard over the centuries.

Moving across the river into the City, you can find the tiny Mitre Tavern (1 Ely Court, EC1N 6SJ, 7405 4751) down an alley between Hatton Garden and Ely Place. Built in 1547 as a London base for the servants of the Palace of the Bishops of Ely, until recently this pub was officially considered to be part of Cambridgeshire, and therefore became a regular loophole refuge for thieves escaping the frustrated City police. The recently deceased tree built into the wooden frontage is said to have been used as a maypole by Elizabeth I.

Meanwhile, although the Viaduct Tavern (126 Newgate St, EC1A 7AA, 7600 1863) gin palace stands right opposite the Old Bailey (once Newgate Prison), it features a landlady's token kiosk aimed at preventing staff thievery. Its cellars boast four vaulted, barred cells from the long-gone Giltspur Street Compter debtors' prison.

Over in the West End's theatreland, the Salisbury (90 St Martin's Lane, WC2N 4AP, 7836 5863) is even more magnificently showy.

All cut-glass chandeliers and eyecatching mirrors, with fabulous light fittings decorating the bar, it's a Victorian art nouveau gin palace that manages to mimic the experience of walking directly into your great gran's jewellery box.

Down on Millbank, the cells in the cellar of the riverfront Morpeth Arms (58 Millbank, SW1P 4RW, 7834 6442) remain an intriguing mystery. Now the neighbour of Tate Britain, this was once the site of the miserable Millbank Penitentiary megastructure, to which the pub cells are supposedly related. However, hard fact on the subject seems to be as scarce as the long-rumoured tunnels linking the pub, prison and foreshore.

Finally, a change of pace up at the Spaniards Inn (Hampstead Heath, NW3 7JJ, 8731 8406, www.thespaniardshampstead.co.uk), effectively a wood-beamed and -floored country pub in zone three, knee-deep in Dick Turpin 'lookout' legends and a full set of Romantic ex-locals in the form of the poets Shelley, Keats and Byron. It's great for Hampstead Heath and the garden is heaven on a sunny summer afternoon.

877

Tour Wilton's Music Hall
Wilton's Music Hall (Graces Alley, E1 8JB (7702 2789, www.wiltons.org.uk) is the world's oldest and last remaining grand music hall. It was built by John Wilton in 1858, and still has a programme of plays, concerts and performances. You can also tour the Grade II-listed building, in which a great many of the original Victorian features remain intact. Tours cost £6.

878

Chill in St Pancras Crypt Gallery

Under the watchful gaze of the caryatids of St Pancras Parish Church, young, emerging artists exhibit their work in what used to be the last resting place of the local Bloomsbury gentry back in the 1800s. Opened as an exhibition space in 2002, the Crypt Gallery's echoing corridors, low ceilings and uneven cobbled floor are constant reminders of the building's past, but despite being chilly and a little damp, it avoids being too creepy, thanks to some soft lighting and almost no trace of its former occupants. In fact, the musty alcoves now act as enclosures for individual artworks: paintings, installations and sculptures whose inspiration is often the setting itself. The gallery hosts a year-round programme of group shows that rotate frequently and are often curated by the artists themselves, so opening times may vary.

St Pancras Church *Euston Road, NW1 2BA (7388 1461, www.cryptgallery.org.uk). Free.*

879 *Walk a city ley line*

Regardless of your views on paranormal energy fields, walking a ley line through London's backstreets is a great way to explore the hidden city and a neat medieval antidote to the 21st-century world. Follow in the footsteps of Alfred Watkins – who first defined leys as prehistoric sighting lines conceived from high viewpoints and maintained by ground-level markers – by grabbing a map, drawing a straight line from St Martin-in-the-Fields in Trafalgar Square to Arnold Circus in Shoreditch, and walking the roughly two-and-a-half mile (as the crow flies) Strand Ley. The line spookily falls through three other City churches (St Mary le Strand, St Clement Danes and St Dunstan-in-the-West) before finishing up at the Victorian bandstand in Arnold Circus in the grand Victorian Boundary housing estate.

880 *Get the real deal at Ridley Road Market*

While so many markets go trendy and/or upscale, Ridley Road in Dalston has hung on to its roots. It is gloriously cheap: fresh fruit and vegetables sold in giant buckets go for a quid a throw and the fresh red snapper is the cheapest you'll find this side of Billingsgate. Whether it's watch straps, giant snails or saucepans you need, there's sure to be someone flogging them for next to nothing. Conclude your visit with a wander round Turkish superstore TFC – the onsite bakery is particularly tempting.

Ridley Road Market *Ridley Road, E8.*

881 *Watch classic films for free*

A hi-tech peep show for the capital's cineastes, the British Film Institute's Mediatheque offers the chance to explore the entire digitised National Film Archive for free. Users are given their own private booth in which to browse hundreds of British films from David Lean's *Brief Encounter* to Shane Meadow's *Dead Man's Shoes*. Check out the monthly updated Pandora's Box collection, an oddball mix of celluloid quirks. It includes a 1920s shock drama about STDs and what are thought to be the first words ever recorded on film: a bashful Alfred Hitchcock toying with Anny Ondra, the Czech-Polish star of his 1929 thriller *Blackmail*.

BFI Mediatheque *BFI Southbank, Belvedere Road, South Bank, SE1 8XT (7928 3232, www.bfi.org.uk).*

882 *Invest in a Wedge Card*

Save money and help keep your favourite independent shops independent with this loyalty card. It costs £10 per year (£5 of which goes to various different charities) and entitles you to a multitude of discounts from traders across London. Partcipating businesses include everything from trendy Soho hairdressers to hip Hoxton sex shops, along with larger institutions such as the Barbican and Cargo. See the www.wedgecard.co.uk for a full list.

883 *Get kitted out with some lovely lashes*

Glam up instantly for less than a tenner with a pair of MAC false eyelashes. Buy a pair at the MAC store on the King's Road and get them professionally applied too.

MAC *109 King's Road, SW3 3PA (7349 0022, www.maccosmetics.com). Lashes £7.50.*

884 *Knit for nowt*

A fun yet (potentially) frugal pastime, and one that's easy to turn into a social event, whether you want to learn to knit or simply enjoy knitting in a convivial environment. The new generation of modish yarn shops are friendly and inclusive in a way that seems to be typical of the craft. All the ones we list here offer advice, drop-in sessions and a sense of community (as well as classes, though these usually break the £10 barrier – an exception is the crochet taster sessions on Sundays at All the Fun of the Fair in Soho); they also tend to be run by self-confessed knitting fanatics. I Knit London in Waterloo describes itself as 'a shop and a sanctuary' and the same ethos is true of east London's Prick Your Finger, Crouch End's Nest, and Islington's Loop (which runs a drop-in SOS clinic once a month – check the website for date). There's even an informal Tuesday Knit Club at south London florist and café You Don't Bring Me Flowers. Have a look at www.castoff.info, www.knitchicks.co.uk or www.stitchldn.com for an idea of the number and variety of events out there.

All the Fun of the Fair *Unit 2.8 Kingly Court, off Carnaby Street, W1B 5PW (07905 075 017, www.allthefunofthefair.bigcartel.com).*
I Knit *106 Lower Marsh, SE1 7AB (7621 1338, www.iknit.org.uk).*
Loop *15 Camden Passage, N1 8EA (7288 1160, www.loopknitting.com).*
Nest *102 Weston Park, N8 9PP (8340 8852, www.handmadenest.co.uk).*
Prick Your Finger *260 Globe Road, E2 0JD (8981 2560, www.prickyourfinger.com).*
You Don't Bring Me Flowers *15 Staplehurst Road, SE13 5ND (8297 2333, www.youdont bringmeflowers.co.uk).*

Loop

Get out of town

Despite soaring rail fares, there are still places you can get to from London for less than a tenner that really do feel like they're a world away (rather than just at the end of the northern line). The train stations listed below all cost less than £10 to get to if you travel at off-peak times (after 10am Mon-Fri and all day at the weekend).

Coulsdon South station (£6.10) is less than 30 minutes from London Bridge or Victoria, but you'll soon be walking in unspoilt country, in particular the belt of ancient hedgerow (home to more than 20 different tree varieties) and Farthing Down, designated a Site of Special Scientific Interest.

From Marylebone station, the village of Great Missenden (sometime home of both Roald Dahl – his house is now a museum – and Robert Louis Stevenson) is around 40 minutes away (£8.50). Nestled in a valley in the Chilterns, it makes a great starting point for walks. Maps and routes are available from www.chilternsaonb.org.

The dormitory town of Oxted in Surrey is half an hour from both London Bridge and Victoria stations (£9.40) and a good jumping off point for walks on the North Downs. We recommend walk No.2 from the reliable Saturday Walkers Club – one of many free downloadable walks (www.walkingclub.org.uk).

Purfleet in Essex is within walking distance of the RSPB reserve Rainham Marshes, where you can spot all manner of wading species as well as the odd peregrine falcon. Purfleet is around 30 minutes from Fenchurch Street station (£7).

For something a little less rural, discover what a garden city is all about by making your way to Welwyn Garden City in Hertfordshire. The mile-long stripe of green at its centre, known as Parkway, has been described as one of the world's greatest urban vistas. A tad far-fetched? You decide – it's 25 minutes on the train from King's Cross station (£10).

Splash out at Hunga Munga

'Make stuff, make friends, make a mess!' is Hunga Munga's motto. This rag-tag art collective organises evenings of monthly mayhem and alternative creativity usually at the Bethnal Green Working Men's Club, which it transforms into an arty wonderland. It's a bit of a handmade cabaret night – with dancers, performers, a game show, paint-a-thon and raffle as well as quirky bands, DJs and some temptingly inexpensive drinks (not to mention free scones!). While you watch, use the arts table to create a your own masterpiece. Anything goes.

Organiser Lloyd Ellis says, 'There are art clubs that take themselves too seriously and there are others that encourage people to splatter paint around everywhere. We're somewhere in-between … not too messy, not too boring … just right.'
www.hungamunga.co.uk. From £6.

887

Chow down in Eat.St

King's Boulevard is a recently constructed walkway connecting King's Cross and Euston stations with the relocated Central St Martins College of Art to the north. At the north end, from Wednesdays to Fridays (10am-3pm), you'll find a huddle of food vans serving lunch. They all belong to the eat.st collective (www.eat.st), founded by Petra Barran and Giles Smith; part of the appeal is that the vendors rotate. You might find a line-up that includes Luardo's burritos, dispensing from the bright pink retro van; Anna Mae, who is all about chilli; and Tongue n Cheek selling Italian-style ox cheek with polenta (check the website for that day's featured vans). One of our favourites is Kimchi Cults, with their Korean-style filled baguettes. Most of the dishes here cost around a fiver, are filling, and – if the sun is out and the wind not whistling by too hard – the funky plastic seats on King's Boulevard are a nice spot for a quick lunch.

888 *Visit W...*

Across the road from North Lambeth tube
is a plaque marking the sometime home of
William Blake, the writer, artist and rebel
the Romantic age. Until recently, this was t
only evidence of Blake's presence in Lambe
despite him spending ten productive years
living and working in what in his time was
'new suburb'. Today, Blake is finally getting
some recognition in south London with the
help of the Southbank Mosaics and the Willi
Blake Heritage Project.

Blake always wanted his works enlarged
and put on the streets where the public could
see them and it seems that he's finally getting
his wish: on the brick walls of the railway
bridge running over Centaur Street and low

889 *Trace the New River*

The New River was constructed
17th century to bring fresh w
from Hertfordshire. Desig
Myddelton – commemo
on Islington Green –
it was the first fr
n the city, and
walked, cou
In Islin
over i
a l

ach 10cm
square costs just £3.)
www.projectblake.org and
www.southbankmosaics.com.

Spring like redeemed captives whe
their bonds & bars are burst

891

See deep space in Hampstead

The capital's would-be astronomers may think of Greenwich as the ultimate place to star gaze in London – or they may not bother at all, given the city's light pollution – but Hampstead's observatory, with its six-inch Cooke refracting telescope, opens up the night sky to both curious beginners and keen amateurs. Located at the highest point of London, on a clear night it allows fascinating views of not just the moon, but also planets, stars, double stars (like Alpha Centauri), as well as eclipses and comets when they occur. The observatory is open to the public on clear nights and visits are free. It's run by the Hampstead Scientific Society charity and a member is always on hand to help navigate visitors round the sky.

Hampstead Observatory *entrance on Lower Terrace, by Whitestone Pond, NW3 (www.hampsteadscience.ac.uk).*

892

Eat at one of Brick Lane's oldest curry houses

Successive waves of immigration have shaped Brick Lane, and any walk from north to south is pungent with the fragrance of different cuisines – most famously the curries. The restaurants can be hit and miss, but because pretty much all are BYO and most will offer you decent discounts to get you through the door, it's easy to keep the bill low. The Aladin has been around for a while, and even got a look-in from Prince Charles when he toured the East End.

Aladin *132 Brick Lane, E1 6RU (7247 8210, www.aladinbricklane.co.uk).*

...in the early ...ter into London ...ed by Hugh ...ated with a statue ...and some 20 miles long, ...sh water supply of its type ...most of its route can still be ...tesy of Thames Water. ...gton itself, where it has been covered ...most parts, the Council have constructed ...vely sliver of a park along a half-mile open stretch: New River Walk runs from Canonbury Road (near Essex Road station) upstream to St Paul's Road, where the river disappears beneath Wallace Road and Petherton Road. A small section of it can also be seen further north in Clissold Park, where it has been converted into a duck pond in front of the café.

Back nearer Highbury, as it winds its way behind ranks of gentrified mansions, the walk along the river park can easily include a diversion to Canonbury Square – once home to George Orwell (No.27B) and also Evelyn Waugh (No.17) – or even the Estorick Collection of Italian Art (No.39A). The maintenance of the waterway is undertaken by the New River Action Group who can be contacted via the Chair, Frances Mussett, at 27 Elm Park Road, N21 2HP.

890

Save on interior design fees at the Geffrye Museum

The Geffrye, housed in a set of converted almshouses, is a quite marvellous physical history of the English interior. It recreates living rooms through the ages – from refined Georgian drawing rooms to cool Stateside-style 'living spaces' beloved by local Shoreditch DIY-obsessives. If you can't afford an interior designer, this is the perfect place to steal ideas. There's also a series of lovely gardens designed on similar chronological lines. Special exhibitions are mounted throughout the year.

Geffrye Museum *Kingsland Road, E2 8EA (7739 9893, www.geffrye-museum.org.uk). Free.*

Geffrye Museum

Transports of delight

Peter Watts rides the buses – each and every one.

London is unimaginable without its buses. They flow through the city's veins like little red blood cells, travelling along more than 500 different daily routes, dispensing Londoners around every limb and organ of the city. A couple of years ago, in a moment of recklessness, I decided to travel every single one of them, in order, end-to-end, starting at No.1 Tottenham Court Road to Canada Water and finishing at No.499, the Gallows Corner loop service via Becontree Heath. After that there are the weekday-only Red Arrow services (507, 521, 549), the school bus services (600-699) and the mobility buses (900-999) that take OAPs to local shopping centres. When you take into account all the night buses and the letter-prefixed local routes, from A10 (Heathrow Airport-Uxbridge) to X68 (West Croydon-Russell Square express service), it looks like I'll be kept on the move by the bright red behemoths until the day I die from excessive exhaust fume inhalation.

As a Londoner, I've always been a fan of buses, but I became particularly attached to them during a period of fallow employment, when I was cash poor and time rich, and therefore happy to pay a quid to take an hour to travel from A to B rather than £1.50 for the faster, more direct Tube. Travelling above ground, seeing how London unfolds and how postcodes knit together, was a key part in my London education. Every Londoner carries about in their head a mental map of the city, with the unexplored bits, usually those between Tube stations, left blank. The bus fills in the gaps. Cheaply.

London's routes cover plenty of ground and offer different things for different users. So if you are serious about buskateering, you need to be prepared. Start with the London Transport Museum (Covent Garden Piazza, WC2E 7BB, 7379 6344, www.ltmuseum.co.uk) or Ian Allen's transport bookshop in Waterloo (45-46 Lower Marsh, SE1 7RG, 7401 2100) to get Quickmap's *London By Bus* map, which shows you every London bus route for a bargain £3.95. From the same venues, you should also get the *Greater London Bus Map* (£2), which isn't quite as pretty, but has a very handy list of destinations, from 1 to X68, for every route on the reverse (Quickmap doesn't list routes, it only shows them on the map, so it can be difficult picking out individual routes from the mass of figures that march cheerfully across the page). Finally, crucially, get yourself an Oystercard pay-as-you-go, capped at £4.20 a day). Now you're ready to ride.

EMERGENCY EXIT
TO OPEN

76
MUDCHUTE

London's busy morning buses are hellish for the unprepared, but one thing we'd heartily recommend is swinging by Waterloo – there are numerous usable routes – at around 8am to see the old-fashioned British queue in all its glory. Gaze down from the top deck as commuters, fresh off the train from the sticks, line up in sober crocodiles waiting for their bus to the City. You won't see neater queues outside of the Post Office and it's interesting to speculate on why they occur here of all places – the bus stations outside London Bridge and Victoria stations, by contrast, are screaming scrums of Metro-wielding ne'er-do-wells, and have none of the decorum and 1950s after-you-isms of the Waterloo brigade. Such good behaviour was clearly set in stone by commuters many years previously and has never been unbuilt by the generations that followed.

The top floor of the London bus is great for this sort of people-watching, and makes the double-decker London's answer to European café culture. Ride any of the dozen buses that shuffle along Oxford Street like scarlet pachyderms and, if you're lucky, you might see one of the great British scams in progress. It works like this: an Arthur Daley type sets up a trellis table on the pavement selling boxes of shady perfume. He starts up his patter and attracts a middle-aged woman, who, after some toing-and-froing, hands over a twenty to pay for a couple of bottles of the stuff. This initial purchase then convinces a further flurry of buyers to give up their hard-earned, and between them fill Arthur's suitcase with lovely lolly. Watch from a bus backed-up in Oxford Street traffic, though, and you'll have a bird's eye view of the fiddle in action as you catch the initial buyer – the woman that prompted the gold rush in the first place – returning to the vendor as soon as things have quietened down. She returns the perfume and cash to her partner, and then they'll both get ready to start the process again. If the traffic is really bad, you can watch the dodgy duo work the scent scam in tandem a couple of times before the police get wind of it.

The bus is also the perfect place to see the finer, forgotten points of London architecture, such as the impeccable first-floor detailing you find in the older parts of the City. Try the 21 or 43 north along Moorgate and you'll see a succession of delights: a carved lighthouse on the side of a Swiss bank; the bas-relief of two Tube trains entering a tunnel above a doorway; an old fire insurance plaque on the corner with London Wall; the fine stained glass window of the City campus of the London Metropolitan University; and, where the street feeds into Finsbury Square, the strident art deco Triton Court with its secular spire topped by the statue of a man, standing astride a globe, with one arm raised to shield his eyes from the sun as he stares into the distance. Most central London streets conceal similar treats.

'...the big question: what buses should you catch for pleasure?'

Top decks are also the best place to witness another London ritual: school going-home time. In a 2008 transport policy document, the Conservative Mayor Boris Johnson argued that 'Free travel for kids has brought a culture where adults are too often terrified of the swearing, staring in-your-face-ness of the younger generation.' But it's really not as bad as all that, and 'free' has nothing to do with it. For decades, schoolchildren have gone home by bus and in exactly the same manner – they swarm on, stampede upstairs, then spend the short duration of their journey shouting at each other about pop music and clothes, fighting and snogging, and occasionally waving wildly/gesticulatingly crudely to their peers who are doing exactly the same thing on the top decks of neighbouring buses. Sure, it might get a bit noisy, but it's only intimidating if you've never been a schoolchild on a London bus. So, ignore Boris's nannying and catch any London bus at around 3pm (the No.4 is particularly exciting) – you will, if nothing else, be able to impress your

friends with some sensational new slang. You might even be pleasantly surprised: I was recently on a 68 when a gang of hoodies slouched on and stomped towards the back of the bus. Commuters nervously eyed each other – was this the dreaded 'in-your-face-ness' Boris had warned them about? However, teenage gang war on the 8.47am to Euston seemed increasingly unlikely as the kids started an enthusiastic discussion about the best way to present a Thai green curry – they were catering students, threatening nothing but our tastebuds.

Most tourists won't go anywhere near buses that serve the inner-London schools though; they'll be too busy getting gushy over the Routemaster. Yes, these still survive, rattling along two 'heritage' routes, the 9 and 15. Both buses serve tourism hotspots – the 9 covers South Kensington and the West End, while the 15 goes from the Tower of London to Trafalgar Square. Tourists love them – and who can blame them? Boris Johnson has introduced a new generation 'Routemaster' to replace the articulated 'bendy buses' (at the time of writing, just the one, on the 38 route from Victoria station to Hackney). The bendy buses were a disappointment for many reasons, one of which was no top deck – meaning no chance to get above the London streets. Nobody would catch a bendy bus for pleasure.

Which leads us to the big question: what buses should you catch for pleasure? One of the best for seeing the sights is the 11, which goes from Fulham Broadway to Liverpool Street, taking in everything from the boutiques of Sloane Square to the national monuments of Westminster and the City. The 360 is a good way of getting from the museums of South Kensington down to the brilliant Imperial War Museum, albeit by entertainingly circuitous means. The 73 is a London icon, being one of the capital's most regular services. The 24 is the most scenic way of getting from central London to Hampstead Heath. The 3 will take you down south to London's magical Crystal Palace Park. And the 22 allows you to finish your journey in the charming surrounds of the Spencer Arms on Putney Common, where the tables are big enough for you to get out your maps and contemplate your next voyage on London's best and cheapest form of transport.

894

Cheer, boo and hiss at a Mystery Play

For the last decade, the pale cream walls of St Clement's in the heart of the City have served as a backdrop for medieval Mystery Plays given a new lease of life by voluntary drama group the Players of St Peter. Back in the 15th century, the plays, which could go on for as long as 20 hours, were performed in the streets of London by guildsmen and craftsmen on pageant wagons that were moved around the city, each company or guild performing a different play. Based on biblical texts, the plots range from the story of Creation to the Last Judgment. These days, having tweaked the language just a bit, the Players select scenes from the plays and edit them to form an Advent production. They tell the story of the birth of Christ right through to the Ascension.

Dressed in elaborate and lovingly crafted costumes that resemble those originally worn in the 15th century, the audience is transported back to medieval London. 'We don't use any materials that wouldn't have been used originally', says Edward Weedon, stage manager and bit-part actor in the production. 'Even our stage hands are in costume.' The scene from the Shepherds' play features an excellent and very life-like sheep, while the shepherds themselves sup on 'a sheep's head soused in ale' (actual sheep's head not included).

Members of the audience are encouraged to join in with the performance: make sure you hiss and boo at the bad guys (that's Satan and his helpers) and clap and cheer on the good (Christ and Mary). With 50 volunteers involved in each production every year, the Players welcome new members. The entrance fee to the productions costs £6 and all profits from the venture go the church fund.

The Players of St Peter *PO Box 3040, E1W 3TQ (www.theplayersofstpeter.org.uk). St Clement Eastcheap, Clements Lane, EC4N 7AE.*

895 *Browse under Waterloo Bridge*

Stroll along the South Bank and before long you'll find the second-hand book fair under Waterloo Bridge, a venerable London institution and a great place to browse for literary classics, out-of-print books and old magazines and prints (many of which you'll get for less than a tenner).

896 *Taste vintage wine at the Sampler*

Wannabe wine buffs need look no further than the Sampler in Islington, an independent wine shop that offers 80 of its more than 900 wines for you to try, whether it's an inexpensive Chardonnay from Australia or a fancy bottle of Château Latour from Bordeaux. The wines are rotated every two to three weeks so there's always something new to savour, starting at just 30p for a slug of fino sherry. Browse at your own pace or get some expert help from the staff.

The Sampler *266 Upper Street, N1 2UQ (7226 9500, www.thesampler.co.uk); 35 Thurloe Place, SW7 2HP (7225 5091).*

897 *Marvel at the boat that made it to South Georgia*

Tucked away in a corridor of grand Dulwich School in south London, the *James Caird* might look like any old boat, but this 26-foot whaler is the one in which Sir Ernest Shackleton and five companions sailed over 800 miles to South Georgia during the Antarctic winter of 1916 in a bid to rescue their men from Elephant Island. They took stores to last one month, reckoning that if it took longer they would be dead anyway. In fact they reached their destination after 16 days – a voyage 'of supreme strife among heaving waters', Shackleton recalled. Amazingly, all members of the expedition were saved. To view this piece of history at Shackleton's old school, get a visitor's pass from reception.

Dulwich College *Dulwich Common, SE21 7LD (8693 3601, www.dulwich.org.uk). Free.*

898 *Follow the Artangel*

Londoners generally consider themselves spoilt when it comes to art shows but they have Artangel to thank for some of the bolder exhibitions in the capital. Working with a range of different artists, the production company (not a gallery in itself) stages one-off projects in temporary spaces around the city, placing priority on powerful concepts. Anything goes – thousand-year musical compositions, detritus sculptures, or recreated battles between miners and police. One of the most popular was Roger Hiorns' extraordinary copper sulphate crystalline installation *Seizure* in a derelict building near Elephant and Castle. **Artangel** *(7713 1402, www.artangel.org.uk). Usually free.*

899
Brush up your Polari

Hosted by author and *Time Out*'s gay & lesbian editor, Paul Burston, 'London's peerless gay literary salon' recently celebrated four years of literary loucheness and the launch of the Polari First Book Prize. Attracting a truly mixed crowd of all ages, from 18 to 70, there are different guest authors each month (Neil Bartlett, Stella Duffy, Christopher Fowler, Ali Smith and Will Self have all graced the stage). Readings are followed by a book signing, courtesy of Foyles bookshop. As well as authors, there have been performances from singers such as David McAlmont and Marcus Reeves, and cabaret from the likes of David Hoyle and Michael Twaits. No wonder the *New York Times* called Polari 'London's most theatrical literary salon'. There's also a bar. Tickets tend to sell out fast, so book early to avoid disappointment.

Polari *Southbank Centre, SE1 8XX (0844 875 0073, www.southbankcentre.co.uk). Monthly (various days), 7.45-10pm. £5.*

900

Have a pie and a pint

In a world of smart gastropubs and espresso martinis, it is comforting to find a back-to-basics watering hole where life's essentials – 'Ale. Cider. Meat.' – are exalted and scrawled across the outside wall. This Kentish Town boozer offers beers and ciders from independent UK breweries (Crouch Vale, Dark Star, Slaters, Redemption, Sambrooks, Twickenham and many more); once the barrel's run out you'll just have to try a different one. Snacks are pig-based. There's pork pie or the more-ish hot pork and crackling bap – a steal at £3.80. And note – a tenner means a tenner. This pub is hard cash only.

Southampton Arms *139 Highgate Road, NW5 1LE (07958 780073, www.thesouthamptonarms.co.uk).*

901
Think positive in the West End

Rubbing shoulders with trendy hair salons and minimalist boutiques, Covent Garden-based meditation centre Inner Space offers the kind of spiritual free lunch we're told doesn't exist: you can take courses in Raja Yoga meditation or try workshops in effective stress resistance, heightened self-esteem techniques and progressive relaxation methods. Alternatively, drop in to its curious, mood-lit quiet room, listen to piped Zen music and sit among London's enlightened ones.

Inner Space *36 Shorts Gardens, WC2H 9AB (7836 6688, www.innerspace.org.uk). Free.*

902
Get the most out of your Mac

If you've splashed out on a Mac, it makes sense to take advantage of the free in-store aftercare and learn more about getting the most out of your investment. Check the website for details of the frequent workshop sessions.

Apple Store *235 Regent Street, W1B 2EL (7153 9000, www.apple.com/uk/retail/regentstreet).*

903
Visit the eighth wonder of the world

The grand entrance hall of the Thames Tunnel can be found at the Brunel Museum. Built by the father and son team of Marc and Isambard Brunel, it was hailed as the eighth wonder of the world when completed in 1843 and Isambard held probably the world's first underwater dinner party here – complete with 50 guests and tunes from the Coldstream Guards. Access varies as museum expansion works go ahead.

Brunel Museum *Railway Avenue, SE16 4LF (7231 3840, www.brunel-museum.org.uk). £3.*

904-908 *Celebrate New Year*

Baishakhi Mela

Pohela Boishakh (Bengali New Year) happens in Bangladesh on 14 April but its London incarnation isn't celebrated here until the second Sunday of May. The main thrust of this vibrant, cross-cultural event is a grand street procession and party in the heart of the East End's buzzing Banglatown. Food, rather than alcohol, is central to festivities and many of the curry houses bring their kitchens on to the (pedestrianised) streets to offer samples of their native cuisine. For the most authentic, head towards the smaller cafés such as Meraz (56 Hanbury Street, E1 5JL, 7247 6999, www.themeraz.co.uk). Finish with a trip to traditional Bangladeshi sweet shop Madhubon (42 Brick Lane, E1 6RF, 7655 4554, www.madhubonbricklane.co.uk) for some jalebis (deep-fried orange sugar spirals) or rasgullas (soft, spongy balls).

Chinese New Year

Based on the lunar and solar calendar, the date of this festival ranges from late January to mid February and usually coincides with the capital's annual China in London festival. Flagship events include a parade of contemporary arts and traditional lion dance across the West End and a spectacular fireworks display in Leicester Square.

Diwali

Fortunately, the Chinese haven't installed their own version of a western-style midnight countdown piss-up – rather, celebrations are spread out across the restaurants and bars of Soho and Chinatown, which are adorned with low-slung lanterns and duilián. For Chinatown on a budget try Baozi Inn (25 Newport Court, WC2H 7JS, 7287 6877) for satisfying noodles, dumplings and feather-light 'dragon' won tons.

Diwali

This five-day 'Festival of Lights' is celebrated in October and is one of the most important religious occasions for Hindus, Jains and Sikhs. Trafalgar Square usually plays host to a day of lively festivities and is typically closed with traditional prayers and a moving and tranquil lamp lighting finale (known as Aarrti). But by far the best celebration is at the celestial Neasden Shri Swaminarayan Hindu Temple (*see p210*) where thousands of Londoners queue to enter the grand prayer hall to see a kaleidoscopic display of over 1,000 artisanal vegetarian dishes known as an annakut. Alternatively, head to Ealing Road in Wembley, a unique hub of Indian shops and cafes. The best budget meal here is at Sakonis (129 Ealing Road, Wembley, Middx HA0 4BP, 8903 9601, www.sakonis.co.uk), always heaving with local Gujju families. Try the masala dosa or dahi wada – and don't expect to pay much for it.

Nowruz

Iranian New Year lands on 21-23 March on the Gregorian calendar and is best celebrated in London's little Middle East – Edgware Road. Home to a large number of the capital's Arabic and Iranian population, a variety of languages, including Farsi, can be heard outside the street's many kebab shops and shisha lounges. Persian New Year here can feel like a central Tehran bazaar. For some of the cheapest and most authentic cuisine head to Patogh (8 Crawford Place, W1H 5NE, 7262 4015). It doesn't stand on ceremony – the decor is basic, the menus laminated and main courses come served on simple metal plates. Try starters of freshly baked Persian bread with masto khiar (yogurt with cucumber and mint) or masto musir (yogurt with diced shallots) or houmous followed by lemon and saffron-marinated chicken or lamb kebabs. The fact that no alcohol is served is not only in keeping with the native

tradition but anoth[...]
though you can alwa[...]

Russian 'Old' New[...]

The Soviet Union adopted [...]
calendar in 1918 but Russian[...]
'Old New Year' (that is New Y[...]
to the Tsarist calendar), which fa[...]
January. Since 2005, an annual Ma[...]
London-sponsored Russian Winter F[...]
has taken place in Trafalgar Square an[...]
includes a free bill of dance and entertai[...]
It serves as a neat excuse, should any be
needed, to get into Russian pop music.
Traditional food on offer includes blinis,
borscht and piroshkis (small pies). After
that, head north to East European bolthole
Trojka (101 Regent's Park Road, NW1 8UR,
7483 3765, www.troykarestaurant.co.uk), where
violinists or accordion players are sometimes on
hand to further liven up the party atmosphere.

Chinese New Year

pianist Stan Tracey (he appears once a month) and sax maestro Peter King.
373 Lonsdale Road, SW13 9PY (8876 5241, www.thebullshead.com).

Charlie Wright's International Bar

A newly refurbished jazz bar in the heart of trendy Hoxton, Charlie Wright's has quickly established itself as one of the most exciting new jazz venues in the capital. London's equivalent of New York's legendary 55 Bar, this is very much a 'players' club, attracting a new generation of jazz virtuosos, as well as quite a few international heavyweights, both in the diverse modern jazz programme and also at its high-energy late night jam sessions.
45 Pitfield Street, N1 6DA (7490 8345, www.charliewrights.com).

Crypt in Camberwell

There's something both magical and mysterious about walking into this basement jazz club, situated under an imposing church a stone's throw from the centre of Camberwell. Attracting

£6. Featuring ...ions of cello/voice/ ...ms/bass each night, the ...ut friendly atmosphere is enhanced ͻy poetry readings from the likes of David Lee Morgan and Ronnie McGrath.
Temple Pier, Victoria Embankment, WC2R 2PN (8133 6045, www.boat-ting.co.uk).

Bull's Head

A venerable Thames-side pub that won a reputation for hosting modern jazz in the 1960s, but today specialises in mainstream british jazz and swing. Regular guests include ace veteran

a loyal, and knowledgeable jazz audience, this charming, quirky venue hosts many high-calibre (and often cutting-edge) jazz and world music acts. The no-nonsense food is a real plus, as is the well stocked (and cheap) bar.
St Giles Centre, 81 Camberwell Church Street, SE5 8RB (07791 873 183, www.jazzlive.co.uk).

Lord Rookwood, East Side Jazz Club
This lovely, atmospheric pub venue has consistently booked big jazz names from the UK scene. Yet the USP here is seeing the likes of Acoustic Ladyland's Pete Wareham playing 'straight ahead' jazz without any post-modern irony in a relaxed 'pick up' band setting.
314 Cann Hall Road, E11 3NW (8989 8219, www.eastsidejazzclub.blogspot.com).

Ronnie's Bar, Upstairs at Ronnie Scott's
Once destined to be an exclusive member's bar under the old management regime, this is now the hippest late-night hangout in central London thanks to the club's new, inclusive attitude. With its plush decor and funky vibe, general admission is a steal. Musicians can get in free on the now-packed jam nights, while themed vocal, Latin and funk jazz nights make

up a lively late night weekly programme (free-£10). Expect to queue if you arrive late.
47 Frith Street, W1D 4HT (7439 0747, www.ronniescotts.co.uk).

606 Club
Now over 35 years old, the 606 is still run by flautist/saxophonist Steve Rubie (who took over in 1976). As well as retaining its original street number it's also hung on to its intimate but swinging atmosphere. Programming mainly classic hard bop jazz artists such as sax greats Peter King, Bobby Wellins and Mornington Lockett, the club also features fine blues, soul and funk artists. Note that on Friday and Saturday nights, the entrance fee rises to more than £10.
90 Lots Road, SW10 0QD (7352 5953, www.606club.co.uk).

Spice Of Life
Another stalwart of London's Soho music scene, the Spice has been around for more than 60 years, taking in blues, funk and trad jazz (with a regular Friday afternoon big band session). It's also nurtured many of the new generation of jazz musicians, and every Wednesday and Thursday nights there are jazz sessions.
6 Moor Street W1D 5NA (7437 7013, www.spiceoflifesoho.com).

Upstairs at the Ritzy
The beautiful Ritzy cinema is further enhanced by a well-designed upstairs café area that offers an intimate space for a huge selection of jazz-orientated (and mainly free) music nights. The likes of Polar Bear drummer Seb Rochford and Portico Quartet have been regulars among the constant stream of emerging talent.
Brixton Oval, SW2 1JG (0871 902 5739, www.picturehouses.co.uk).

Vortex
Widely regarded as London's hippest jazz club, this cosy venue puts on the cream of today's contemporary jazz scene. While international luminaries such as Tim Berne, Vinicius Cantuaria and John Taylor have all played at Vortex, the imaginative and eclectic nightly programme ensures speculative visits are rewarded with a diverse selection of artists from the top drawer of the jazz spectrums.
11 Gillett Street, N16 8JN (7254 4097, www.vortexjazz.co.uk).

919-922
Get some wickets

London landmarks such as White Conduit Street in Islington, Lincoln's Inn Fields and, of course, Lord's, are key locations in cricket's venerable history. However, until recently the game was almost extinct in inner London (though a common sight out of the city). Things only began to change when the charities Cricket 4 Change (www.cricketfor change.org.uk) and Capital Kids Cricket (www.capitalkidscricket.co.uk) started campaigns to restore the game to urban areas. You'll now find thriving cricket leagues in Regent's Park and Victoria Park, with many inner-city schools involved. See the websites for details.

Club cricket remains, on the other hand, quintessentially suburban. The sport is organised on a county basis, and top clubs play in Premier Leagues where recreational and professional teams compete. The season runs from late April to mid September and games are free for spectators, plus there's usually a bar to help jolly the afternoon along. For all the details of both clubs and fixtures, consult the following websites: Essex League (www.essexcricket.com), Middlesex League (www.middlesexccl.com), Kent League (www.kcl.uk.net) and Surrey Championship (www.surreychampionship.com).

If you're after something more bucolic, simply head off into the countryside around the capital. You won't have to go far before you find a village green with two sets of stumps pitched – and possibly even a welcoming pub on the corner.

The following are all good grounds within London at which to catch matches:
Wanstead Cricket Club *(Essex) Overton Drive, E11 2LV (8989 5566, www.wanstead.hitscricket.com).*
Blackheath Cricket Club *(Kent) Rectory Field, Charlton Road, SE3 8SR (8858 1578, www.blackheathcc.com).*
Finchley Cricket Club *(Middlesex) East End Road, N3 2TA (8346 1822, www.finchley.play-cricket.com).*
Dulwich Cricket Club *(Surrey) Burbage Road, SE24 9HP (7274 1242, www.dulwichcc.com).*

923-924
See (bits of) Buckingham Palace

The State Rooms and garden of Buckingham Palace cost more than £10 to see *and* they're only open in August and September. However, throughout the year two lesser known, and in some ways more rewarding, bits of the Queen's official London residence can be visited – each for less than a tenner.

The Royal Mews are the Queen's stables (and garage), complete with Georgian riding school and magnificent horses, as well as a pungent saddlery, impressively sumptuous state carriages and the odd customised Rolls Royce (aka Her Majesty's motor). The Queen's Gallery, erected in the 1950s on the ruins of the palace's bomb-damaged private chapel, and recently renovated at great expense, shows changing selections from the Royal Collection of fine art, sculpture, furniture and porcelain.

Royal Mews & Queen's Gallery
Buckingham Palace, SW1A 1AA (7766 7301, www.royalcollection.org.uk). £8.25 and £7.50 respectively.

925

Rethink science at the Dana Centre

Think science and scientists are dull, irrelevant and best confined to labs? Think again. An evening spent at the Science Museum's Dana Centre, an adult-only venue exploring issues in contemporary science through dialogue, performance and art, should be enough to convince you otherwise. Every night the creative minds behind this innovative venture roll out something different: from haute couture catwalk shows, video gaming cabaret nights and stand-up comedy to no-kids-allowed fun and games in the Museum's Launchpad gallery. Come with an open mind, prepare to participate and enjoy a drink or two at the café-bar.

Dana Centre *165 Queen's Gate, SW7 5HD (7942 4040, www.danacentre.org.uk). Free.*

926-930

Indulge in tea and cake

Tea at the Ritz and other 'ritzy' London hotels will set you back anything up to £40 – here we pick some of our favourite tearooms where you'll come away with change from a tenner.

Bea's of Bloomsbury

Dusky blue walls and plush velvet chairs add a glamorous contrast to the bakery that sits at the back of this friendly café. Teas from prestige specialist Jing (earl grey, english breakfast, green tea and a couple of herbal options) are offered alongside excellent coffee and chai lattes made with Cordon Bleu-trained Bea's own concoction of organic darjeeling tea and spices. Cakes are in the French and American traditions: chocolate truffle, cheesecakes, red velvet and pretty cupcakes.

44 Theobald's Road, WC1X 8NW (7242 8330, www.beasofbloomsbury.com).

High Tea of Highgate

Tea cosies illustrated with dogs, hearts and Union Jacks, cow-shaped milk jugs, cute aprons, porcelain jelly moulds and bags of humbugs provide a colourfully retro take on the traditional village tearoom in this most traditional of London villages. You can hear the hand-mixer whirring away behind the counter as owner Georgina Worthington whips up a fresh victoria sponge or carrot cake. Organic butter and eggs are used in the baking. A cream tea costs £6.50.

50 Highgate High Street, N6 5HX (8348 3162, www.highteaofhighgate.com).

Orange Pekoe

A pretty tearoom huddled neatly among the boutiques of Barnes, Orange Pekoe offers pleasing river views and a shop boasting over 100 high-quality teas. Owner Marianna Hadjigeorgiou uses teapots with a removable filter, so you can brew your tea to the perfect strength. Spectacular cakes are provided by esteemed bakery Konditor & Cook, but check out the big, warm own-made scones too.

3 White Hart Lane, SW13 0PX (8876 6070, www.orangepekoeteas.com).

Le Chandelier

Both tea and cake are in plentiful supply at Le Chandelier. More than 30 varieties of loose leaf tea by Jing are stacked in jars while the cakes cause passersby to ogle from the window. Piled high and wide, they cover the gamut of confections from cupcakes and brownies to billowing meringues and grown-up cheesecakes and are ordered daily from various local suppliers. Scones, however, are baked in-house. The salon setting – a sort of grand French, British and Middle Eastern fusion – is a suitably special backdrop.

161 Lordship Lane, London, SE22 8HX (8299 3344, www.lechandelier.co.uk).

Tea Smith

Spitalfields' premier tearoom – with its distinctly Japanese aesthetic – might not have the homely charm of some of its contemporaries, but it is undeniably stylish. Owner John Kennedy sources exquisite teas direct from the Far East and brews them with precision. The pâtisserie's offerings are innovative, fusion combos such as jasmine truffles or dark chocolate infused with oolong tea.

6 Lamb Street, E1 6EA (7247 1333, www.teasmith.co.uk).

931

Why limit fireworks viewing to fifth November? Other pyrotechnical highlights of the capital's calendar include Diwali, Chinese New Year, the Lord Mayor's Show, the Thames Festival and, of course, New Year's Eve on the river.

932

See the poetry in modern architecture

The heart of the City doesn't necessarily feel like the most auspicious spot for a poetic experience, but if you sit on the stone benches that circle the base of the 'Gherkin' (30 St Mary Axe, EC3) that is exactly what you'll have. Incised on each bench, one line at a time, is 'Arcadian Dream Garden' by eccentric, neo-classical Scottish modernist Ian Hamilton Finlay. Could he have been thinking about the Gherkin itself when he wrote: 'A slender stone vase…', 'A tree, pierced right through by a bronze arrow'?

933

Rise with the birds

London's bird-lovers have taken to International Dawn Chorus Day with enthusiasm since it was initiated for the UK (in Birmingham) back in 1984. There are two approaches to the event, neither of which need cost a brass razzoo. Those who can already tell a tweet from a twitter often go it alone in their local park or back garden, then feed their findings back to the official website (www.idcd.info). Sociable coves and the blissfully ignorant can set the alarm early on the designated Sunday in early May (check the website for this year's date) and head out to one of London's organised events. The prime location (the London Wetland Centre) is out of our price range, notwithstanding the group breakfast, but many local reserves – notably Tower Hamlets Cemetery Park and Roundshaw Downs Local Nature Reserve – are enthusiastic participants, offering free tours. You'll probably have to be up at 4am… but you can always go back to bed afterwards.

934

Play in Coram's Fields

You have to be accompanied by a child to gain entry to Coram's Fields in Bloomsbury. Set up in 1936 as London's first public children's playground, the seven sprawling acres of playgrounds and park are exclusively for the use of children living in or visiting London. There are massive lawns for free play and family picnics, sports pitches, a paddling pool, sandpits, a flying fox and other slides, a pets' corner (sheep, goats, ducks and hens), a sensory play area designed for children with disabilities and a branch of lovely Austrian café Kipferl.

Coram's Fields *93 Guilford Street, WC1N 1DN (7837 6138, www.coramsfields.org).*

935 Listen to the best songs about London

Have a look at *Time Out*'s list of the 100 Best London Songs and see if you agree. In at number one we have 'Waterloo Sunset' (The Kinks, 1967), followed by 'London Calling' (The Clash, 1979), 'West End Girls' (Pet Shop Boys, 1984), 'LDN' (Lily Allen, 2004) and 'Streets of London' (Ralph McTell, 1969), but there are plenty of lesser known gems in the top one hundred, including tunes by Des O'Connor and Barry Manilow. Log on to the website and you'll be able to listen to every tune, from 'London Pride' (Noel Coward, 1941) to 'New Cross Massakah' (Linton Kwesi Johnson, 1981). *www.timeout.com.*

936 Stand at the pagan heart of the City

Set low in the wall opposite Cannon Street Station is a strange glass case protected by an ornate wrought iron grille. It contains the bare stump of a stone which once stood tall, a pagan menhir at the centre of the Roman city from which all measurements in the land were once taken. It said that if the stone ever leaves London, the city will fall.

A few of my favourite things

937-943

Anna Robertson, market trader

I love Borough Market (7407 1002, www.boroughmarket.org.uk) because pretty much everyone who comes there – the sellers and the buyers – are complete foodies. And despite its image, it's still an inexpensive place to get your fruit and veg. I buy mine from a stall called Ted's Veg. The seasonal stuff tastes like it comes straight out of the ground and into your hand – the freshness is amazing. Last week there were some beautiful pink, orange and gold beetroots. The one you should really look out for is called chioggia beetroot, which has pink and white spirals. I just made a salad with it and it looked stunning.

If you're ever in town late at night and want to grab a cheap veggie takeaway, go to Maoz (43 Old Compton Street, W1V 6SG, 7851 1586, www.maozveg.com) in Soho. You get falafel in pitta bread and there's also a whole salad bar with things like couscous, chilli carrots, fresh vegetables and sauces that you can pile on top. It's absolutely gorgeous – and feels quite healthy for fast food.

There's a wonderful vegan restaurant near Old Street called Saf (152-154 Curtain Road, EC2A 3AT, 7613 0007, www.saf restaurant.co.uk). It's quite expensive for dinner, but if you go there at lunchtime it's cheaper. It does all kinds of foods that you would never imagine could be vegan – I love the beetroot ravioli, which has beetroot instead of the pasta and, inside, vegan cheese made with nuts and herbs. I wouldn't normally go anywhere near vegan cheese, but the cheesecake is also quite possibly the best I've ever had.

We live near Hither Green, and really try and keep everything as local to there as possible. One place we go to a lot is Royal Teas (76 Royal Hill, SE10 8RT, 8691 7240, www.royalteascafe.co.uk), a vegetarian coffee shop in Greenwich. It does classics like eggy bread, but staff just do them really well. All the cakes and juices are made on site and every day there's a special soup of the day.

Another local favourite is a nice little Lebanese café called Levante (11 Lewis Grove, SE13 6BG, 8355 3522), in Lewisham. It does a vegetarian special that has falafel, houmous, tahini, salad and olives.

Also nearby is the Greenwich Picture House (180 Greenwich High Road, SE10 8NN, 0870 755 0065, www.picturehouses.co.uk). It's £9 to see a film on a Monday night and it shows everything from blockbusters to world cinema and children's films. There's a bar there too and you can buy drinks and take them into the cinema, with its comfortable, relaxing chairs.

When we were starting up the business, I went everywhere by bike, and I still have a lot of fun cycling around London. One of my favourite cycle rides is around Greenwich Park (8858 2608, www.royal parks.org.uk). There are paths throughout, which means that there are always lots of other people cycling, rollerblading and skateboarding here. And because it's on a hill you have fantastic views over the whole of London.

Anna Robertson is the owner of the Veggie Table market stalls (www.the veggietable.co.uk).

944

Check out London's classiest convenience store

It's official. Britain's best corner shop is in E17 (though it isn't actually on a corner). The Walthamstow Village Stores Spar was named Britain's Best Convenience Store at the 2011 Convenience Retail Awards. And this is no ordinary Spar. You can pick up a pizza made fresh by its Italian chef; home-made bread; or some own-brand artisan jam (the bacon jam is gaining speedy notoriety). Post-pub munchies shopping never tasted so good.

The Village Store *24 Orford Road, E17 9AJ (8521 8187).*

945 *Let off steam at Kew*

For those who usually associate steam engines with the railways, it may come as a surprise to learn that they were also used to supply water to the city. The Victorian pumping station at Kew, now Kew Bridge Steam Museum, is a significant piece of industrial architecture in its own right but it is now also home to an extraordinary collection of different engines and is one of London's most engaging visitor attractions – particularly at weekends when the great pieces of machinery are in steam. The museum illustrates how the rapidly expanding city met the challenge of delivering water to its citizens – and of removing their effluvia. With plenty of hands-on exhibits for children, including a small steam train, the stars of the show remain those beam engines – four of them in all – gleaming behemoths whose mighty pistons and whirring wheels fill the building with an unearthly, rhythmic whooshing sound. The £10 entrance fee buys admission for a year.

Kew Bridge Steam Museum *Green Dragon Lane, Brentford TW8 0EN (8596 4757, www.kbsm.org).*

Art for art's sake

Mindful of our ten pound budget, Robin Saikia takes a tour round the West End's finest – and most expensive – galleries.

Spending time visiting the lush lairs of London's leading art dealers, either for private views (easier than ever to gatecrash, *see p156*) or simply in search of warmth and edification, is a time-honoured pursuit of the cash-strapped Londoner. It may require a steely frame of mind to ignore the sometimes withering glances of the starchy front-of-house concierges in Bond Street, but the effort is well repaid, because London's leading commercial galleries and auction houses routinely exhibit works of art that are as good as – if not better than – the art on show in the national collections. The West End (for our purposes, both sides of Piccadilly) remains the core of the art world and the following itinerary is easily walkable and manageable within a day (two, if you're taking your time).

Choose a busy auction house as your first port of call – they're slightly less daunting than an intimate and dimly lit old master gallery. Saunter purposefully into Sotheby's (34-35 Old Bond Street, W1Y 9HD, 7923 5000, www.sothebys.com) or Christie's (8 King Street, St. James's, SW1Y 6QT, 7839 9060, www.christies.com) and disarm the resident

ice maiden by asking her what's 'on view' – it could be next week's sale of old master paintings or next month's sale of Oriental Art. Unless you resemble a Texan oil magnate or a Russian oligarch, refrain from making loud and disparaging remarks about the prices or quality of the goods on offer. Instead, muse your way thoughtfully around the exhibits, pausing to inspect the occasional lot. If there is, say, a marvellous piece of Fabergé locked in a cabinet, you may ask to see it or handle it. Don't drop it or steal it.

One of the grandest, most civilised and most welcoming galleries in London is Philip Mould (29 Dover Street, W1S 4NA, 7499 6818, www.philipmould.com). Mould specialises in museum-quality portraits of important people from the Tudor period to the present day, and a visit to his gallery is every bit as instructive as a visit to the National Portrait Gallery. There is always a chance (if you're lucky) that Mould will have made one of his now celebrated 'discoveries' of a long-lost portrait and that it will be on view. The frisson afforded by these twice- or thrice-yearly unveilings is nothing less than addictive: past triumphs

Philip Mould

have included a fire-damaged Charles II, Elizabeth I in the first flush of youth, Bonnie Prince Charlie's brother, Cardinal Henry, and a sensitive early portrait of Henry VIII, yet to become the harsh, unbending tyrant of later years. Next door at 27 Dover Street, W1S 4LZ (7290 1540, www.andrewwyld.com) is the affable Andrew Wyld, formerly top dog at Agnew's and now a leading dealer in British and Irish paintings. 'Nothing over £5,000' is a down-to-earth watchword of one of this gallery's annual exhibitions.

On the other side of Piccadilly, in St James's, is the Portland Gallery (8 Bennet Street, SW1 1RP, 7493 1888, www.portlandgallery.com), representing the unimpeachable face of British contemporary art. Here, the pictures and sculpture are unlikely to frighten, unnerve or annoy you; instead a visit should prove an appropriate antidote, should one be needed, to the hurly-burly of the YBA scene – and a cost-effective alternative to tea in Fortnum and Mason. Expect masterly London scenes by Nick Botting, glimmering and glittering visions of Venice by Alexander Creswell, sexually charged couples by Jack Vettriano, and meditative seascapes by Sophie Macpherson.

Nearby is Chris Beetles (8 & 10 Ryder Street, SW1Y 6QB, 7839 7551, www.chrisbeetles.com), a leading specialist in British watercolours and illustrators. There is always entertaining work to be seen here: a drawing of a steely and self-assured Kenneth Clark by Ronald Searle, for instance; genially mad contraptions by Heath Robinson; pop-eyed cats playing golf by Louis Wain; dashing Italian views by Brabazon and Winnie the Pooh as Roman emperor by EH Shepard. In recent years Beetles has shown photography too: some elegant work by Snowden (Jack Nicholson, David Bowie, the Queen, Anthony Blunt) and Terry O'Neill (Frank Sinatra, Robert Redford, Pierce Brosnan, Bowie again, Bridget Bardot and a strikingly provocative Marianne Faithfull).

Arguably the best dealer in Dutch old masters in the world is Johnny van Haeften (13 Duke Street, SW1Y 6DB, 7930 3062, www.johnnyvanhaeften.com). Here you can enjoy Brueghel's skating peasants, drink-crazed boors or desperate alchemists by Teniers or a magnificent tulip by Bosschaert. Next door is Derek Johns (12 Duke Street, SW1Y 6BN, 7839 7671, www.derekjohns. co.uk) who deals in important Italian, Spanish and French old masters – there is a fair chance

of seeing work by Canaletto, Guardi, Francesco Zanin, Tiepolo, Goya, Murillo and Ingres.

Finally, on the other side of Piccadilly again, there are about two dozen galleries in Cork Street, a location that has successfully managed to preserve its reputation as a cradle for contemporary art. Favourites include the Mayor Gallery (22a Cork Street, W1S 3NA, 7734 3558, www.mayorgallery.com), the Medici Gallery (5 Cork Street, W1S 3LQ, 7495 2565, www.medicigallery.co.uk) and Waddington Custot Galleries (11 Cork Street, W1S 3LT, 7851 2200, www.waddingtoncustot.com). At the Mayor you can see the latest multi-million pound art phenomenon – contemporary Chinese art by painters such as Chang Xugong and Chen Weimin. Medici has at any given time a selection of solid and pleasing figurative work by Alan Kingsbury (the thinking man's Jack Vettriano), Dylan Lisle (stimulating nudes) and Ray Donley (who has acquired a cult following through painting, with startling effect, like an old master). A visit to the unassailably cosmopolitan Waddington's should give you a firm grounding in most of the things that really matter in the art world on either side of the Atlantic: Picasso, Moore, Robert Indiana, Barry Flanagan (refer knowingly to his 'hares', for under no circumstances are they rabbits), Josef Albers (yes, very like Rothko) and many more.

Chris Beetles

957 Have a drink in a car park

Forget the West End – for a truly London sky-high cocktail experience, head to a multi-storey car park in Peckham. The slightly ramshackle bar and barbecue is open July to September – if it starts to rain you can huddle under a large red canopy.

Frank's Café & Campari Bar *Level 10, Peckham multi-storey car park, 95A Rye Lane, SE15 4ST (07582 884574, www.frankscafe.org.uk)*

958 Go on a singles night with a difference

Slagbox is the 'singles night for people who don't like singles nights'. It's a pound on the door – for this you get a number on your way in. Wear this with pride, have a scout around for potential beaux, write them a note and pop it in the 'slagbox'. It's up to you how smutty you go. At points throughout the night a trusty compere will read out notes from the box. And it's up to you to take it from there.

Dolphin *163 Mare Street, E8 3RH (0871 984 4885).*

959 Take in the calm of Chiswick House and Gardens

For a gasp of earthly paradise amid west London's urban bustle, head to graceful Chiswick House and Gardens. This is the birthplace of the English landscape movement, which bulldozed formal gardens in favour of sweeping elegance. The magnificent neo-Palladian villa was conceived as a kind of giant cabinet to display its owner's art and book collection and the garden's grand vistas and hidden pathways influenced designs as far afield as New York's Central Park. Lord Burlington, who completed the villa in 1729, entertained such luminaries as Handel, Alexander Pope and Jonathan Swift, while in the swinging sixties, the Beatles filmed promos for *Paperback Writer* and *Rain* here. Why not join them?

Chiswick House *Burlington Lane, W4 2RP (8995 0508, www.chgt.org.uk). £5.50.*

960 Pound the streets

OK, so running is always free. But if you do it with others it feels like an event, and offers you the chance to take to the streets with a supportive crew who'll prick your pride to run that extra mile or slow their pace if you flag. The Nike + Run clubs happen almost every weeknight, and there are different run lengths, so you can choose the one that suits your fitness or mood. *www.nike.com.*

961-962 Check out London's mosques

There's no mistaking the London Central Mosque in Regent's Park, with its golden dome and stout 140-foot minaret. The main prayer hall is as grand as one might expect – lush red carpets, mosaics and an impressive chandelier – but this centre for British Muslims also houses a library, offices, an events venue and a bookshop. Its history goes back to World War II, when Churchill's War Cabinet put aside £100,000 for the site, but the mosque was actually built in the 1970s.

Up to 50,000 Muslims visit during the two main Islamic festivals, or eids, and at lunchtime on Fridays, the main day of worship, the mosque is usually overflowing. Visitors are allowed in any time the mosque is open, though women must cover their heads (headscarves are available from the bookshop) and both sexes must cover their legs to below the knee. Guided tours are also available if you call ahead.

Also impressive is the towering complex of the East London Mosque in Whitechapel – one of the biggest mosques in Britain. Building work began in the 1980s and it has continued to grow steadily since – the latest part, London Muslim Centre, opening in June 2004. If you'd just like to visit the building, ring ahead first.

London Central Mosque & Islamic Cultural Centre *146 Park Road, NW8 7RG (7724 3363, www.iccuk.org).*
East London Mosque & London Muslim Centre *46-92 Whitechapel Road, E1 1JX (7650 3000, www.eastlondonmosque.org.uk).*

963-968
Take advantage of Wi-Fi

Why work from home (wandering aimlessly from room to room then grazing on the contents of your fridge) when some of London's most impressive cultural centres, quirky little cafés and world-class museums are more than happy for you to pitch up, log on and generally make like their gaff is your very own office for the day? And, what's more, most won't charge you a penny.

Barbican Centre

Accommodating hordes of culture vultures during weekends and evenings, the Barbican Centre is often eerily empty on weekdays – working here can seem like stepping on to a near-deserted Kubrickian film set. Nevertheless, you'll come across the odd writer, a few students and creatives and as well as business types. A word of warning though: the complex lies within a Wi-Fi hotspot, but because its walls are six feet of solid concrete, the signal can sometimes be unreliable (the library on the second floor has internet terminals if you get stuck).
Silk Street, EC2Y 8DS (7638 4141, www.barbican.org.uk).

Camden Arts Centre

The Camden Arts Centre's café is light and airy and has free Wi-Fi and big tables. There's also a gallery and bookshop stocked with quirky little publications that you'll struggle to find anywhere else. The café tends to be populated by twenty- and thirtysomething creative types but there's also usually a healthy smattering of gossiping pensioners to liven things up. The café opens on to a garden, where you can work among the various temporary artworks.

Arkwright Road, NW3 6DG (7472 5500,
www.camdenartscentre.org).

Camera Café

Idiosyncratic Camera Café near the British
Museum is a perfect example of the many
quirky little cafés around town that love having
people pitch up for the day but won't hassle you
to keep buying coffees. In the front there's a
shop selling second-hand cameras (lovely old
Leicas and restored Hasselblads), out back is a
cosy café with photographs covering the walls.
You can use the Wi-Fi all day for free and you'll
no doubt run into a character or two.
44 Museum Street, WC1A 1LY (07887 930 826,
www.cameracafe.co.uk).

Leon

At this Spitalfields branch of Leon there's
free Wi-Fi and a massive table if you need to
spread out. It attracts City folk, art directors
and copywriters from the nearby advertising
agencies, as well as young artists. It tends to
get very busy at lunchtime but before noon and
after 3pm you'll have the place pretty much to
yourself. Bear in mind a rumour we once heard:
arty types sit to the right, suits to the left…
3 Crispin Place, E1 6DW (7247 4369,
www.leonrestaurants.co.uk).

Peyton and Byrne

This bright, airy branch of Peyton and Byrne
on the ground floor of the Wellcome Collection
is great for a light lunch or an indulgent
afternoon tea. You can potter away on your
laptop using the free Wi-Fi while enjoying
superb scotch eggs, pastries, pork pies and
salads or sticky cakes, sponges and crumbles
made fresh daily. If you're lacking inspiration
have a wander round the (free) museum.
Wellcome Collection, 183 Euston Road, NW1 2BE
(7611 2138, www.peytonandbyrne.com).

Royal Festival Hall

The Royal Festival Hall has a little more hustle
and bustle than the Barbican, but it does have
fabulous views and a better range of snack
options. Head for Level 2 for Wi-Fi.
Southbank Centre, Belvedere Road, SE1 8XX
(0844 875 0073, www.southbankcentre.co.uk).

969-970

Collect bits of old London Bridge

The medieval, 19-arch London Bridge, once cluttered with houses, shops and heads on sticks, was finally demolished in 1831, but you can still catch a glimpse of a few of its ancient fixtures and fittings. Most incredible of all of them is the royal coat of arms that adorns the front of the King's Arms pub in Newcomen Street, off Borough High Street. It was salvaged from the stone gateway that stood at the southern end of the old bridge until 1760, and duly shows the arms of George III.

From 1762 comes a collection of stone alcoves, which were installed at regular intervals on the bridge to prevent pedestrians being trampled under hoof by the traffic when the last of the teetering buildings were cleared from the bridge. Needless to say, they were quickly pressed into alternative service by dossers, beggars, footpads, thimble-riggers and their dog-eyes, street hawkers and tuppenny molls. Two of them survive in Hackney's Victoria Park, and you'll find another closer to its original home in the grounds of Guy's Hospital.

971

Eat at the home of Reggae Reggae sauce

Super charismatic marinade maverick and *Dragon's Den* slayer Levi Roots opened his own restaurant in Battersea in 2007. Definitely one for the frugal, the Papine Jerk Centre offers a small but uncomplicated menu of Caribbean staples: Jamaica's national dish, ackee and saltfish (£3 per portion) is a crowd-pleaser (expect queues at lunchtime), or try the richly seasoned mains of jerk chicken, curried goat or oxtail (£5 small, £6 large), with a side of fried plantain or saltfish fritters (£1 per portion). The Guinness punch (£1.50 small, £2.50 large) is also a big draw, as, of course, is the entrepreneurial chef himself – real name Keith Graham – who you'll sometimes see here.

Papine Jerk Centre *8 Lavender Road, SW11 2UG (7924 2288, www.100acres.com/papinejerk).*

972

Reconnoitre the City's less familiar Wrens

St Paul's Cathedral has been in the news a lot in 2012, but Sir Christopher Wren was a notably prolific architect and there are many other fine churches in the vicinity that can be visited for free. If you start on the west side of Ludgate Circus and look up to St Paul's, the black spire to the left of the dome is St Martin Ludgate, while St Bride's is hidden behind. The latter's steeple is the tallest of any Wren church and was supposedly the model for tiered wedding cakes. Turn right in front of the Cathedral and you pass through Temple Bar, another Wren creation. It originally stood at the western end of Fleet Street to mark the boundary between the Cities of London and Westminster, but now it marks the entrance to the new Paternoster Square. Cross the square, emerging on Newgate Street, and Christ Church is opposite. Almost destroyed during World War II, the ruined nave is today a lovely rose garden. Head east to Gresham Street for the Wren motherlode: first, St Anne & St Agnes, with its leafy churchyard; then a glimpse of the tower of St Alban, Wood Street; next you pass St Lawrence Jewry, the church of the Corporation of London; and finally, when Gresham Street becomes Lothbury, St Margaret Lothbury. This has one of the loveliest interiors of any Wren church, and the impressive wood screen is by Wren himself.

Over at Bank tube station, take the Mansion House exit and turn left for St Stephen Walbrook, Wren's most grandiose church, a mass of creamy stone with a soaring dome, fabulously bulbous pulpit and a slightly incongruous modern altar by Henry Moore. Near Cannon Street station, on Abchurch Lane, you'll find St Mary Abchurch, a real gem with a shallow, painted dome and a beautiful carved reredos by Grinling Gibbons. It was shattered into 2,000 pieces by a wartime bomb but painstakingly pieced together again afterwards.

973 *Bob on Apple Day*

Despite sounding like more like an ancient pagan ritual, or perhaps a corruption of the Christian harvest festival, this celebration of apples, orchards and locally grown food actually only dates from 1990 (though bobbing for apples has been around for much longer). There are events all over the country and in London, with Borough Market (7407 1002, www.boroughmarket.org.uk) a great place to dunk, bob, eat and drink this quintessentially English fruit, in all its many varieties. It all takes place around the nearest Sunday to 21 October.

www.commonground.org.uk.

974-983 *Follow some vintage advice*

In search of cheap thrills from an earlier era, Derek Hammond plunders some old London guidebooks.

The *London Spy* was London's first-ever guidebook, published in 1703 to shout up the pleasures of dog-tossing, gaming and baiting lunatics in Bedlam. But it isn't just the long-disappeared aspects of Dickensian/Swinging/Thatcher's London that stand out when you pick up an old guide for pennies from a second-hand bookshop – there's also a surprisingly broad swathe of places, possibilities and things to do that remain strangely constant – and affordable.

Pop in to the Anchor, Bankside

'What more would you have than a tankard of ale where the greatest of all Englishmen used to have his?' demands HE Popham in his brilliantly swashbuckling *Guide to London Taverns* (Claude Stacey, 1927). 'If you prefer a West End hotel, with gold-laced flunkeys to bow you in, and a drink that costs five shillings a glass, for goodness sake leave us here and take yourself westward in the first cab that you can find, or swim up river if you prefer it. We don't care. We are for a game of darts with our riverside friends in the taproom'. Shakespeare may be no more likely to turn up now than he was 80-odd years ago but, on the plus side, the Anchor has added a smart new(ish) drinking area right by the river that's glorious on a summer's day.

Gaze through misty glass at a 'Roman' curio

'At 5 Strand Lane is an antiquarian's mystery,' teases Harold F Hutchinson, author of London Transport's *Visitor's London* (1954), 'and no reputable authority will vouch for its latinity. But it is an interesting relic.' It remains a thrill to dodge down this dingy alley off the Strand and shade your eyes in order to see into this spring-fed plunge bath – still in working order, and handling around 2,000 gallons of fresh spring water a day. 'The oval lead overflow pipe is considered to be genuinely Roman,' Harold stuck his neck out, 'but the bricks are more probably Tudor'.

Buy your own hanky on Petticoat Lane

'Thousands pack into Petticoat Lane between the sweatshops and bomb sites on Sunday morning, and it is the nearest thing London can offer to an Oriental bazaar.' So reckoned VS Pritchett in 1962, when Harvest published *London Perceived*. 'They used to say that you could walk through this market and see your own handkerchief on sale on a stall by the time you got to the end. I was brought up on scandals of a similar kind sold at the dog market in Bethnal Green: you met your own dear Airdale painted black and offered as a retriever'.

Get into ironwork at Leadenhall

'Leadenhall Market is solid and reassuring, and it asserts the Victorians' belief in the virtues of cast iron. The entire market with its adjoining alleys is of the greatest interest to the London virtuoso...' Londonologists don't come any more cultish than the great writer/sketcher Geoffrey Fletcher. *The London Nobody Knows* (Hutchinson, 1962) was his debut outing and subsequently made into a documentary film starring James Mason. Leadenhall Market features in both: 'The ironwork is highly elaborated with ornament and the griffins which support the City's coat of arms... discreetly sober. One of the most attractive buildings is the Lamb Tavern, with its large hanging lamps and engraved glass. All is Victorian here, apart from the human element and the delivery vans.'

Let's all go down the Strand... on the green

'A picturesque stretch of tree-lined riverside walk with Georgian houses, a boatyard and a couple of pubs. The City Barge was granted a charter for 500 years by Queen Elizabeth I, and the river entrance has to be sealed up with clay and boarding during high tides.' Brilliantly grumpy American tourist Betty James went for a stroll down Strand on the

Green in Chiswick the very year the Beatles filmed scenes from *Help!* in the City Barge pub. Her *London on £1 a Day* (Batsford, 1965) is truly evocative of the times – and timeless. 'The Bull's Head has an underground tunnel to an island known as Oliver's Eyot. It is said that this tunnel was used by Oliver Cromwell and his Roundheads, which is decidedly peculiar because, as everybody knows, they didn't drink.' Actually, there are three more-than-decent riverside pubs on Strand on the Green, and it's the Bell and Crown that has come to the fore in claiming the tunnel myth today and Oliver's Eyot is now a haven for herons and cormorants.

Be very scared... at a cult leader's spooky Gothic house

'At 12 Langford Place, sheer horror: a Francis Bacon shriek in these affluent, uncomplicated suburbs at the end of Abbey Road. It looks like a normal St John's Wood villa pickled in embalming fluid by some mad doctor...' That's how Ian Nairn described the Victorian charlatan John Hugh Smyth-Pigott's pad in his witty, opinionated architectural bible, *Nairn's London*. The book was published by Penguin in 1967, but he could have written this particular entry yesterday.

Take a perfect London photo

Len Deighton's *London Dossier* is the essential guide for clawing back the mood of London in 1967. Len's own chunks are masterly, but the book also benefits from the multiple perspectives of specialist buddies roped in to write odd chapters – like Adrian Flowers on photography: 'Some foreigners are most struck by the effect of twilight,' he wrote. 'Certainly some of London's special moments are at this time, as the artificial lights slowly take over... All along the Embankment is good for night shooting, especially the Victoria Embankment and the promenade between Westminster and Lambeth Bridges on the south side.'

Tune in, drop out

Nicholas Saunders was an anarcho-hippy self-publisher with plenty of vital information to pass on about drugs, dole, sex and squats in his psychedelic-covered *Alternative London*, from 1972. 'There are millions of things you can do in London,' he wrote, 'like yelling at people in Speaker's Corner, climbing every tree in every park, flying kites just about anywhere, but it's best in the middle of Oxford Street or outside Buckingham Palace... See the second half of any play for free, simply by walking in at the interval... Drop in for free entertainment when the light is on over Big Ben: the entrance is the arch in the car park: you can leave your car where it says "Peers only"...' Saunders went on to found Neal's Yard wholefood empire and later wrote another underground classic, *Ecstasy and the Dance Culture* (1995).

Go 'window shopping' at an auctioneer's

The high-tension atmosphere of auction houses is great fun to drop in on, whether you're bidding on outlandish art yourself – or just watching others sweat it out. 'But they have their own set of rules,' warned Martin Lightfoot in his *Visitor's Guide to London Shopping* (Martlet, 1982), 'and it is well to know roughly how they work before venturing into them. If you watch an auction you will often find it difficult to see who is actually bidding, one reason for this being that the auctioneer may have recorded bids by people not actually present, and is therefore pushing up the bidding by taking a slightly higher bid "off the wall", as they say. There are horror stories of someone sneezing or scratching his ear and finding himself with a £20,000 lot. These stories are complete myths.'

Visit the birthplace of indie

Richard Jobson was the singer in punk band the Skids before he drifted into TV, and so to novels and directing films: no wonder he dealt in muso mythology with a lasting quality. 'The most independent record shop in Britain, Rough Trade was the place where the alternative music scene, born off the back of punk, really matured,' he wrote in the Virgin *Insider's Guide To London* (Virgin, 1993). 'Covered with posters from seminal punk and post-punk releases and gigs, the Rough Trade shop is the meeting place for people interested in new music. Now that CDs seem to have taken over completely, it's one of the few places you can get new releases on vinyl.'

984-993

Buy brilliant British beer at London's finest real ale pubs...

We know, we know: it's hard to spend less than £4 on a pint in central London these days, but at least at the following places your money will buy you a great British gourmet treat.

Greenwich Union
The Greenwich, flagship pub of Alistair Hook's laudable Meantime Brewery, makes the most of the training and recipes its founder gleaned at age-old institutions in Germany. Meantime produces London Stout, Pale Ale, Helles, Kölner and Union, plus chocolate and raspberry varieties, all on draught and at reasonable prices. *56 Royal Hill, SE10 8RT (8692 6258, www.greenwichunion.com).*

Jerusalem Tavern
Located in the alleys behind Farringdon station, this creaking and cosily tatty little pub serves the sought-after ales of Suffolk's St Peter's Brewery. Almost hidden between timber divides, the bar is backed by barrels, their names and ABVs chalked on a board: Suffolk Gold, Organic and even a Whisky Beer. A rag-tag and decidedly loyal crowd muses over the *Evening Standard* crossword or tucks into their moreish roast pork and apple sauce sandwich. *55 Britton Street, EC1M 5UQ (7490 4281, www.stpetersbrewery.co.uk).*

Lamb

Founded in 1729, this Young's outpost in Holborn found fame as a theatrical haunt when the A-list included Sir Henry Irving and assorted music hall stars; they're commemorated in old photos and surrounded by well-worn seats, much polished wood and a few vintage knick-knacks. Punters range from discerning students to Gray's Inn barristers, supping from half a dozen pumps – expect real ale from Young's and Wells (the two breweries combined operations in 2006), plus a guest beer (perhaps St Austell Tribute).

94 Lamb's Conduit Street, WC1N 3LZ (7405 0713, www.youngs.co.uk).

Market Porter

Few market bars stock this range of beers. In an invariably cramped main bar area – there's more room in the back, but the bustle can be off-putting – Borough Market traders and sundry other regulars gather around the likes of Okell's Maclir, Vale Brewery Best, Acorn Brewery Kashmir, Harveys Best and Lund's Bitter. There are choices from Meantime Brewery too – in all it adds up to around 40 ales a week.

9 Stoney Street, SE1 9AA (7407 2495, www.markettaverns.co.uk).

Pembury Tavern

Drinking in this vast, overlit Hackney bar room feels like rattling round a youth hostel canteen, but the 16 handpumps – mostly fine real ale from Cambridge's Milton Brewery (Pegasus, Sparta, Justinian and their stout Nero on our last visit) – are a delight. Bar billiards and a red-baize pool table on one side give way to bookshelves and boardgames on the other. Beer festivals take place in February, July and November.

90 Amhurst Road, E8 1JH (8986 8597).

Royal Oak

The Royal Oak off Borough High Street seems wonderfully trapped in time, complete with its unused hatch for off sales. Serving the great works of Lewes brewery Harveys, the ales – Mild, Pale, Old, Best and Armada – are nicely priced (the cheapest is Mild at £3.10), and a felt-tipped menu offers classics such as rabbit casserole and Lancashire hotpot. Music hall stars Harry Ray and Flanagan & Allen, celebrated in framed hand bills, would have tucked into the same.

44 Tabard Street, SE1 4JU (7357 7173).

Sultan

In the backstreets of south Wimbledon lies an ale-drinking nirvana, named after an 1830s racehorse. A much-loved, if rather antiseptic locals' boozer, the Sultan is the only London pub owned by Wiltshire's Hop Back Brewery; on the weekly beer club evenings, chattering middle-aged locals enjoy the delights of GFB, Entire Stout and Summer Lightning (cheapest pint, £2.80). Carryouts are also available.

78 Norman Road, SW19 1BT (8542 4532, www.hopback.co.uk).

Wenlock Arms

From the outside, the Wenlock doesn't look like much. To be honest, it doesn't look like much inside either, but god forbid it should ever tear out its carpet or gastro-up its menu of doorstep sarnies. On any given night, you might find yourself sitting next to a table of beer-bellied ale-hunters going through the excellent and ever-changing range of beers and, of course, the eccentric, ever-talkative regulars.

26 Wenlock Road, N1 7TA (7608 3406, www.wenlock-arms.co.uk).

White Horse

This stupendously popular stalwart does what it does best exceptionally well: it serves a fantastic, even mind-boggling, array of beers. There are over 200 (count 'em) available at any one time, including 30 on draught, eight of them cask ales (the likes of Harveys Sussex Best, Adnams Broadside and rotating guests). And there's always a cask mild, stout and porter on offer, as well as regular beer festivals.

1-3 Parsons Green, SW6 4UL (7736 2115, www.whitehorsesw6.com).

Ye Olde Mitre

Its secluded location requires you to slink down an alleyway just off Hatton Garden, and as you do so you're transported to a parallel pub universe where the clientele are friendly and the staff (in pristine black and white uniforms) briskly efficient. A Monday-to-Friday joint, it opens for just one weekend a year – happily that's to coincide with the British Beer Festival. Ales are certainly the speciality – Deuchars and Adnams are regulars, with frequently changing guest beers beside them – but the proprietors don't turn their noses up at wine either. Historic, but never dusty.

1 Ely Court (Ely Place side of 8 Hatton Garden), EC1N 6SJ (7405 4751).

994

...or direct from a brewery

Go direct to the brewer for your ale: the Griffin Brewery (Chiswick Lane South, W4 2QB, 8996 2063, www.fullers.co.uk) sells the full Fuller's range.

995

Check out the MPs' secret tunnel

In the grand baroque lobby of the St Ermin's Hotel in Westminster, it's easy to overlook the small door given unusual prominence halfway up the grand staircase. Down a tight spiral staircase lies a vaulted four-metre tunnel – now definitively blocked – which once carried MPs to and from the Houses of Parliament, some 650 yards distant. The Division Bell still sounds in the hotel when it's time for members to return to work and cast their vote.

996

Spot secret creatures at the Natural History Museum

The 70 million specimens housed in the Natural History Museum's galleries – from immense pickled squids to tiny lichens pressed by Charles Darwin – are, of course, mind-boggling: but when did you last look at the building itself? Monkeys scamper up arches in the central hall, huge columns resemble fossilised trees, and outside there are more statues of animals and plants (the extinct above the east wing, the living to the west). In a final flourish, beautiful paintings of gilded plants – many of them chosen for their economic value to the Empire – look down from the high, broken-arched ceiling.

Natural History Museum *Cromwell Road, SW7 5BD (7942 5000, www.nhm.ac.uk).*

997

Hear a free steel band concert

Do yourself a favour and avoid Notting Hill Carnival crowds by heading instead to the incredible steel drumming of the National Panorama Championship. Every year on the Saturday before carnival (which is always on the August Bank Holiday weekend), an enthusiastic crowd converges in Hyde Park to watch the cream of UK steelpan talent battling it out to be named national champions. The music begins at noon, with the contest proper kicking off at teatime and running into the evening.

998

Be welcomed into a government office

Want to see London government in action? The 25 London Assembly members call the mayor to account ten times a year at Mayor's Question Time – and anyone can watch: check www.london.gov.uk/get-involved/public-meetings/mayor's-question-time to find out what's next up for discussion. Even if the hurly-burly of live politics doesn't appeal, Lord Foster's motorbike helmet of a building might. The first two floors of City Hall are, subject to a security search on entering, open to the public 8.30am-6pm Monday-Thursday, 8.30am-5.30pm Friday, as well as some weekends. You can walk up the spiral ramp to visit the temporary exhibitions and view the Assembly Chamber, or descend to the café and – best of all – the London Photomat (on the lower ground floor). Most recently updated in April 2008 (although some source photos date to summer 2006), this is a walk-on aerial photo of the whole of Greater London, at sufficiently high resolution for you to be able to identify your own house. London's Living Room, located on the top floor and offering fabulous views, is also occasionally open too.

City Hall *Queen's Walk, SE1 2AA (www.london.gov.uk/gla/city_hall/index.jsp).*

999

Take it all in at Somerset House

You can see all of Somerset House for less than a tenner if you plan things right: the trick is to turn up on Monday between 10am and 2pm when entry to the Courtauld Gallery is free.

Start from the river side of the building and head downstairs from the new Embankment Galleries. You'll find a free exhibition on the history of Somerset House, complete with ceremonial Thames barge and the strains of Handel's *Water Music*. Next, explore the Studio and Terrace Rooms, which hold intriguing temporary exhibition. Done? Then it's time to make your first investment: cough up £8 to get into the Embankment Galleries themselves, where changing exhibitions highlight the connections between art, architecture and design under inviting titles like 'Wouldn't it be nice…: Wishful thinking in art and design'.

Once you've had your fill of the contemporary, cross the brilliant fountain court – lingering among the choreographed water jets in summer or laughing at the tumbling ice-skaters in winter – and head into the Courtauld Gallery (7848 2526, www.courtauld.ac.uk/gallery). This is one of the country's best collections of paintings – diverse and compelling, yet on a more manageable scale than, say, the National Gallery. Sensational old masters, Impressionists and post-Impressionists are displayed in atmospherically creaky rooms, alongside prints, drawings and sculpture. Key works here include Cranach's *Adam and Eve*, Manet's *Bar at the Folies-Bergère*, Van Gogh's *Self-Portrait with Bandaged Ear* and Gauguin's *Nevermore*.

Snack options include a big branch of Fernandez & Wells, or Tom's Deli; in warm weather, there are outdoor tables and chairs ranged around the courtyard.
Somerset House *The Strand, WC2R 1LA (7845 4600, www.somerset-house.org.uk).*

1000 *Get to the top...*

… of the Monument (Monument Street, EC3R 8AH, 7626 2717, www.themonument.info). The recipient of an impressive £4.5 million refurbishment, Sir Christopher Wren and Robert Hooke's memorial to the Great Fire of London is the world's tallest free-standing column and, unlike other high points in the city, (such as the London Eye or St Paul's Cathedral, to name just a couple) it'll only cost you three quid to get to the top. Scaling the internal spiral staircase, with its 311 steps, may make you a little tired and dizzy, but what the hell – you'll have London at your feet.

A-Z index

Thematic index

Note: number refers to page, not list entry.

T

V

W

Z

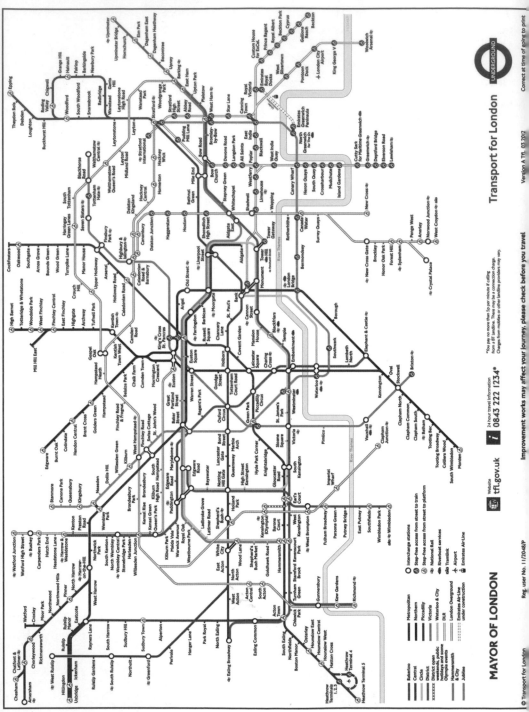

MAYOR OF LONDON

Transport for London

tfl.gov.uk

0843 222 1234*

Improvement works may affect your journey, please check before you travel

© Transport for London   Reg. user No. 11/2048/P   Version A Tfl. 03.2012   Correct at time of going to print